The Personal Writings of
Eliza Roxcy Snow

Eliza Roxcy Snow. Courtesy Historical Department, The Church of Jesus Christ of Latter-day Saints.

The Personal Writings
of
Eliza Roxcy Snow

Edited by
Maureen Ursenbach Beecher

University of Utah Press
Salt Lake City

Copyright © 1995 University of Utah Press
All rights reserved.

Book design by Richard Firmage.

LIBRARY OF CONGRESS CATALOGING-IN-PUBLICATION DATA

E. R. S. (Eliza Roxcy Snow), 1804–1887.
   [Selections.   1995]
   The personal writings of Eliza Roxcy Snow, 1804–1887 /
edited by Maureen Ursenbach Beecher.
       p.   cm.
   Includes bibliographical references and index.
   Contents: My variegated life : the "Sketch of my life"—
A day of much interest : The Nauvoo journal and notebook—
A growling, grumbling, devilish, sickly time : The trail diary,
February 1846–May 1847—Truly a glorious time : The trail
diary, June 1847–September 1849.
   ISBN 0-87480-477-9 (alk. paper)
   1. E. R. S. (Eliza Roxcy Snow), 1804–1887—Diaries.
2. Mormons—United States—Diaries. 3. Women in the
Mormon Church—History—19th century—Sources.
I. Beecher, Maureen Ursenbach. II. Title.
BX8695.E18A3   1995
289.3'092—dc20
[B]   95-10403

Contents

Acknowledgments

That these diaries have been preserved, prepared, and presented is their own miracle, aided by many people. First, of course, is Eliza herself, who spent her last dime to purchase ink with which to record her western journey. Her heirs followed; they valued her memory and saved her diaries until they could be permanently deposited. The Henry E. Huntington Libraries, San Marino, California, who hold the trail diaries; the Bancroft Library, Berkeley, California, where the "Sketch of my Life" is deposited; and the Historical Department of the Church of Jesus Christ of Latter-day Saints, where the Nauvoo journal is now housed, and *BYU Studies*, where it was first published—all have been most cooperative in this publication venture, both in granting permissions for the publication and in assisting in its preparation. Their staffs, Peter Blodgett, Irene Moran, Ronald Barney, Stephen Sorensen, and Pauline Musig in particular, have been helpful. Cynthia Snow Banner, granddaughter of Eliza Snow's brother Lorenzo, has been a moving spirit behind this work and generous with information as well as with her family's papers.

Professor S. George Ellsworth, long ago recognizing my interest in Eliza, surrendered both his intent to publish and his typescript of the two trail diaries to me. I'm sure he thought I'd have completed the task long before this. Leonard J. Arrington, as church historian, and his assistants Davis Bitton and James B. Allen encouraged the task when I worked with them in the History Division of the Church of Jesus Christ of Latter-day Saints. As director of Brigham Young University's Joseph Fielding Smith Institute for Church History, Ronald K. Esplin continued that support. Colleagues in the institute, Jill Mulvay Derr, Carol Cornwall Madsen, Richard Jensen, Ronald W. Walker, and William G. Hartley, have encouraged and assisted me. My lodestone in the particularities of editing documents has been Dean C. Jessee, whose work with Joseph Smith papers set new standards in the treatment of Mormon materials. Marilyn Rish Parks checked and formatted the manuscript. I appreciate them all.

Several other people also have assisted over the years: Cheryl McClellan and her teenagers Christian and Sunny; my neighbor Jean Greenwood; Susan McClelland; Scott Kenney; Norlyn Snow Torres; Sonoma Snow Wilson; James Kimball; Marjorie C. Gardner; Todd Compton.

Financial aid came in the form of grants from Brigham Young University's Women's Research Institute, Religious Studies Center, and the David M. Kennedy Center for International Studies. I am most grateful for their confidence.

I most appreciate Nana Anderson and Linda King Newell of the University of Utah Press. They are well aware of both the financial risk and the inestimable worth of such publications as this. Richard Firmage acted well his part as editor and designer.

Editorial Methods

Since the 1987 publication of Mary-Jo Kline's *Guide to Documentary Editing*,[1] editors have had a handbook for a uniform method in transcribing handwritten manuscripts. Accordingly, since the increase in public interest in such edited works, readers have become accustomed to the apparatus which distinguishes personal writing from writing created for publication.

The intent of editors of such documents is both to preserve the immediacy of a handwritten page and to simultaneously provide the accessibility of a printed volume. Readers and scholars alike deserve to know as nearly as possible what the writer wrote, and how s/he wrote it. In preparing these documents for general readers, we will follow guidelines based on the premise that readers can and will interact most directly with the diarist/autobiographer if editor and designer present their work silently and unobtrusively. Rather than scatter bracketed spelling corrections throughout the text, for example, we trust the reader to "sound it out," assuming that the sometimes phonetic spelling of nineteenth-century writers will not be that foreign to our ears. There are advantages to the very strangeness of the spelling: when Eliza Snow writes of a "canion" we not only can see a natural gorge but can also hear the overtones of the transition into English of a term brought to the American West by Spanish explorers. When, however, she renders as "Nationa Botana" the Native American name "Nishnabotna," a small river in Iowa, we will spare the reader the need to consult an atlas by providing an explanation.

The flexibility of handwriting creates a fluidity and immediacy of expression, however, that print cannot reproduce. In typesetting, for the sake of simplicity, letters superscribed in the original are brought to the line, and strokes, however long they might be, are reduced to dashes. Capitals cannot always be distinguished from lower-case letters; a midrange emphasis available to the pen must be compromised in print, so editors must make a judgment on the basis of context and the writer's usual practice. Words struck through, however, can be shown as such, and words inserted are indicated by enclosing them in angle brackets < >. Where it is necessary or helpful to add letters to a word, or words to a sentence, the editor encloses them in square brackets [ ]. Explanations provided by the editor will be in italics and enclosed within brackets.

Punctuation is very difficult to render accurately. Not only do ink marks fade but flaws in the writing paper sometimes resemble dots or strokes. Where there is doubt, we have chosen the most logical interpretation, ignoring slips of the pen, and, by their context, rendering as a comma or a period marks which otherwise are indistinguishable. Where there is an obvious sentence break but no period, we have inferred haste on the part of the writer and have retained her breathlessness. Eliza Snow's shortening of "Tuesday, March 3rd," to "tu 3d," and "miles" to "m.s" will soon become familiar to readers—her abbreviations remain as she wrote them. Where contemporary usage required an apostrophe, Eliza used a period, as in Bm.s for Brigham's. This we retain. Her quotation marks, however, appear generally directly above a comma or period, a placing impossible to duplicate with contemporary technology. These we have standardized. Her dashes—Eliza used them frequently—provide a sense of thoughts not quite ordered, a flow not quite in control. Eliza Snow's diary jottings are, after all, not prose compositions; the difference between them and her more finished autobiographical sketch is made more readily apparent by the transcription's adherence as much as possible to the handwritten manuscript—how it "looks."

A most difficult problem in preparing vernacular writings for an audience unfamiliar with the context is the identification of proper names. In Eliza Snow's two tiny trail diaries, for example, where time and available space were limited, this problem is pronounced, even when the transcriber is familiar with most of the people named. Editors in the past have guessed, sometimes in error, whom Eliza meant by "E," or "S.M.K," or "br. N" in a given context. Rather than identify these references each time, even when I feel certain, I have provided a register of names in which the identifiable people are noted, their abbreviations listed, and some details about them provided. The index provides the actual pages on which their names appear.

While some background material is provided in the endnotes to each chapter, there has been no attempt to summarize the entire history of the times of which the author wrote. There is purpose in such paucity of textual explanation: we present this series with the intent that, in this reading, the focus be upon the writer herself and her intimate circle. As Laurel Thatcher Ulrich invited, presenting diarist Martha Ballard to the reading public, "Opening a diary for the first time is like walking into a room full of strangers. The reader is advised to enjoy the company without trying to remember every name."[2] The people most significant to our diarist, and therefore to our readers, will soon become known. It is our intent here to provide in the introduction and notes sufficient background of people, places, and events for most practical purposes, and to let readers gradually acquaint themselves with the diarist and her world.

Introduction

The Life Writings of
Ordinary Women

"AND NOW THAT I HAVE WRITTEN this long disconnected rambling remembrance of the past," wrote Mormon pioneer Margaret Judd Clawson in the late nineteenth century, "I Scarsly know what to do with it For who Can be interested in the little things of [the] Common, everyday life of another?"[1] It would appear from the recently increasing publication of just such life writings—the autobiographies, diaries, and letters of ordinary women—that a great many people can be interested in the everyday life of another.

Since the nascence in the 1960s of the study of women's history, historians have unearthed hundreds of women's personal manuscripts, often valuing them for the richness of their details, their "little things." From just such "rambling reminiscences" as those of Margaret Clawson we have been able to extract details which, analyzed and synthesized, help us to construct and amplify the history of the frontier past, and of women's past.

As I have worked with archive collections abstracting an overall picture, though, I realized that my own excitement was not in the generalizations I could draw but in the glimpses I had of each particular life I was reading. Something in the handwritten, sometimes pencilled, often rough, misspelled, and unpunctuated account each woman gave of herself drew me in and held me fast. The gathered data became a by-product of what was now to me a much more satisfying focus: a search for the life writings of ordinary women, frontier women, Mormon women, and a view that such writings constitute a literary genre of their own.

Some of the manuscripts defy analysis by any of the criteria by which I was taught to recognize good writing. Simple sentences, run-on sentences, or sentence fragments appear frequently. So too interjections, dangling modifiers, and common expressions characteristic

xiii

of the spoken language, often spelled as they were pronounced. But at times these naive writings have the same power to move me that I find in a Hopkins sonnet or a John Donne sermon. The literary canon must expand to allow them place.

These manuscripts are the explication of those parts of a woman's life which she chose to tell, in a way which suited her telling. Their form is as idiosyncratic as their content. They are frequently fragmentary, and are often inaccurate. Daily accounts and letters are short-sighted, while autobiographies telescope events and often sweep over or confuse details. Diaries and journals can reveal circumstances often overlooked, events having little importance in the larger society, people whose names history has lost. Puzzling through their interlacing of domestic and community life can be as engrossing as reading a mystery, as rewarding as completing an acrostic, . . . with the difference that these texts are real. Their subjects lived; the events occurred.

However, for all their simplicity and honesty, the life narratives of women are very incomplete representations—we see only traces. Yet that is surely part of their appeal: the intimation of the complexity of real life which connects the bits we see. For how, from writing which is at best only conditionally referential and is subject to a great play of meaning, can one recreate a life? a year? a day? Some have seen a further difficulty occasioned by gender: a woman having as literary models those works created mainly by men, about men's lives, in a society dominated by male values. Despite the fact that the first extant autobiography in English was written by a woman, the genre has been essentially male: Augustine, Goethe, Rousseau, Bunyan, Franklin. Even that noble first, *The Book of Margery Kempe,* written in about 1450, lay undiscovered until the mid-twentieth century.

Two centuries after Kempe, Margaret Cavendish, duchess of Newcastle, penned "A True Relation of My Birth, Breeding and Life" as an appendage to her much longer biography of her husband. In her story, anticipating the criticism of her peers in seventeenth-century England, she asked the rhetorical question, "Why hath this lady writ her own life?" But the question was real—in publishing her autobiography, Lady Cavendish was exploring largely unknown territory. "I hope my readers will not think me vain for writing my life," she began, adding that of herself "none care to know whose daughter she was or whose wife she is, or how she was bred, or what fortunes she had, or how she lived, or what humour or disposition she was of." Margaret's hope for her text was that it both reveal and preserve her identity, "lest after-ages should mistake in not knowing I was daughter to one Master Lucas of St. Johns, near Colchester, in Essex, second wife to the Lord Marquis of Newcastle; for my Lord having had two wives, I might easily have been mistaken, especially if I should die and my Lord marry again."[2]

Lady Cavendish was right. Historically she had no individuality separate from that of her father and her husband, and the existence of other daughters and other wives might obscure from memory her very being. "Ultimately," writes critic Sidonie Smith, "the issue is one of identity versus anonymity. Cavendish is writing for her very life."[3]

Later women autobiographers likewise struggled to justify their efforts at life writing. "Who Can be interested?" apologized Margaret Clawson. "It has been a passtime and pleasure to me recalling the little incidents, And occurrences of the long ago, And this is my only excuse for these lengthy reminiscences."[4] Few, at the time, seemed to be interested, discouraging some from writing, while much of the work of others who did was neglected and lost to posterity. It should not surprise us, then, that in Davis Bitton's *Guide to Mormon Diaries,* a listing of over three thousand diaries and autobiographies of the American West, the ratio of women's to men's life writings in Utah repositories is about one in ten—a discrepancy, I suggest, created as much by our failure to value and preserve women's life writings as by their failure to write.[5]

Fortunately, however, our manuscript collections do contain some writings of ordinary women of our recent past. Local repositories, state historical societies, and church and university archives frequently have such gems packed away in fiberdex boxes, often untouched from year to year. And other narratives emerge from time to time from trunks and boxes in attics and cellars where families have kept them, not knowing what treasures they are. These are not works written for publication by famous women; they are daily jottings of mothers, wives, daughters, or they are attempts of mature women to set their lives in order, to explain themselves—not to the world, as the great and famous ones might—but to their children and to their children's children in the Puritan tradition of testimony bearing and lasting testament. In loose sheets or bound notebooks, they are as imperfect as the lives they represent, as incomplete as a peek through a keyhole.

As we broaden the literary canon to include these texts, we face certain questions. How do we then approach them critically? What principles can guide our reading? What expectations should we bring to these private pieces?

First there is the question of genre. For diaries and journals differ from autobiographies, memoirs, or reminiscences—and both differ from letters or recorded conversations. Let me use a homely image to illustrate some of the distinctions. Mary White was one of the West Texas quiltmakers interviewed by Patricia Cooper and Norma Bradley Buferd for their 1978 book *The Quilters.* For Mary, quilting was a way to see a woman's life:

> You can't always change things. Sometimes you don't have no control over the way things go. Hail ruins the crops, or fire burns you out. And then you're given so much to work with in a life and you have to do the best you can with what you've got. That's what piecing is. The materials is passed on to you or is all you can afford to buy . . . that's what's given to you. Your fate. But the way you put them together is your business. You can put them in any order you like.'[6]

The image works as well to explain the writing of a life as its living. Each recorded moment, each diary entry, is a piece saved from the fabric of a woman's day. Ragged, incomplete, misshapen—only its color and its pattern are left to show how it fits with its mates. A diary or a journal can be seen as a jumble of unconnected pieces tossed together into a box and pushed under the bed.

Having survived the greater demands of her life, a woman might in her later years pull out her box of swatches and arrange them into a full quilt top. "You can put them in any order you like," as Mary White said. A woman could now create a work in which every piece connected artistically and permanently to its neighbor and every block had its partner; emergent patterns become fixed, each piece part of the whole. Each piece that the collector still liked, that is, or would acknowledge as hers. That is an autobiography. Its intricacy or simplicity tells more about the woman at the time of its quilting than it does of the parts at the time of their origin. It uses the stuff of the past as raw material out of which the present is ordered and represented.

Take Annie Clark Tanner, for example. Under the title *A Mormon Mother,* her autobiography was edited and published by her son Obert in 1969.[7] In it, from first to last, we have a later account of the child Annie growing up, the girl Annie attending Brigham Young Academy, the young woman Annie marrying into polygamy, the mother Annie rearing her children alone in Farmington, Utah. Each part is cut to shape and placed in the whole to reveal the mature, reflecting Annie and her present view of the meaning of the events of her life. In composing the autobiography, Annie drew on her diaries and letters, which, her son later told me, were afterwards destroyed. What she left, her autobiography, is her recreation of her life as she wanted her children and others to perceive it (for in encouraging her to write Obert must have suggested the possibility of publication).

What we might have had for Annie, diary accounts of events as they happened, we do have for Rhoda Dykes Burgess, whose diary as typed by her granddaughter recently came to hand. Begin anywhere—it hardly matters. Try 15 January 1882, Pine Valley, Utah.

> It is snowing very hard today   there has been no meeting nor Sunday School   most of the men are away at work   I am not well today   Eliza has been writing   the young folks are having a sleigh ride   oh how I miss my Dear Mother when I am sick. . . Aunt Amanda . . . came and spent the evening with us.[8]

Patch after patch, the quilt pieces jumble into Rhoda's box. Life. Raw life. Day by tedious day. "I have been piecing a flannel quilt and tearing carpet rags all day." The fabric of a woman's life.

Eliza Roxcy Snow left both a brief autobiography and occasional diaries. The contrast between the two is characteristic. The "Sketch of My Life" is a carefully crafted gloss over some seventy years of its author's life. At the time of its writing, the 1870s, Snow was queen among Mormon women. Wife of Brigham Young, president of the women's Relief Society comprising nearly three hundred chapters, published poet and author, she felt herself, with some justification, to be a role model for her peers and their daughters. Her story is shaped to their needs, her virtues those they might well emulate, her vices the little peccadillos of youth easily forgiven. But a second agenda also underlies the story: the work will be published in New York, to an audience critical of Mormons, most especially of their practice of polygamy. Her account of her 1842 marriage to Joseph Smith, for example, is carefully presented in the light of the prejudices she imagines her readers to espouse, prejudices she herself had initially held, and her witness of the spirit by which she overcame them. At the time of writing, her account was tailored to fit both audiences. When, however, the "Sketch" was edited for serial publication to a Mormon audience in the 1940s, when Latter-day Saints were putting on an acceptable American face, the whole section on her plural marriage significantly was omitted.[9]

In contrast, the diary account of Eliza's plural marriage from the Nauvoo 1842–44 journal reveals more about its times than about the event itself. Secrecy was essential at the time because of the threat of persecution, so no direct mention of the ceremony or its participants was appropriate. Far different from the reasoned statement of the autobiography, the diary entry recording the marriage is jumbled, its meanings obscured, the whole lurching through a confused allusion to living arrangements to an impassioned metaphor of a rain storm, and concluding in a statement of faith which seems more a plea for succor than a convincing affirmation. It bears no resemblance to the account composed thirty years later for the autobiography. It would seem that in life writings truth is a matter of purpose and point of view.

Personal texts thus are the fictions we create in order to make our lives acceptable to ourselves and our imagined readers. Our memories are often flawed and distorted, as people discover when they share their version of a particular event with that of a sibling or a spouse. In addition, by omissions, by evasions, or by outright untruths we reshape events to our liking. "I don't remember why I was lying here," observed a young friend on reading her own teenage diary, "but I know this is a lie." Within every text, I believe, is imbedded a deeper truth, a reality the researcher may try to reconstruct.

"While there's nobody here but Eliza and I," ends one of the few personal poems of Eliza Roxcy Snow. One would hope to glimpse both the external "Eliza" and the intimate "I" in her diaries, in her verses, and in her autobiographical reflection. The public Eliza R. Snow, later familiarized as "Sister Eliza" or "Aunt Eliza," never just "Eliza," and more often formalized as "Sister Snow," lives in Mormon history as the most significant woman of its past. The "I," the inner woman, remains in relative obscurity, hidden intentionally under the coverings of a propriety which protected Eliza from the curious, the antagonistic, even from her friends, and, in large part, from us. Only rarely does a phrase or entry reveal the soul so determined on its own concealment.

Diaries, those personal accounts in which many writers reveal themselves to themselves and to intimate others, were to Eliza Snow historical documents. She seldom used them as outlets for her inner struggles, and then usually only in veiled prose or bits of verse to be deciphered at great risk of misinterpretation. It is almost as though Eliza were consciously concealing her "I" even from herself, as though she feared the revelation would show her somehow other than she expected herself to be. And yet that inner "I" must occasionally out.

There are those bits of overlap, those junctures where "Eliza" and "I" meet and interact. Perhaps they were troublesome or perplexing to Eliza Snow. Perhaps she could in the end no longer distinguish between the "Eliza" and the "I." Neither, usually, can we.

The separation of the "Eliza" and the "I" is not unusual. Consciously or unconsciously, all life writers make choices between the self revealed and the self concealed. Certainly Eliza Snow intended to tell the truth, though she must have been conscious that she would not tell "the whole truth." We can but guess at the event which drew from her pen the sad complaint: "Alas! that Saints of God can be so full of selfishness as to sacrifice the source of others' happiness to gratify their own enthusiastic notions." Only the "I" could fill between the lines, though the reader perhaps can intuit the depth of some nameless hurt inflicted upon Eliza.

The idea that the whole truth can be told is itself a fiction. In the attempt to re-create the past, the writer selects only those bits which seem to fit a particular audience, a specific occasion, a definite purpose, a significant moment. Each recounting of the same event may well be different. So it is, for instance, that when Eliza recorded in her 1848 Utah diary that frost threatens the grain and the crickets are devouring the crops, there was no mention of seagulls, and no talk of miracles. Twenty-eight years later, she retold the story with the familiar trappings of the miracle every Mormon child learns: crickets, seagulls, divine intervention, and all. To Eliza Snow and much of her audience there was no ultimate discrepancy here, no falsifying of the earlier account. Rather, time had lent a new perspective, and the unspoken fear of destruction in 1848 had become in 1874 an assurance that God does indeed protect His people.

We all wish to control the view others have of us. Frequently we omit from our manuscripts those details which contradict the persona we are trying to present. Some diaries and autobiographies come down to us with pages missing, bits excised with scissors or a razor blade, words or names crossed out. Spaces. Silences. The most interesting part of the autobiographical record can be what is left out, and why. Perhaps certain details reflected ill on another person; perhaps they spoke a truth which could be damaging to family, friends, church; perhaps they simply compromised the self the writer wished to portray. Women, for example, have been known not only to suppress parts of their records but to destroy the entire record.

More often, what happens in a woman's world seems to her simply too mundane, too routine, too insignificant to warrant mention, let alone preservation. The "dailiness" of a woman's life, Laurel Ulrich calls it: the ongoing "woman's work" which creates the core around which the household members build their lives, the "little things" Margaret Clawson deemed of no interest.[10]

Quilts, embroideries, tapestries, fabrics of women's lives are these personal narratives. They may be loosely woven, or still on the loom, bobbins dangling, colors yet to be interwoven; or they may be tightly bound and neatly finished, ends tucked in, seams hidden. They are unique as the minds that conceived them, the hands that made them. They warm us, elicit our sympathy, delight our sensibilities, evoke our admiration.

And so with Eliza Roxcy Snow. Her life writings here reproduced are likewise varied: the tentative Nauvoo diary, blending the chronicler's narrative with the confessional utterance; the cryptic plains journals; the neat and finished "Sketch of My Life." The same life, seen from differing points of view. The "Eliza" and the "I" interwoven. They do not present a finished portrait or even a gracious and candid interview. They give us close-ups, details, as when a student of art focuses on one small section of a masterwork. They do furnish enough, however, for yet another approach to that woman whose life experience finds echoes in our own.

Chapter 1

"My Variegated Life"
The "Sketch of My Life"

THE GENESIS OF ELIZA ROXCY SNOW'S "Sketch of My Life" lies in the strange and extended interweaving of three lives: Eliza's own, that of British author Edward Tullidge, and that of English convert Fanny Warn Stenhouse.

Eliza first learned of young Jersey-born Fanny presumably through letters from Eliza's brother Lorenzo, serving in the early 1850s as European mission president of the Church of Jesus Christ of Latter-day Saints. Snow had persuaded a charismatic young Scot, Thomas Stenhouse, to leave his bride of four months in England in the care of the Southampton Latter-day Saints and to accompany him to Italy. An ardent missionary, Stenhouse agreed. Fanny, already pregnant, concurred, "although," she later wrote, "I thought that my very heart would break."[1] The local Saints, most of whom Stenhouse had converted, wept as their young leader left them. He arrived in Geneva in June 1850 and began his labors among the French-speaking Swiss.[2]

In December Fanny bore their daughter. Mother and child were living in cold, hunger, and loneliness, the Saints having neglected their duties to her, when Lorenzo Snow returned the following spring. "On his arrival," Fanny wrote, "he came directly to my house. He seemed much shocked to see the change in my appearance." Snow called young Stenhouse home, and then in June dispatched the couple to Geneva where, with Fanny's facility in French, the two could labor more effectively as missionaries.

Lorenzo Snow must have kept his sister Eliza apprised of these events, for she wrote and later published a poem, "To Mrs. Stenhouse, Switzerland." In the rhetoric of the faith she sympathized with the young woman, promising her "Grace according to your day," and, commensurate with her faithfulness, "Wreaths of honor, crowns of

1

glory, / Robes of pure, celestial white." It would be nine years before the two women actually met.

Finishing their missions in Switzerland and later in New York, the Stenhouses finally gathered to the center of Zion in Salt Lake City, Utah. Bright, attractive, and devout as they were, Fanny and "T.B.H.," as he came to be called, quickly rose to the top of Salt Lake City society. In 1867 their daughter Clara married Brigham Young's oldest son, and by 1868 T.B.H. was editor of Young's newspaper, the *Salt Lake Telegraph*, and betrothed in plural marriage to one of the most popular of Young's daughters.

Eliza R. Snow also had arrived at a position of prominence in Mormon society. In 1842, just before she was married in polygamy to Joseph Smith, the founding prophet of Mormonism, she had become an officer in the church's Female Relief Society of Nauvoo. Four months after Joseph Smith's death, she wed his successor Brigham Young, under whose direction she arrived in the Salt Lake Valley in 1847. From its completion in 1856 to her death, Eliza resided in the Lion House as chief among Young's plural wives. In 1866 Young called her to reestablish the Relief Society in the intermountain Mormon communities and to preside over the women of the church. She was the obvious choice; her co-religionists knew her not only as "Zion's poetess," the title Joseph Smith had given her, but also by the 1870s as "priestess" and "prophetess" for her ministry of ordinances and blessings in the Endowment House, forerunner of the temple, and as "presidentess" for her role in the Relief Society. In the meantime, Fanny, with her English accent and facility in French, often found herself official hostess and guide to educated and influential visitors to Utah. Eliza as the dignified matron and Fanny as the cultured young lady were the prize and pride of Utah society.

Enter Edward W. Tullidge, an English journalist praised in the Utah press as "one of the most gifted literary men of America."[3] Enigmatic, mercurial, individualistic, he would later introduce himself to New York readers of his biography of Brigham Young as "an apostate," but in Utah he considered himself one among the Saints. Siding first with Brigham Young, then with the Godbeite faction of economic and theological reformers, Tullidge admired Mormonism's social order while doubting its doctrinal singularity. His Mormon associates, among them Eliza Snow, remained surprisingly loyal to their inconstant friend, forgiving him his lapses, perhaps in deference to his literary gifts.

A good friend of the Stenhouses, Tullidge enticed them into the liberal Godbe-Harrison circle. At about the same time, Zina Young declined T.B.H.'s suit of marriage and her father Brigham packed Stenhouse off to Ogden to relocate his newspaper there. The Stenhouses' allegiance wavered, and in 1870 the couple moved to New York.[4]

Bitter about her life in Mormonism, and especially about what she now saw as outrages perpetrated on women by polygamy, Fanny wrote the first draft of her autobiography, published variously as *An Exposé of Mormon Polygamy*, and *A Lady's Life Among the Mormons*. She toured with the book, lecturing against Mormonism and its leaders.[5] Encouraged by the book's success, she enlarged her small volume into what became, with a foreword by Harriet Beecher Stowe, *"Tell It All": The Story of a Life Experience in Mormonism*, long a best-seller on the national market. Her intent was less to defame the Mormon people than to vilify their leaders, but the effect on Mormon women was devastating.

Whether Eliza R. Snow, as president of the Relief Society, approached Tullidge, or whether he, fresh from his success with the Brigham Young biography approached her, it was agreed between them that she would use her influence to support a book he would write as a "set-off to Sister Stenhouse's."[6] They were strange comrades-in-arms—the rock-solid Snow and the unpredictable Tullidge. Whether she trusted his allegiance to the Mormon Church or not, she obviously felt that his approbation of Mormon women gave them common cause enough. He envisioned a slim book of 150 pages; she had typically grander ambitions. Their collaboration was a success by all counts, and *The Women of Mormondom* appeared in New York in 1877. It was a 552-page compilation of the simply written life accounts of some forty Mormon women, woven together by the ostentatious Victorian prose of the author/editor.

It was for that project that Eliza Snow composed the first draft of her "Sketch of My Life," reprinted here in a later form. Tullidge cut-and-pasted Eliza's original memoir for use in his book, so the version printed there is incomplete, though enough crossover exists to identify it as the ur-text of the extant "Sketch."

The handwritten text from which her story is reproduced here is of later derivation. In the early 1880s came unbidden another opportunity for the Saints, eager to offset continuing bad press, to tell their story. Ambitious historian Hubert Howe Bancroft proposed to spearhead the research and writing of a series of histories of the western territories. He enlisted the support of Mormon leaders for the volume on Utah. The Mormon church presidency assigned Apostle Franklin D. Richards the task, and he recruited his wife Jane Snyder, a Relief Society leader, to encourage women to submit their stories. Eliza R. Snow was quite likely the first one Jane Snyder Richards approached. Fortunately Eliza had a text already written: a quick revision and updating of the Tullidge manuscript would serve. Eliza's forty-page sketch, neatly copied on lined foolscap, resides now among its sister stories in the Bancroft Library in Berkeley, California.

For reasons of her own, probably as simple as lack of time and energy—she was by now in her eightieth year and still traveling extensively as Relief Society president—Eliza cut several long sections from the Tullidge draft for the Bancroft manuscript. Because of the additional details they provide, I have included the most significant of these in indented sections in the narrative. Other excerpts from the Tullidge book deemed interesting but less important are added as notes.

The handwritten text is transcribed here without emendation. Eliza wrote carefully, seldom erring in grammar or spelling. Her second audience was much like her first: American readers unfamiliar with Mormonism and Mormons, or predisposed to scorn their practices. Selecting purposefully, she related those parts of her life experience calculated to invoke sympathy for the Saints, to justify their doctrines, and to defend their actions.

The times also helped determine the pro-polygamy slant Eliza put on her words. As she wrote her first draft for Tullidge, as well as when she revised it for Bancroft, federal officers armed with ever more rigorous legislation were mounting increasingly zealous campaigns against the practice. Eliza and her sisters in the church hoped their stories, simply and honestly told, would win public support for what they considered their constitutional right to contract plural marriages and live in "the principle."

Eliza's conflict between her allegiance to the U.S. Constitution and her sense of betrayal by the government which had refused to protect her people is apparent throughout her essay. "A born patriot," she mourned what she perceived as the "stained escutcheon" —the flag dishonored by the treatment of the Saints at the hands of their enemies. An agenda apparent in both drafts of the "Sketch" is Eliza's desire to show herself, and by implication her sisters, as genteel, well-spoken, educated daughters of Puritan foremothers and revolutionary forefathers. Her self-portrayal modestly affirmed what her life work demonstrated: Mormon women were every whit as talented, as able, as diligent, and as politically astute as their Eastern counterparts. And probably more so, one reads in whispers between the lines.

The Eliza of the "Sketch of My Life" is well aware of her worth. Her story did not need to tout her fame; it could rather simply relate her accomplishments: her presidency of the Relief Society, her publications, her mission abroad, and her parts in the children's Primary Association, the Woman's Commission Store, and the Deseret Hospital. In her retelling, the woman herself seems to be swallowed up in her accomplishments, a victim of her own abilities. The human Eliza is lost; in her place we have mainly a collection of roles. Although she seems at the first of the sketch a living, seeking, accepting person, by the end she appears a vast, efficient business machine, polite and intelligent, but remote and unapproachable. The stereotype is hard to crack.

The "Sketch of My Life" looks back with modest pride over a life well lived. Written well after the events it related, it remembers no more the ladder of loneliness, fear, self-doubt, and insecurity by which its author ascended. So is it with reminiscences—they use the past as a camera through which to depict the present. We here read Eliza Snow as what she believed she became, not as how she became it; we begin, as it were, at the end—a good place to begin if we wish to witness with understanding the becoming.

Sketch of My Life

I was born in Becket, Berkshire Co., Mass. Jan. 21, 1804.

My parents were of English descent—their ancestors were among the earliest settlers of New England. My father, Oliver Snow, was a native of Massachusetts—my mother, Rosetta L. Pettibone, of Connecticut.[1]

In my early childhood, my parents moved to that section of the State of Ohio bordering on Lake Erie on the North, and the State of Pennsylvania on the East, known as the "Connecticut Western Reserve"; where they purchased land, and settled in Mantua, Portage County.[2]

I am the second of seven children—four daughters and seven sons:[3] all of whom were strictly disciplined to habits of temperance, honesty, and industry; and our parents extended to us the best educational facilities attainable at that time, without preference to either sex.

Although a farmer by occupation, my father performed much public business—officiating in several responsible positions and, as I was ten years the senior of my eldest brother, so soon as I was competent, he employed me as Secretary in his Office.[4] This experience has proved of great benefit to myself and to others, at different periods of my variegated life.

Whether my mother anticipated or originated the wise policy of Queen Victoria, concerning the training of girls, does not matter—at all events, my mother considered a practical knowledge of housekeeping the best, and most efficient foundation on which to build a magnific<e>nt structure of womanly accomplishments—that useful knowledge was the most reliable basis of independence. Hence ~~my sisters~~ <her> daughters were early trained to the kitchen and housekeeping in general; then to various kinds of needlework <u>etc</u>. Two years in succession, I drew the prize awarded by the Committee on Manufactures, at the Portage County Fair, for the best manufactured Leghorn.[5]

My parents carefully imprest on the minds of their children, that useful labor is honorable—idleness and waste of time disgraceful and sinful; and, with us, book-studies and schooling were ever present—intermingling with every other industry, not omitting music and singing: Thus we never knew what it was to be idle. I mention these items as constituting a key to ~~to~~ my subsequent life, showing that the impressions made in childhood and youth give indelible stamp to character.

My apparently inherent fondness for reading was encouraged by my parents. I was partial to poetical works, and when very young frequently made attempts at imitations of the different styles of favorite authors. In school I often bothered my teachers by writing my dissertations in rhyme, thereby forcing <from them> acknowledgments of inability to correct my articles, through lack of poetical talent; and yet, my teachers were uniformly too indulgent to protest against my rhyming practice.

On one occasion, my versatility occasioned me intense mortification. I was a small girl in a "Grammatical Institution" of young gentlemen and ladies, taught by a Presbyterian clergyman.[6] Up to this time, the Professor had uniformly read before the school, the compositions written by the students; but it so happened that a change was to commence that very day, and each student must read his and her own production. Unfortunately for me, without surmising any change, I had indulged my mirthfulness in a humorous poetical article, written in a peculiar measure, which I copied from a war-song in one of the periodicals of the day—the extreme oddity of the measure rendered the article so exceeding amusing, I was well aware that it would create laughter among the students, and I should break down if I attempted to read it. I could have listened composedly had the Prof. read as I anticipated; but for me to read it before that audience! How could I? I tearfully told the Prof. I could not. But an equitable law must not be sacrificed to my timidity, and the Prof. compassionately helped me out of the dillemma by proposing to excuse me for the present, provided I would come the next morning, before the students assembled, and read it to him; to which I responded with all promptitude.

When quite young, I commenced writing for publication in various Journals, which I continued for several years, over assumed signatures—wishing to be useful as a writer, and unknown as an author.

During the ever memorable contest between Greece and Turkey, I watched, with deep interest, the events of the war, and after the terrible destruction, by the Turks, of Missolonghi, I wrote an article enti-

tled "The fall of Missolonghi."[7] <Soon> after its publication, the
deaths of Adams and Jefferson, almost simultaneously occurred, on
the Fourth of July, just at the time when, in honor of the glorious day,
the nation was chanting songs of Liberty. I was requested, through
the Press, to write their requiem, to which I responded, and, to my
regret found myself ushered into conspicuity; and not long after,
eight volumes of "Godey's Lady's Book" were awarded me for a first
prize poem published in one of the Journals.[8]

That "men are born poets" is a common adage—I was born a patriot—at least, a warm feeling of patriotism inspired my thoughts as
evinced in many of the early productions of my pen. I can even now
recollect how, with beating pulse and with fond emotion I listened,
when but a small child, to narratives of the Revolution. My Grand-
father on my mother's side, when fighting for the freedom of his
country, was taken prisoner, and confined in a dreary cell, and so
scantily fed, that when a fellow prisoner, incarcerated with him, died
from exhaustion, he reported him sick, in order to obtain the usual
amount furnished for both—keeping him wrapped in his blanket as
long as he dared to remain with a dead body. This with many other
incidents of revolutionary sufferings recounted by my grand parents,
so deeply impressed my mind, that, as I grew up to womanhood, I
fondly cherished a pride for the Flag which so proudly waved o'er
the graves of my brave and valiant ancestors.[9]

My parents were Baptists in their religious profession—free from
bigotry and intolerance, their hospitality was proverbial, and their
house a welcome resort for the honorable of all denominations. As a
natural result, my acquaintance became extensive.

I was early taught to respect the Bible, and in Sabbath-Schools re-
cited much of the New-Testament—at times reciting seven of the
long chapters in the Gospels, at a lesson. When studying the<se> interesting narratives, my mind, many times, was filled with reflections
of the deepest type, and my heart yearned for the gifts and manifestations of which those ancient Apostles testified. Sometimes I wished
I had lived when Jesus Christ was on the earth, that I might have witnessed the power of God manifested through the Gospel; or that I
could see, and listen to a true Prophet of God, through whom He
communicated His will to the children of men. But, alas! that day
and those blessings had forever gone by! So said the clergy of my own
time, and the clergy <u>professed to know</u>.[10]

Although my parents adhered to the Baptist creed, they extended to their children the right, and afforded us every opportunity we desired, to examine all creeds—to hear and judge—to "prove all things." Through being conversant with priests and people of different sects, I found them widely differing from each other; and all, more widely differing from that "form of doctrine," and practice described in the New Testament, with the writings in which, I grew more and more familiar year by year.

Feeling that religion was necesssary, I sought for it; but, when I asked, like one of old, "What shall I do to be saved?" and was told that I must have a change of heart, and, to obtain it, I must feel myself to be the worst of sinners, and acknowledge the justice of God in consigning me to everlasting torment, the common-sense with which God had endow<ed me,> revolted, for I knew I had lived a virtuous and consciencious life, and no consideration could extort from me a confession so absurd. Some told me one thing and some another; but there was no Peter, "endowed from on high."

I heard Alexander Cambell advocate the literal meaning of the Scriptures—listened to him with deep interest—hoped his new light led to a fulness—was baptized, and soon learned that, as well they might, he and his followers disclaimed all authority, and my baptism was of no consequence. During my brief attachment to that church I was deeply interested in the study of the ancient Prophets, in which I was assisted by the erudite A. Cambell, Walter Scott whose acquaintance I made, but more particularly Sidney Rigdon who was a frequent visitor at my father's house.[11]

In the autumn of 1839 [*either* 1829 *or* 1830] I heard of Joseph Smith as a Prophet to whom the Lord was speaking from the heavens; and that a sacred ~~history~~ Record containing a history of the origin of the aborigines of America, was unearthed. A Prophet of God—the voice of God revealing to man as in former dispensations, was what my soul had hungered for, but could it possibly be true—I considered it a hoax—too good to be true.[12]

In the winter of 1830 and 31,[13] Joseph Smith called at my father's, and as he sat warming himself, I scrutinized his face as closely as I could without attracting his attention, and decided that his was an honest face. My <adopted> motto, "<u>prove all things and hold fast that which is good</u>," prompted me to investigation, as incredulous as I was; and the most impressive testimonies I had ever heard were given by two of the witnesses to the Book of Mormon, at the first meeting of the believers in Joseph Smith's mission, which I attended.[14]

Early in the spring of 1835, my eldest sister, who, with my mother was baptized in 1831, by the prophet, returned home from a visit to the saints in Kirtland, and reported of the faith and humility of those who had received the gospel as taught by Joseph,—the progress of the work, the order of the organization of the priesthood and the frequent manifestations of the power of God.

The spirit bore witness to me of the truth. I felt that I had waited already a little too long to see whether the work was going to 'flash in the pan' and go out. But my heart was now fixed; and I was baptized on the 5th of April, 1835. From that day to this I have not doubted the truth of the work.[15]

On the 5th of April, 1835, I was baptized by a "Mormon" Elder, and <in> the evening of that day, I realized the baptism of the Spirit as sensibly as I did that of the water in the stream. I had retired to bed, and as I was reflecting on the wonderful events transpiring around me, I felt an indescrible, tangable sensation, if I may so call it, commencing at my head and enveloping my person and passing off at my feet, producing inexpressible happiness. Immediately following, I saw a beautiful candle with an unusual long, <bright> blaze directly over my feet. I sought to know the interpretation, and received the following, "<u>The lamp of intelligence shall be lighted over your path</u>." I was satisfied.[16]

In December I went to Kirtland—was happy in an association with the Saints, fully appreciating their enlarged views and rich intelligence from the fountain of Eternal Truth, through the inspiration of the Most High; and was present on the ever memorable occasion of the Dedication of the Kirtland Temple, <(the building of which was commenced in June 1833, and completed in 1836)> the first superstructure erected by command of God, and under His immediate direction, for many centuries. In that Temple, after its dedication, I witnessed many manifestations of the power of God.[17]

In the Spring of 1836, I taught a select school for young ladies, and boarded with the Prophet's family: at the close of the term I returned to my parental home, where friends and acquaintances flocked around me to enquire about the "strange people" with whom I was associated. I was exceedingly happy in testifying of what I had both <u>seen and heard</u>, until the 1st of Jan. 1837, when I bade a final adieu to the home of my youth, to share the fortunes of the people of God.

By solicitation, on my return I resided in the family of Joseph Smith, and taught his family school, and had ample opportunity to mark his "daily walk and conversation," as a prophet of God; and the more I became acquainted with him, the more I appreciated him as such. His lips ever flowed with instruction and kindness; and, although very forgiving, indulgent, and affectionate in his temperament, when his God-like intuition suggested that the welfare of his brethren, or the interests of the kingdom of God demanded it; no fear of censure—no love of approbation could prevent his severe and cutting rebuke.

Though his expansive mind grasped the great plan of salvation and solved the mystic problem of man's destiny—though he had in <his> possession ~~of~~ keys that unlocked the past and <the> future with its succession of eternities; in his devotions he was humble as a little child.[18]

Previous to the completion of the Temple, I proffered a Cash donation to the "Building Committee," which they very much needed, but insisted on my acceptance of a note of hand for the amt. This, they subsequently redeemed by deeding to me a valuable <city> Lot, very favorably situated under good cultivation—containing a house which accommodated two families: one part opportunely made a home for a widowed sister with two children—the other, I rented. This, like many other trivial events in human life, proved to be one of the little hinges on which events of immense weight occasionally turn.[19]

My Brother Lorenzo was in a Presbyterian College.[20] From his letters I learned that he was investigating their orthodoxy. At length he wrote me, saying, "If you have nothing better to offer than ~~I find here~~ this, then good bye to all religions". I feared he was approaching the vortex of infidelity, and felt that the only rescue was in the unadulterated Gospel of Jesus Christ; and was anxious to induce him to come where he could see its workings and judge for himself. I wrote him he could have a home with my sister, if he would spend his College vacation with us. He came, and to improve the time, he engaged in study under an efficient Hebrew Teacher, who had opened a school for the benefit of the Saints in Kirtland;[21] and while studying a dead language, he also studied the eternal principles of a living faith. He was baptized—ordained an Elder, and is now one of the Twelve Apostles. Although this belongs to my brother's history, I consider it one of the events of my life, inasmuch as he has been a great benefit to me, as well as having been energetically useful in the Cause which I esteem dearer than my mortal life.[22]

In the Spring of 1838, when through persecution, the Saints were compelled to leave Kirtland; with my father's family I moved to Adam-ondi-Ahman, Daviess Co. Mo., where we arrived on, or about the last of July. But our stay was short—a fierce mob violence, with which all departments of the State authorities, civil, judicial, and military participated, so soon manifested itself, that before the year closed, in submission to the Governor's order, we moved from Daviess Co., to Caldwell; and, on the 5th of March, started enroute for Illinois.[23]

A few days before leaving Adam-ondi-Ahman, the former owner of the house, for which my father had paid in full, came in, and impudently enquired how soon we should be out of it. My American blood warmed to the temperature of an insulted, free-born American citizen, as I looked at him and thought, poor man, you little know with whom you have to deal—God lives. He certainly over-ruled in that instance, for the original owners of two homesteads which my father paid for, although they had made arrangements for mobbing us, previous to the purchase, they never regained possession.

The Governor gave us ten day's notice to prepare and leave Daviess County, and in the mean time, subservient to his order a posse of Militia was to remain in the vicinity, ostensibly to protect the Saints; but we could not decide which was most to be dreaded the Militia or the mob—no property was safe within the reach of either.

It was December and very cold when we left our home,[24] and, after assisting in the morning arrangements for the journey, in order to warm my aching feet, I started on foot and walked until the teams came up. When about two miles out, I met one of the so-called Militia who accosted me with "Well, I think this will cure you of your faith". Looking him squarely in the eye, I replied, "No, Sir, it will take more than this to cure me of my faith." His countenance dropped, and he responded, "I must confess you are a better soldier than I am." I passed on, thinking that, unless he was above the average of his fellows in that section, I was not complimented by his confession.

In recording the following incident, I wish to perpetuate the remembrance of the only expression of sympathy which, to my knowledge, ~~was~~ was uttered by the former citizens of Mo. in our behalf, from the commencement of our persecutions in that State, till our final expulsion. On our outward journey, after a night of rain, which changed to snow and covered the ground in the morning; we thawed our tent which was stiffly frozen, by holding and turning it alternately before a blazing fire, until it could be folded for packing, and, while we all shivered and shook with cold we started. As the sun mounted upwards the snow melted and increased the depth of the mud with which the road before us, was previously amply stocked, and rendered travel almost impossible. The teams were puffing and the wagons dragging so heavily that we were all on foot, tugging along as best we could, when an elderly gentleman on horseback overtook us, and, after riding alongside for some time, apparently absorbed in deep thought, as he (after enquiring who we were) with apparent interest, watched women and ~~children~~ girls, men and boys, teams and wagons slowly wending their way up a long hill, enroute from our only earthly homes, with no prospect before us, he said emphatically, "If I were in your places, I should want the Governor of the State hitched at the head of my teams." I afterwards remarked to my father that I had not heard as sensible remark from a stranger since entering the State. In my memory, from that time to this, I have cherished a filial respect for that gentleman, and fancy I see a striking resemblance of him in the portrait of Sir Von Humbolt, now hanging on the wall in front of me.[25]

We were two days on our way to Far West, and stopped over night at what was called the Half-way House, a log building perhaps twenty feet square, with the chinkings between the logs, minus—they probably having been burned for firewood—the owner of the house, Brother Littlefield, having left with his family to escape being robbed; and the north wind had free ingress through the openings, wide enough for cats to crawl through. This had been the lodging place of the hundreds who had preceded us, and on the present occasion proved the almost shelterless shelter of seventy-five or eighty souls. To say lodging, would be a hoax, although places were allotted to a few aged and feeble, to lie down, while the rest of us either sat or stood, or both, all night. My sister and I managed so that mother lay down, and we sat by (on the floor, of course), to prevent her being trampled on, for the crowd was such that people were hardly responsible for their movements.

It was past the middle of December, and the cold was so intense that, in spite of well packing, our food was frozen hard, bread and all, and although a blazing fire was burning on one side of the room, we could not get to it to thaw our suppers, and had to resort to the next expediency which was this: The boys milked, and while one strained the milk, another held the pan (for there was no chance for putting anything down); then, while one held a bowl of the warm milk, another would, as expeditiously as possible, thinly slice the frozen bread into it, and thus we managed for supper. In the morning, we were less crowded, as some started very early, and we toasted our bread and thawed our meat before the fire. But, withal, that was a very merry night. None but saints can be happy under every circumstance. About twenty feet from the house was a shed, in the centre of which the brethren built a roaring fire, around which some of them stood and sang songs and hymns all night, while others parched corn and roasted frosted potatoes, etc. Not a complaint was heard—all were cheerful, and judging from appearances, strangers would have taken us to be pleasure excursionists rather than a band of gubernatorial exiles.

After the mobbing commenced, although my father had purchased, and had on hand, plenty of wheat, he could get none ground, and we were under the necessity of grating corn for our bread on graters made of tin-pails and stove-pipe. I will here insert a few extracts from a long poem I wrote while in Davies county, as follows:

> Twas autumn—Summer's melting breath was gone,
> And Winter's gelid blast was stealing on;
> To meet its dread approach, with anxious care
> The houseless saints were struggling to prepare;
> When round about a desperate mob arose,
> Like tigers waking from a night's repose;
> They came like hordes from nether shades let loose—
> Men without hearts, just fit for Satan's use!
> With wild, demoniac rage they sallied forth,
> Resolved to drive the saints of God from earth.
> Hemm'd in by foes—deprived the use of mill,
> Necessity inspires their patient skill;
> Tin-pails and stove-pipe, from their service torn,
> Are changed to graters to prepare the corn,
> That Nature's wants may barely be supplied—
> They ask no treat, no luxury beside.
> But, where their shelter? Winter hastens fast;
> Can tents and wagons stem this northern blast?

The scene presented in the city of Far West, as we stopped over night on our way to our temporary location, was too important to be omitted, and too sad to narrate. Joseph Smith, and many other prominent men, had been dragged to prison. Their families, having been plundered, were nearly or quite destitute—some living on parched corn, others on boiled wheat; and desolation seemed inscribed on everything but the hearts of the faithful saints. In the midst of affliction, they trusted in God.

After spending the remainder of the winter in the vicinity of Far West, on the 5th of March, 1839, leaving much of our property behind, we started for Illinois.[26]

We arrived in Quincy, Illinois, where many of the exiled Saints had preceded us, and all were received with generous hospitality.

My father moved to one of the northern Counties.[27] I stopped in Quincy, and while there wrote for the Press several articles, for which I received many encomiums, with urgent solicitations for effusions, which, probably were elicited by the fact that my articles were productions from the pen of a "Mormon girl."[28]

From Quincy, my sister, her two daughters and I went to Lima, Hancock Co., where we found a temporary home under the roof of an old veteran of the Revolution, who, with his family, treated us with much kindness; although through ignorance of the character of the Saints, their feelings were like gall towards them, which we knew to be the result of misrepresentation.[29] Occupying as we did, an upper room with a slight flooring between us and the occupants below, we were obliged to hear bitter aspersions against those whom we knew to be the best people on earth. Frequently our host, after vilely traducing our people, of whom he knew nothing, suddenly changed his tone and boasted of the "two noble women" he had in his house—"no better women ever lived" etc., which he would have said of the Mormons" generally, had he made their acquaintance. We were pilgrims, and for the time had to submit to circumstances. Almost anything innocent is preferable to dependence—with these people we could earn our support at the tailoring business: thanks to my mother's industrial training, for which, even now I bless her dear memory.

In May, the Saints commenced gathering in Commerce, (afterwards Nauvoo) and on the 16th of July following, I left our kind host and hostess, much to their regret, Elder Rigdon having sent for me to teach his family school in Commerce, and, although I regretted the separation from my sister, I was truly thankful to be again associated with the body of the Church.[30]

The location of the city of Nauvoo was beautiful, but the climate was so unhealthy that several efforts had been made to build it up; and as many times abandoned. It seemed to have been held in reserve to meet the occasion, for none but Saints full of faith, and trusting in the power of God, could have established that city.[31] Through the blessings of our Heavenly Father on the indefatiguable exertions of the Saints, it was not long before Nauvoo excited the envy and jealousy of many of the adjacent inhabitants, and, as "the accuser of the brethren" never sleeps, we had many difficulties to meet which ultimately culminated in the most bitter persecution.

To narrate what transpired within the seven years, in which we built and occupied Nauvoo, the beautiful, would fill many volumes. That is a history that never will, and never can "repeat itself." Some of the most important events of my life transpired within that brief term, in which I was married, and in which my husband, Joseph Smith, the Prophet of God, sealed his testimony with his blood!

Although in my youth I had considered marriage ordained of God; and without vanity can say, I had what was considered very flattering proposals, I remained single; and why, I could not comprehend at the time. But, when I embraced the fulness of the Gospel, in recalling to mind the events of my past life, I felt, and still feel to acknowledge the kind, overruling hand in the providences of God in that circumstance, as fully as in any other in my mortal existence; I do not know that one of my former suitors have received the Gospel, which shows that I was singularly preserved from the bondage of a marriage tie which would, in all probability, have prevented my receiving, or from the free exercise of the religion which has been, and now is dearer to me than my life.

In Nauvoo I first understood that the practice of plurality was to be introduced into the church. The subject was very repugnant to my feelings—so directly was it in opposition to my educated prepossessions, that it seemed as though all the prejudices of my ancestors for generations past congregated around me. But when I reflected that I was living in the Dispensation of the fulness of times, embracing all other Dispensations, surely Plural Marriage must necessarily be included, and I consoled myself with the idea that it was far in the distance, and beyond the period of my mortal existence. It was not long however, after I received the first intimation, before the announcement reached me that the "set time" had come—that God had commanded His servants to establish the order, by taking additional wives—I knew that God, who had kept silence for centuries, was speaking—I had covenanted in the waters of baptism to live by every word He should communicate, and my heart was firmly set to do His bidding.[32] As I increased in knowledge concerning the principle and design of Plural Marriage, I grew in love with it, and today esteem it a precious, sacred principle—necessary in the elevation and salvation of the human family—in redeeming woman from the curse, and world from corruptions.[33]

I was sealed to the Prophet, Joseph Smith, for time and eternity, in accordance with the <u>Celestial Law of Marriage</u> which God has revealed—the ceremony being performed by a servant of the Most High—authorized to officiate in sacred ordinances. This, one of the most important circumstances of my life, I never have had cause to regret.[34]

From personal knowledge I bear my testimony that Plural Celestial marriage is a pure and holy principle, not only tending to individual purity and elevation of character, but also instrumental in producing a more perfect type of manhood mentally and physically, as well as in restoring human life to its former longevity.

When in March, 1842, Joseph Smith, assisted by some of the leading Elders, organized the "Female Relief Society of Nauvoo," I was present, and was appointed Secretary of the Institution. In the following summer, I accompanied Mrs. Emma Smith, the President, to Quincy, Illinois, with a Petition signed by several hundred members of the Society, praying His Excellency, Governor Carlin, for protection from illegal suits then pending against the Prophet, Joseph Smith. We met with a very cordial reception—presented our petition, which the Governor received with manifestations of sympathetic sincerity, pledging his word and honor that he would use his influence to protect Mr. Smith, whose innocence he fully acknowledged. But alas! soon after our return, we learned that at the time of our visit, and while making protestations of friendship, the wily Governor was secretly conniving with the basest of men to destroy our leaders.[35]

The awful trajedy of the 27th of June 1844 is a livid, burning, scathing stain on our national escutcheon. To look upon the noble, lifeless forms of those brothers, Joseph and Hyrum Smith, lying side by side after having been brought home from Carthage, where they had been slaughtered in their manhood and in their innocence, was a sight that might well appal the heart of a true American citizen: but what it was for loving wives and children, the loyal heart may <u>feel</u>, but let <u>language keep silence</u>![36]

This scene occurred in America, "The land of the free, and the home of the brave," to which our ancestors fled for religious freedom—where the "<u>Dear old Flag</u>" yet waves; and under which not one effort has been made by the authorities of either County, State, or General Government, to bring the perpetrators of that notorious murder to justice. The expulsion of the Saints from the State of Ill. soon followed after the deaths of the Prophet and Patriarch.

On my first arrival in Nauvoo, (then Commerce) I resided in the family of Elder Rigdon—taught his family school—was with his mother (who lived with him) at her death—attended her funeral on the 6th of Oct., the first Conference held in Ill.[37] In the following winter my father came for me—I went home with him—found my mother suffering from hardships and exposures through mobocracy. The next Spring my father moved to La-harpe, 30 ms. from Nauvoo—remained there one year, then moved to Nauvoo. My home was with the family until father exchanged his home for one in Walnut Grove, 75 ms. from Nauvoo; a settlement where a Stake of the church had been apointed. After my parents moved, I lived with the Prophet's first wife, and taught a school of 65 scholars. Before its close, I went and boarded with brother and sister Holmes for a short time, and previous to the exodus of the Saints from Ill. I lived in the family of Col. Stephen Markham. Much of the winter of 1845-6, I spent officiating in the Temple—the upper part of which was sufficiently completed for administering the sacred ordinances of the holy Priesthood as God had revealed them.

On the 13th of Feb. 183<4>6, with sister Markham, I crossed the Mississippi on a ferry-boat, and joined the camp of the Saints, three miles from the river, where we found wood and water in abundance. I was informed that on the first night of the encampment of those who preceded us, nine children were ushered into the world; and from that time, as we journeyed, mothers gave birth to offspring under almost every variety of circumstances except those to which they had been accustomed—in tents and wagons—in rainstorms and in snow-storms. I heard of one birth occurring in the rude shelter of a hut—the sides formed of blankets fastened to poles stuck in the ground—a bark roof, through which the rain was dripping: Kind sisters held dishes and caught the water—thus protecting the mother and her little darling from a shower-bath on its entrance to the stage of human existence. Had not this, as well as many others, been a case of necessity, no other result than death could have been anticipated, to both mother and child.[38]

Let it be remembered that the mothers referred to, were not savages, accustomed to roam the forest and brave the storm and tempest—those who had never known the comforts and delicacies of civilization and refinement. They were not those who, in the wilds of nature, nursed their offspring amid reeds and rushes, or in the obscure recesses of rocky caverns. Most of them were born and educated in the Eastern States—had there embraced the Gospel as taught by Jesus and His Apostles, and for its sake had gathered with the Saints; and under trying circumstances, assisted by their faith, energies and patience in making Nauvoo what its name indicates, "<u>The beautiful</u>." There they had lovely homes—decorated with flowers, and enriched with choice fruit trees, just beginning to yield plentifully. To these homes, without lease or sale, they had bid a final adieu, and, with what little of their substance could be packed into one, two, and perhaps in a few instances, three wagons, had started out desert-ward, for where? To this question, the only response at that time was, <u>God knows</u>.

From the 13th. to the 18th. several snow-storms occurred, and the cold was so intense as to bridge the Mississippi river sufficiently for the passage of heavily loaded wagons. The men built huge fires, and when not necessarily otherwise engaged, warmed themselves around the crackling blaze. The women, when the labors of cooking and other <u>etceteras</u> did not prompt them outside, huddled with their small children, into wagons and carriages for protection from chilling breezes.

My dormitory, sitting-room, writing office, and frequently dining-room, was the buggy in which Mrs. Markham, her little son David, and I rode. With the best I could do for myself, I frosted my feet which occasioned me considerable inconvenience for several weeks.[39]

On the 28th we moved out. Previous to breaking camp, (all who designed traveling in the first company had crossed the river, numbering from six to seven hundred,) they were <partially> organized into tens, fifties, and hundreds, which afterwards completed for the order of traveling; with <Captains,> Pioneers, Superintendents, and Commissioners, to each Hundred, and Captains over each ~~Hundred~~ Fifty, and Ten.

We traveled four miles and put up for the night where the prospect, at first sight was dreary enough. It was nearly sun-set—very cold, with four or five inches of snow on the ground: but with brave hearts, strong hands, and plenty of spades and shovels, the men removed the snow, and suddenly transformed the bleak desert into a joyous town of cloth houses with log-heap fires, and a multitude of cheerful inhabitants. The next day the <Nauvoo> Band came up, and its stirring strains were wafted abroad and re-echoed on the responsive breeze.

From time to time, companies of men either volunteered or were detailed from the journeying camps, and by going off the route, found jobs of work, and obtained food for the people and grain for the teams. As we passed through a town on the Des Moines, the inhabitants manifested as much curiosity as though viewing a managerie of wild beasts. Their levity and apparent heartlessness was proof of profound ignorance. How little did they comprehend our movement and the results which the Almighty had in view!

On the 2d of March we again moved forward, and our encampment ~~this~~ this night may truly be recorded as a miracle on natural principles, and yet, very strikingly peculiar—a city reared in a few hours, and everything in operation that <u>living</u> required, and many additional ones, which if not extravagances were conveniences. The next day, great numbers of people in companies were in from the adjacent country patroling our anonymous streets, viewing our unique city, with astonishment visible in their countenances. In the evening sister Markham and I took a stroll abroad, and in the absence of street names, and tent No.s we lost our way, and had to be piloted within sight of our own domicil.

At this point Col. Markham exchanged our buggy for a lumber wagon, in order to assist others in carrying freight; and in performing this act of generosity, so filled the wagon, as to give us barely room to sit in front. This wagon, with bags piled on bags, was my sleeping room—the family lodged in other wagons and in a tent. Instead of comfort, necessity was the order of the move, and the best faculty for adaptation to circumstances, the best inheritance. We were thankful to be so well off—fleeing from persecution, we were in pursuit of a land of peace. The mob in the vicinity of Nauvoo, knowing that I wielded the pen, had threatened my life, lest, as they said, I should write about the tragic scene at Carthage.[40] Altho' I had neither fear nor dread of death, I felt as I expressed in the following,

<u>Let us go</u>.[41]

Let us go—let us go to the ends of the earth—
Let us go far away from the land of our birth;
For the Banner of Freedom no longer will wave
O'er the patriot's tomb—o'er the dust of the brave.

Let us go—let us go from a country of strife—
From a land with oppression and cruelty rife—
From a country where justice no longer remains
From which virtue is fled, and iniquity reigns.

Let us go—let us go from a Government where
Our just rights of protection we never can share—
Where the soil we have purchased, we cannot enjoy,
Till the time when "<u>the waster goes forth to destroy</u>."

Let us go—let us go to the wilds for a home
Where the wolf and the roe and the buffalo roam—
Where beneath our own vines, we in peace, may enjoy
The fruits of our labors, with none to annoy.

Let us go—let us go where our Rights are secure—
Where the waters are clear and the atmosphere pure—
Where the hand of oppression has never been felt—
Where the blood of the prophets has never been spilt.

Let us go—let us go where the Kingdom of God
Will be seen in its Order extending abroad—
Where the Priesthood of heaven, unopposed will go forth
In the regeneration of man and of earth.

Let us go—let us go to the far western shore
Where the blood-thirsty "christians" will hunt us no
  more—
Where the waves of the ocean will echo the sound,
And the shout of salvation be heard the world 'round.

When we started again, Mrs. M. and I were seated on a chest with brass-kettle and soap-box for our foot-stools, and were happy, and well might be, in comparison with some of our sisters who walked all day, rain or shine, and at night prepared supper for their families, with no sheltering tents; and then made their beds in, and under their wagons that contained their earthly all. Frequently with intense sympathy and admiration I watched the mother when, forgetful of her own fatique and destitution, she took unwearied pains to fix up in the most palatable form the allotted portion (most of the time we were rationed) of food, and as she dealt it out, was cheering the hearts of her children, while, as I truly believed, her own was lifted to God in fervent prayer that their lives might be preserved, and, above all, that they might honor Him in the religion for which she was an exile from the home once sacred to her, for the sake of those precious ones which God had committed to her care.

We were traveling in the season, significantly "between hay and grass," and the teams feeding on browse obtained by felling trees, wasted in flesh and had but little strength; and at times, it was painful to see the poor creatures straining every joint and ligature—doing their best, and looking the very pictures of discouragement. When crossing the low lands, where Spring rains had soaked the mellow soil, they frequently stalled on level ground, and we could move only by coupling teams, which made very slow progress. From the effects of chills and fever, I had not strength to walk, or I would not have been guilty of riding after those half-famished animals. Most of the time I was obliged to ride, no ~~matter~~ matter how dangerous it might be on roads formed by the hand of nature.

In some instances, a cow and ox—and frequent<ly> two cows were yoked together and these poor animals, after helping draw wagons through the day, at night furnished all the milk with which the family was supplied; but ~~it~~ <the yield> was a small pittance, especially when divided among a number of tired, hungry, houseless, little ones.

It would require a painter's skill and pencil to represent an encampment where we stopped, as we frequently did, to give the jaded teams a chance to recuperate, and the people to straighten up matters and things generally. Here is a slight touch from my journal.

"Our town of yesterday has grown to a city—laid out in a half-hollow square, fronting East & South on a beautiful level, ~~with~~ <on> one side an almost perpendicular, and on the other, a gradual descent into a deep ravine, which defines it on the North and West. At nine o'clock this morning, I noticed a Blacksmith's shop in full blast, and everything, every-where, indicating local industries of real life. Only the sick are idle. Not a stove or cooking utensil, but is called into requisition; while tubs and wash-boards, etc, are taken one half mile distant, where washing is done by the side a stream of water. I join Mrs. M. in the washing department, and get a Buggy-ride to the scene of action, as a spectator, where the boys have the fire in waiting: while other of our mess (21 in number) stop in the city and do the cooking arrangements; and for our dinner, send us a rich portion of their immense pot-pie, made of rabbits, squirrels, pheasants, quails, prairie chicken, etc, etc, trophies of the success of our hunters, of whom, each Division has its quota. Thus, from time to time we are supplied with fresh meat."[42] I will now attempt a description of a prairie fire, and then, as I am writing merely "a sketch," I shall pass hastily forward.

At our encampment at the head waters of the Grand River, we saw a fire in the distance coming rapidly towards us with tremendous fury. Our men turned out <u>enmasse</u>, and set fires to burn a broad extent around our p[r]emises, for the wind was so strong, that, without thist precaution, the fire would have swept over us almost instantaneously. So soon as we felt secured, we gazed with admiration and astonishment at the terrific grandeur of the bewildering scene before us, as the devouring element rolled in awful volumes over the tall, <dry> grass, interspersed with leafless trees as dry as tinder—the flames rising at times, to the height of forty or fifty feet and shooting, as if drawn by powerful attraction, from tree to tree. I had often read and listened to descriptions of "<u>Prairies on fire</u>," with the dangers to which travelers are exposed in consequence, and had thought those accounts overdrawn, but now I can <say> in truth, that the reality "beggars all description."

I now pass hurriedly over the founding of the settlement called Pisgah—the unjust Frequisition of Government in calling out the "Mormon Battalion" and consequent hardships devolving on the women and children, as they have long since become subjects of history.

When we left Pisgah, Col. M. was minus one teamster, and Mrs. M. to avoid having another to cook for, proposed to drive the gentle, well-trained yoke of oxen which was selected for the wagon she and I were to occupy; but soon after we started, she was taken quite ill, and of course, the driving fell to me. Had it been a horse team, I should have been amply qualified, but driving oxen was entirely new business. However, I took ~~the~~ the whip, and very soon learned to <u>haw</u> and <u>jee</u>, and acquitted myself very well in driving most of the way to "Winter Quarters" (now Florence,) the cattle being so pliable that I could sit and drive. At the best, I was ~~at times~~ <often> much fatigued, the family at times having so much sickness, that I had to cook as well as nurse, and I was truly thankful for strength to do for those from whom I received much kindness.

On the 2d [September 1846] we arrived at our "Winter Quarters" where we joined the general Camp. From exposure and hardship I was taken sick soon after with a slow fever, and as I lay sick in the wagon, where my bed was exposed to heavy rains, and, at times, unavoidably wet from head to foot, I realized that I was near the gate of death; but in this suffering and exposed condition, I did not feel that God had forsaken me—my trust was in Him, and His power preserved me. While passing through this trying scene, I not only realized the goodness of God, but experienced many kindnesses from my sisters, whose names are not only written in my Journal, but also are engraven on my heart; and I never shall forget the unceasing kindness of brother and sister Markham, with whom I journeyed from Nauvoo to this winter stopping-point. At the time of which I am writing, many were sick around me, and under the circumstances, no one could be properly cared for. Although exposed to Autumnal rains in the wagon—worse was yet to come.

On the 28th of October, a company starting out for supplies, required the wagon which sister M. and I occupied: and the house we moved into, having been built of logs, with openings only partly chincked and mudded—the wind cold and blustering, found plenty of crevices on the sides through which to play; while the roof was shingled only on one side, with a tent-cloth thrown over the other: and besides, it was minus a chimney, and when a fire was kindled, the smoke so filled the house, that a breathing apparatus was of little use, and the fire was put outside. Mrs. M. had partially recovered from her sickness, but was feeble—I was not able to sit up long, and under the circumstances, having to dispense with a fire ~~not at all, having~~ <I had> to keep my bed.

The men had so much to do in preparing for winter, our circumstances were much the same—cooking done out of doors, <u>etc</u>, until past the middle of Nov., when our chimney was built—the house chinked, and other improvements added, which we were prepared to appreciate.

About the last of December I received the sad news of the death of my mother, in which, altho' accompanied with a feeling of heavy bereavement, [I] realized a sweet, soothing sensation in the thought that she was free from all earthly ills. She had lived to a good age, and been a patient participator in the scenes of suffering through the persecutions of the Saints. Her mortal remains sleep in peace—her grave, and that of my father, whose death preceded hers less than a year, are side by side, in Walnut Grove, Knox Co., Illinois.[43]

The privations, hardships, and exposures to which we had been subjected, combined with the unhealthiness of the climate of our Winter-Quarters, caused much sickness, and sickness increased destitution: but in the midst of all, we enjoyed much of the Spirit of God, and many seasons of refreshing from His presence. My life, as well as the lives of many others, was preserved by the power of God, through faith; and not on natural principles, as comprehended by man.

Our extensive encampment was divided into Wards, and so organized that meetings were held in each Ward. An order was introduced and cheerfully carried into effect, that each able-bodied man, should either give the labor of each tenth day, or contribute an equivalent, for the support of the destitute, and to aid those families whose husbands and sons were in the Battalion, and those who were "widows indeed."

On the 7th of April, 1847, President Brigham Young with his band of pioneer braves, started in search of a home for the Saints, in the mountains of the desert.

The first emigrant company started early in June. Brother and sister Robert Peirce kindly offered me a seat in their carriage, which was left vacant by the death of their daughter Mary, a promising young lady, who had fallen a victim to the sickly climate; and on the 12th of June, we bade <u>Goodbye</u> to many dear friends, and again started on pilgrimage.

Previous to starting for an indefinite point—probably one thousand miles into the interior, and from all supplies, the idea of an <u>outfit</u> was a very important consideration. Some of our brethren had purchased and brought from St. Louis a few articles of merchandize, which supplied our local Store with some of the necessaries and comforts for journeying. I was to start immediately, and what about my outfit? Its extent must be determined by the amt. of means. On examining my purse, I found it contained <u>one dime</u> (ten cents)—I was nearly minus ink—I could not go without that article: one dime was just the price of a bottle, and I made the purchase.

After we started out from Winter Quarters, three or four days were consumed in maneuvering and making a "<u>good ready</u>". At an appointed place for rendezvous, a general meeting was held around a Liberty Pole, erected for that purpose, and an organization effected similar to that entered into after leaving Nauvoo. Also, at our next point, on the Platte River, a Liberty Pole was erected, from which our national Flag floated gracefully on the breeze. How dear to the heart of an American, has that sacred emblem ever been! And, although at that time, it yielded us no protection—although we were homeless exiles, the wave of the "Dear old Flag," seemed fraught with that inspiration which silently breathes a promise of peace.

As we moved forward, one Division after another—sometimes in Fifties—sometimes in Tens—but seldom traveling in Hundreds, we passed and repassed each other, but at night kept as compact as ~~possible~~ circumstances would admit, especially when in the Indian country. Not knowing how our "red brethren" might feel disposed towards us, it was admitted that caution was the parent of safety. East of Fort Laramie, many of the Sioux nation mixed with our traveling camps—sometimes in our front and sometimes in our rear, on their way to the Fort, where their national Council was in Session.

We had no other trouble with them than the loss of a few cooking utensils, which, when unobserved, they light-fingered; except in one instance, when our Ten had been left in the rear to repair a broken wagon, until late in the night. It was bright moonlight, and as we were passing one of their encampments, they formed in a line closely by the road-side, and, when our teams were passing they simultaneously and vigorously shook their blankets to frighten the teams and cause a stampede; however no serious injury occurred, although the animals were dreadfully frightened—cows broke their fastenings, oxen turned their bows, and horses pranced and trembled, while some of the weaker human nerves were not altogether proof against the unanticipated scare.

Those Indians carried their tents and baggage on horses, mules and on drays formed of tent-poles, and drawn by horses, mules, and dogs; covers for the little ones were made by fastening skins over bows fixed to the upper side of the drays.

We had two fearful stampedes while on this journey—the first was in the evening—the animals were in a corrol [corral] formed by placing the wagons and carriages side by side, with the tongues on the outside of the hollow square, to which open spaces were left on two sides, for ingress and egress. The wagon in which I had retired for the night was either second or third from one of these openings, and to this gateway the animals all rushed—bellowing, puffing, and snorting, while they rushed against, and clambered over and upon each other in heaps, above the wagon-tops, and so frightened that it was sometime before they succeeded in breaking through the gateway in making their escape. The scene was horrible! Some animals died of injuries—many had their horns knocked off, which produced pitiful sights. The trouble was occasioned by a person shaking the dust from a buffalo robe, which frightened the near animals—they started others to run, and the contagion spread almost instantaneously thro' the entire herd. The camp necessarily halted for the recovery of the runaways, most of which were found the next day.

The second stampede occurred in the day-time. We had stopped to repair a dilapidated crossing over a broad slough—the teams were standing two, ~~and~~ three <and four> abreast; and from the top, nearly to the bottom of a gentle slope, facing the hands at work, when two men on mules, with blankets swinging, rode galloping past—frightening the back teams, and they started on a rush forward, which started others, and soon <nearly> every vehicle was in motion <with fearful velocity,> the drivers absent; and women and children in wagons, carriages, and others still more exposed, standing where they were in danger of being crushed by the reckless flying wheels. With fearful velocity, heedless of crossings and bridges, those teams whirled their vehicles across the slough where, it was admitted that the most skillful teamster could not have succeeded. I was sitting alone on the back seat of a carriage, holding the reins of a high-spirited span—vehicles were flitting past—the horses made several springs, and I knew very well, if they really got started, no human power could prevent them stripping every thing to strings. While I held them with all my strength, I prayed with all the fervency of my soul. Mrs. Peirce and her daughter Margaret, with whom I was journeying, being out of the carriage when the scene occurred, had been trying to stop some ox-teams, but finding they could not succeed, they came, one on each side, and caught the horses by the bitts: they stopped prancing, but shook all over like a person with the shaking ague. Whatever skeptics may say, I attribute my preservation at that time to the peculiar and special blessing of God. And not only mine, but that of others: in the midst of the many fearful exposures, no one was seriously hurt.

Much of the time we journeyed on untrod ground, but occasionally we struck the track of the Pioneers and read the date of their presence, with an "All well" accompaniment inscribed on a bleached buffalo skull, and had a general time of rejoicing. Those skulls were duly appreciated; but at times, the tremendous herds of live buffalos were very annoying, especially when crossing their watering paths in near proximity to a river, and we were compeled to make a break in a line of wagons, and wait for two or three thousand of those uncompromising animals to pass.

We had many seasons of rejoicing in the midst of privation and suffering—many manifestations of the loving kindness of God. In very many instances the sick were healed, and those who by accidents were nigh unto death, made speedily whole. I will mention one case which was under my immediate observation. Mrs. Love, an intimate friend of mine, fell from the tongue of her wagon, containing sixteen hundred freight; the wheels ran across her breast as she lay prostrate, and to all appearance, she was crushed, but on being administered to by some of the elders, she revived; and after having been anointed with consecrated oil, and having the ordinance of laying on of hands repeated she soon recovered, and on the fourth day after the accident, she milked her cow, as usual.

Many, yes many were the star and moonlight evenings, when, as we circled around the blazing fire and sang our hymns of devotion and songs of praise to Him who knows the secrets of all hearts—when with sublime union of hearts, the sound of united voices reverberated from hill to hill; and echoing through the silent expanse, apparently filled the vast concave above, while the glory of God seemed to rest on all around us.[44]

On one of these soul-inspiring occasions—prompted by the spirit of Song, I wrote the following:

> <u>Song</u> of the <u>Desert</u>.[45]
>
> Beneath the cloud-topp'd mountain—
>   Beside the craggy bluff,
> Where every dint of nature
>   Is wild and rude enough:
> Upon the verdant meadow—
>   Upon the sun-burnt plain—
> Upon the sandy hillock,
>   We waken music's strain.
>
> Beneath the pine-tree branches
>   Which have for ages stood—
> Beneath the humble cedar,
>   And the green cotton-wood:
> Beside the broad smooth river—
>   Beside the flowing spring—
> Beside the limpid streamlet,
>   We often sit and sing.
>
> Beneath the sparkling concave,
>   When stars in millions come
> To cheer the weary strangers
>   And bid us feel at home.
> Amid the cheering moon-light,
>   Fair Cynthia's mellow rays
> In social groups we gather,
>   And join in songs of praise.
>
> Cheer'd by the blaze of fire-light,
>   When evening shadows fall,
> And when the darkness deepens
>   Around our spacious hall;
> With true and warm emotion

To saintly bosoms given,
In strains of pure devotion
We praise the God of heaven.

Had it not been for the rich seasons of refreshing from above which we experienced from to time, with renewing influence; it really seemed as though many must have yielded beneath the weight of fatigue and exposure; who were thus enabled to struggle through. But with all that was so kindly and timely bestowed, death made occasional inroads in our traveling camps. Nursing the sick in tents and wagons, was a laborious service; but the patient faithfulness with which it was performed, is, no doubt, registered in the archives above as a unfading memento of brotherly and sisterly love.[46]

On the 4th. of Aug., we met several of the "Mormon Battalion"—husbands and sons of women in our Division; and to see the care-worn faces of those women, beaming with the glow of exquisite joy in a happy re-union, after a long, toilsome separation, imparted unspeakable pleasure to us all.

On the 17th, a letter brought by brethren returning to Winter Quarters for their families, was publicly read, confirming the cheering report of the first arrrivals, to wit—the Pioneers have found a location in Great Salt Lake Valley—a City site was being surveyed etc. etc., which prompted a feeling that we had a definite point before us—a future peaceful home.

On the 8th. [September], we met the main body of the Pioneers, led by Pres. B. Young and H. C. Kimball, who were returning to Winter-Quarters to spend the winter. It was a joyful time, and so deeply interested and absorbed were all, that no guard was kept, and about forty horses and mules were stolen in the night—some of them were not recovered; which crippled the teams and impeded our progress; for many times, especially in ascending hills, the teams had to be doubled, thus causing much delay. But with all these <and other> impediments, we strung along and reached the valley, one company after another, until all had arrived. Our arrival was on the 2d. of October.

Our first winter in the mountains was delightful—the ground froze very little—our coldest weather was three or four days in November, after which, the men plowed and sowed, built houses (huts.) etc. during the winter—the temperature truly seemed to have been particularly ordered to meet our very peculiar circumstances. Every labor, such as cultivating the ground, and procuring timber

and fuel from the canyons was an experiment—most of us were
houseless: and what the result would have been, had that winter been
as severe as the succeeding ones, the Lord only knows.

The small amount of breadstuff brought over the plains, was dealt
out sparingly; and our beef, made of cows and oxen that drew it, was,
before they had time to fatten on the dry mountain-grass, very inferior. Those to whom it yielded sufficient fat to grease their griddles,
were considered particularly fortunate. But we were happy in the
rich blessings of peace, which, in the spirit of brotherly and sisterly
~~love~~ union, we mutually enjoyed in our wild mountain home, and
what we had, seemed to be multiplied as we carefully and thankfully
used it.

When the men were toiling in the fields and canyons, the women
devoted much time in meeting together—administering to the sick,
and in fervent prayer <to God for assistance from on high,> in behalf
of our brethren who labored hard with but little food to sustain them.
Some large families detailed a portion of their number, who spent
their time in digging the wild "Sego-root," the use of which was taught
us by the Indians, of whom we sometimes purchased it, and proved it
to be a nutritious, substantial article of food, and not unpalatable.

President Young had made arrangements for me to live with his
wife, Clara Decker, who accompanied him with the pioneers, and remained in the valley while he returned to Winter-Quarters for the
other portion of his family. I found her living in a log-room, about
eighteen feet square, which constituted a portion of the East side of
our Fort. This hut, like most of those built the first year, was roofed
with willows and earth, with very little inclination—the first-comers
having adopted the idea that the valley was subject to little, if any rain,
and built their roofs nearly flat. We suffered no inconvenience until
about the middle of March, when a long storm of snow, sleet, and rain
occurred, and then for several days, the sun did not make its appearance. Mrs. Clara Young happened to be on a visit to her mother, (who
lived outside the Fort) when the storm commenced, and did not return until it subsided.

Sally, an Indian girl who had been purchased from a tribe by which
she was held captive, was with me. The roof of our dwelling was covered deeper with earth than the adjoining ones, consequently did not
leak as soon, and some of my neighbors huddled in for shelter. One
evening as several were sitting socially conversing in my room, the water commenced dropping in one place and then in another, and so
on: they dodged it for a while, but it increased so rapidly, they con-

cluded to return to their own wet houses. After they left, Sally wrapped herself in her buffalo robe on the floor, and I spread my umbrella over my head and shoulders as I ensconced myself in bed, the lower part being unshielded, was wet enough before morning. During the night, despite all discomfitures, I laughed involuntarily while alone in the darkness of the night I lay reflecting the ludicrous scene. The earth over head being fully saturated, after it commenced to drip, the storm was much worse inside than out, and as the water coursed through the willows and patterned on the floor, washed the stones from the earth above, and they went clink, clink, while the numerous mice which the storm had driven in for shelter, ran squealing back and forth—the Indian girl asleep on the floor, altogether made the situation rather romantic.

A little now about the Indian girl. The same Indians who brought her, had, a short time previous, brought an Indian boy which they offered for sale, saying they would kill him at sun-down if not purchased. Our people did not credit their threat, but when too late for remedy, learned that it was promptly executed, which prompted some of my neighbors to purchase Sally (whose Indian name was Pidash) when brought in and offered for sale with the same threat; and was placed in charge of Mrs. C. Young, and under our mutual care and cultivation, she very soon became disgusted with her native habits,—became neat and tasteful in dress, and delicate in appetite, although at first she cronched bones like a dog. When she had sufficiently learned to communicate her ideas in our language, she informed us that she was of the Pibandy tribe—that her father died—her mother married again—her step-father was cruel to her and sold her to those of whom she was a captive. She proved to be a good, virtuous woman, and died beloved by all who knew her.[47]

Before we left Winter-Quarters, a Committee, appointed for the purpose, inspected the provisions of each family, in order to ascertain that all were provided with at least, a moderate competency of three fourths pound of fine flour per day, for grown persons, and one half pound for children—a precautionary measure to prevent famishing. A portion of the "Mormon Battalion," having been disbanded on the Pacific coast, destitute of pay for their services, joined us before Spring, and we cheerfully divided our "rations" of flour with them, which put some of us on scant allowance.

Soon after our arrival, a tall Liberty Pole was erected, and from its summit, the "Stars and Stripes" seemed to float with, if possible, more significance than they were wont on eastern breezes.[48]

Many, whose circumstances would not admit of coming the first year, sent seeds for fruit trees by those who came; and as the season advanced, it was highly gratifying to see the multitudes of sprouts starting up in new-born nurseries in various directions. But alas! a tragic fate awaited the luxuriant growth of those trees in embryo.—Precisely corresponding with descriptions of ancient locust raids on the Eastern Continent, the crickets of enormous size, came down from the mountains, moving in a solid phalanx—taking everything before them, while desolation followed, insomuch that had not a host of sea gulls (which we considered a special Providence) come to the rescue, all of our crops would have been destroyed. Those gulls in large swarms, went through the invading army, swallowing the crickets wherever they went—as their stomachs filled, they vomited and filled again until the premises were entirely cleared. The drouth of the summer prevented <its full growth and> the wheat left in the ground after the cricket ravages, was, much of it too short to cut, and was pulled.

In the first winter a company of men was sent from the valley to California for seeds and cuttings. They arrived home early in May, and I gave 75 cts. for 6 or 7 little potatoes, all of which I could hold in one hand. I let them out to raise, and in the fall, my half was a heaping half-bushel of beautiful, well developed potatoes.

On the 20th Sept. 1848 Prest. Young arrived, and with him a large company of Saints, which produced a scene of general joy.

Our public meetings were all held in the "Lord's parlor"—ie. out of doors, where was plenty of room for the new-comers, with sufficient ground-floor to sit or stand upon; with a rustic elevated Stand for the speaker, and as a rallying point for the audience. Quite an improvement on the first year's experience, when our place of gathering was by the side of a wheat or [illegible] stack.

A neat brick building, called "Council House" was early completed: the lower story was occupied as its name denotes, and the upper, in administering in some of the sacred ordinances of the Gospel. Subsequently the "House of the Lord" was erected, and I was present at its dedication—a privilege that cannot be too highly estimated. From that time, when in the city, I have been a constant officiate in that House, [in pencil in a different hand: one, two and four days per week.][49]

Our numbers had so increased that before the close of the second year, representatives of the people met in the Convention and formed what was termed a "Provisional Government of the State of Deseret." A Constitution was adopted and Delegates sent to Washington, asking for admission into the Union. The people elected a Governor, Judges, and members for the Legislature—all of whom, discharged the duties of their several offices, without pay. The General Assembly adopted the following rule—"All non-punctual officers and members shall be subject to fine." And sufficient means was thus realized to furnish fuel, light, and brooms.

In <the Autumn of> 1850 Congress passed an Act by which we were organized into the Territory of Utah. Millard Fillmore then Pres. of the U.S., appointed Brigham Young, who previous to this, was Governor of the State of Deseret, Governor of Utah Territory. He was truly the choice of the people, but the wishes of the people were not consulted in choosing the other officers: with the exception of Marshall, all were appointed and sent; and most of them, especially the notorious Judges, Brocchus and Brandebury, with their colleague, Day, were positively nuisances: and because the Government would not send a possee of soldiers to destroy us, they went howling away.[50]

The Secretary, Mr. Harris with-held the money sent by him to pay the expenses of the Legislature. But to us, money and all, their exit was a good riddance, so long as their sole object was to stir up strife between Congress and the Territory. So much in explanation of our Territorial birth.

From our first settlement in the mountains we celebrated the Fourth of July, our great National birth-day; and the Twenty Fourth of that month, the day of the arrival of the Pioneers in the vallies of the mountains.

In this early time poets were not as plentiful with us as at present, and I was expected to furnish one song, and sometimes more than one, for each of these occasions. It so happened that the Government officers, above referred to, absconded in 1852, just before we had a Mammoth Celebration of the Fourth. Our first Tabernacle having been completed, did honor to the occasion. In composing a song for this celebration, prompted by the circumstances of the times, I indulged in the ludicrous—adopting the measure and also the tune of "Old Dan Tucker," in which it was sung, and called for the second time, creating a considerable merriment in the audience.

I here transcribe the Song for the Fourth of July, 1852, for its novelty.[51]

> All hail the day Columbia first
> The iron chains of bondage burst!
> Lo! Utah valleys now resound
> With Freedom's tread on western ground

Chorus.
Though Brocchus, Day, and Brandebury,
And Harris too, the Secretary,
Have gone! they went! But when they left us,
They only of themselves bereft us.

Here is a people brave and free;
Bold advocates for liberty—
The champions of our country's cause,
And firm supporters of her laws.
    Chorus—Tho' Brocchus, etc.
The Banner which our fathers won—
The legacy of Washington,
Is now in Utah wide unfurled,
And proffers peace to all the world.
    Chorus—Tho' Brocchus, etc.
We'll here revive our country's fame,
The glory of Columbia's name:
Her Constitution's germ will be
The basis of our Liberty.
    Chorus. Though <u>etc</u>.
With hearts of valor, firm and true,
With patriotic ~~valor~~ <ardor> too,
We now commemorate the day
Where Freeedom chants her sweetest lay.
    Chorus—Tho' Brocchus, etc.
Long as the everlasting snows
Upon these mountain-tops respose,
Those rights our vet'ran fathers gained,
Shall in these vallies be sustained.
    Chorus—Tho' Brocchus, <u>etc</u>.
This Territory shall not rate
Inferior to a sister State
For justice, order, harmony,
Peace, virtue, and integrity.
    Chorus—Tho' Brocchus, <u>etc</u>.
Our Motto,—"Truth and Liberty"
As heretofore, will ever be;
And heav'n's strong pillars sooner shake
Than we our Standard will forsake.
Chorus—Though Brocchus, <u>etc</u>.

The "Female Relief Society" was organized by Joseph Smith in Nauvoo on 17th of March, 1842. It was organized after the pattern of the Church of Jesus Christ of Latter-day-Saints, with President and Counselors, and accomplished much good in administering to the sick, relieving the wants of the poor, etc[52] The prophet had donated to the Society a Lot, and the frame of a house, as a commencement for establishing a home for the homeless, but the ruthless hand of persecution thwarted this benevolent purpose—the Prophet was massacred and the Saints driven from their homes.

From the time of the expulsion from Nauvoo, the Female Relief Society remained in <u>status quo</u> until it was reorganized under the direction of Prest. B. Young in the year 1855, commencing in the Fifteenth Ward, S. L. City.[53]

As I had been intimately associated with, and had officiated as Secretary for the first organization, Pres. Young commissioned me to assist the Bishops in organizing Branches of the Society in their respective Wards; for, at that time, the Bishops had not acquainted themselves with the movement, and did not know how to proceed. To me it was quite a mission, and I took much pleasure in its performance. I felt quite honored and much at home in my associations with the Bishops, and they appreciated my assistance. Each Branch of the Society, although constituting a self-governing body, and empowered to create committees and whatever officers may be needed from time <to time> in accomplishing its many and increasing labors, is under the direction of its respective Bishop or presiding officer of the Ward.

Not long after the re-organization of the Relief Society, Pres. Young told me he was going to give me an<other> mission. Without the least intimation of what the mission consisted, I replied, "I shall endeavor to fulfil it." He said, "<u>I want you to instruct the sisters</u>." Altho' my heart went "<u>pit a pat</u>" for the time being, I did not, and could not then form an adequate estimate of the magnitude of the work before me. To carry into effect the President's requisition, I saw, at once, involved public meetings and public speaking—also travel abroad, as the Branches of the Society of the sisterhood extended at that time, through several Counties in Utah, and ultimately, all the vallies of the mountains—numbering, at present date, nearly three hundred; besides other Branches in the U.S., Europe, Asia, Islands of the sea, wherever the "Church of Jesus Christ of Latter-day-Saints" has established its Branches. Some years ago, by mutual consent, the word female was dropped, and the Society called "Relief Society."

Its first duty is to look after and relieve the wants of the poor, to accomplish which committees are appointed to visit each family residing in their respective districts, at least, <once> every month, and report to the presiding officers. The cultivation of the members of the Society (which is composed of aged and middle-aged women) physically, mentally, morally, and spiritually, is another prominent feature of the institution, which has proved very beneficial. At the time of its organization in Salt Lake City, the Saints were very poor, and the funds of the Society were raised by contributions of carpet rags, pieces for patchwork *etc.*, which were converted into carpets, quilts— w<o>ol carded, spun, and knitted into socks and stockings, by the industry of the members, who met together, sometimes weekly, at others, once in two weeks, to work the crude material into wearing and saleable articles.

In 1876 I was called upon to report the charitable Institutions <conducted by women> in Utah, to the "Woman's Department" in the Centennial Fair in Philadelphia. At that time, the number of Branches of the R. S. was very much less than at present, but my financial Report was between ninety 2 and ninety three thousand dollars Disbursed by the Society, including relief to the poor, emigration of the poor, to assist in building Temples, school-houses, meeting-houses, <u>etc</u>. Since that time, <the> favorable circumstances of the L. D. Saints, have added to the facilities of many of the Branches, and they have purchased land and erected houses for their own accommodation in holding meetings—doing business, <u>etc</u>, also Granaries for storing wheat against a day of famine.

In 1867 I organized the first Society of Young Ladies, called "Young Ladies' Retrenchment Association," under the direction of Pres. B. Young.[54] Subsequently the name was changed, and it is now known as "Young Ladies' Mutual Improvement Association," and is <now organized and> in active operation in nearly every settlement in the mountains, and in each Ward in our Cities; and, after the pattern of the Relief Society, <these Branches> are organized in Counties (Stake capacity) with a General or Central Board, presiding over all.

In August 1878, Mrs. Emeline B. Wells and I, after attending a Conference of the Young Ladies in Farmington, Davis Co., spent an hour, waiting for the train, with Mrs. Aurelia Rogers. During our conversation, Mrs. R. expressed a desire that something <more> could be effected for the cultivation and improvement of the children morally and spiritually than was being done through the influence of day and

Sunday-Schools. After consulting together a few moments, I asked Mrs. R. if she was willing to take the responsibility and labor on herself of presiding over the children of that settlement, provided the Bishop of the Ward sanctioned the movement. She replied in the affirmative. The train was near, and no time to consult the Bishop; but directly after arriving home, I wrote the Bishop, and by return Mail received from him a very satisfactory response, in which he, (Bishop Hess) not only gave his permission but hearty approval accompanied with his blessing. I then informed Mrs. Rogers that she might consider herself authorized to proceed, and organize in Farmington, which she did, and I commenced in the eleventh Ward in Salt Lake City. We adopted the appellation of Primary Associations, and admit as members boys and girls from four to twelve, and in some instances, sixteen years of age.[55]

The children are now organized with a Branch in each Ward in our cities and Towns, and one in each settlement—they are also organized in Stake capacity—also with a Central Board. The Branch Associations hold weekly meetings—are presided over by adult ladies for President and Counselors, but the Sec., and Treas. are chosen from the children, and it is surprising to see with what aptitude many of them become proficient.

I have traveled from one end of Utah Ter. to the other—into Nevada & Idaho, in the interests of these organizations—have organized hundreds of the Young Ladies' and Primary Associations since their introduction.

In company of Mrs. Z. D. H. Young, <my 1st Coun. in R. S. Central Board,> I spent the Autumn & Winter of 1880–1 in St. George, officiating in the Temple for the dead, and visiting and organizing Associations in that interesting City, and adjacent country—having traveled one thousand ms. by team over jolting rocks and through bedded sand, occasionally camping out at night on long drives, <before I started for home,> and returned to Salt Lake City in March.

In Nov. 1875 I was notified of an appointment, and not long after received my credentials <from Philidelphia,> requiring me to take charge of the Woman's Department in Utah for the Centennial Fair. I saw at once that the proportions of the work before me, compared better with the elephant than the butterfly, but I never had shrunk from duty, and it was too late to begin. I selected and organized a Committee of twelve, composed of "Mormon" and Gentile Ladies— got up a printed Circular which we sent post-haste to all Presidents of Relief Societies, and Young Ladies' Associations, calling for a united co-operation in preparing & collecting specimens that should be worthy our representation, and do honor to our grand National Centennial Fair. We received a hearty response, and succeeded in collections beyond our most sanguine anticipations. I wrote a Petition which was signed by the Committee, and presented to the Legislature in Session in S. L. City, asking for an appropriation to enable us to defray expenses in forwarding our specimens to Philadelphia which, for reasons satisfactorily explained, was not granted. We made a selection of some hundred dollars worth of choice, light articles and sent to Philadelphia, and directed our energies toward a Territorial Fair—obtained the use of a commodious building—arranged our specimens in two departments including a picture Gallery, which we kept open during the summer of 1876, with grand success.

After closing the Fair, Prest. Young told me he wished the sisters to start a home-industry Store in the building occupied for the Fair: He proposed for us to sell on commisssion & everything sold must be of Home Manufacture. Of course this required a new organization, for all engaged in it must be "Mormon" women, and interested in the developement of Utah.

President Young gave me permission to order as much as I wished of Cloth from his factory, which, with other varieties from the Woolen Mills in Provo, constituted a staple trade at our commencement. As the object of the movement was to promote home-manufacture we placed our commission percentage at low figures, which encouraged & brought to hand a great variety of useful & fancy articles, which gave the store the appearance of an Eastern bazaar, and attracted much notoriety. But experience proved that, no matter how many were obligated to sustain the enterprise, the weight of care and responsibility slid on to my shoulders, and could not be divided without hazarding success. With the many duties devolving on me, <I found that my labors in this directions were too much, and,> after the expiration of one year, with mutual consent, it <the establishment> passed into other hands, and we were honorably released. But the movement was not of the ephemery class—shortlived; it still lives, and <the Store> is in successful operation under the management of two young gentlemen.

Some years before the death of the Prophet, Joseph Smith, and long before the thought had entered the mind of Pres. Young to propose a visit to the "Holy Land," the Prophet said to me, "You will yet visit Jerusalem." I recorded the saying in my Journal at the time, but had not reviewed it for many years, and the, to me, strange prediction had entirely gone from my memory—even when invited to join the Tourist party, although the anticipation of standing on the sacredly celebrated Mount of Olives inspired me with a feeling no language can describe; Joseph Smith's prediction did not occur to me until within a very few days of the time set for starting, when a friend brought it to my recollection, and then by reference to the long neglected Journal, the proof was before us. While on the tour, the knowledge of that prediction inspired me with strength and fortitude.[56]

Accompanied by several dear friends, on the morning of the 26th of Oct. 1872, I left Salt Lake City, en route for Palestine. In Ogden I was joined by my brother Lorenzo Snow, and after an affectionate parting with the friends who accompanied me, we took train for New York via Chicago where we spent one day.[57]

In New York we met George A. Smith, the President of our party, Elders F. Little and Paul A. Schettler, our interpreter and cashier, Miss C. Little, my lady companion, who left home before me, to visit friends in eastern States. After securing our Passports, we steamed out from N. York on the Minnesota—encountered one storm which satisfied my curiosity to witness "a storm at sea," and arrived safely in Liverpool. On leaving London, our party consisted of six gentlemen and two ladies.

We visited principal places in Europe, Asia, [*indecipherable deletions*] Africa, Egypt, Greece, Turkey in Europe etc., and on our return, after a flying trip among our relatives in the States, my brother and I arrived home in July, 1873.

In 1875 I compiled the letters written abroad by Pres. Smith, P.A Schettler, my brother, and myself, and published in a well-bound book, containing nearly 400 pages of <instructive,> truthful descriptive reading matter, making a respectable & useful addition to our home literature.[58] Since that time, I have published seven books, the last and largest, containing nearly 600 pages, was issued, and a few copies bound in September 1884. My first Vol. of poems was printed and bound in Liverpool, Eng., under the supervision of Elder F. D. Richards, at that time presiding over the European Mission. A few years later, I sent the manuscript of the 2d Vol. to the same Office for publication, but through some casualty it was lost, or supposed to be, and was missing until I had relinquished all expectation of it, when it was accidentally found only too safely deposited in an obscure till in the Office. I ordered the manuscript returned, and published it in

Salt Lake City—our printing establishments having, by that time, good facilities for book-making.[59]

Including a "Tune-Book, I have, in all, published nine Volumes, besides second editions to several of them.[60]

In connexion with my literary, social, and sacred labors, I have expended considerable time, labor and means in promoting the culture and manufacture of Silk. In our first organization of our "Silk Association" I was appointed Chairman of a Committee to raise means by donation or investment as capital, for this enterprise. We applied to those who were in possession of wealth, but the prospect of early proceeds were not sufficiently promising for their speculating ambition. But we succeeded in obtaining means sufficient to start the manufacture of the raw material, with simple appliances, to fully test the feasibility of success, provided sufficient interest could be aroused in this direction. Our Cocoons <and> reeled silk were examined by proficients in silk culture who visited us from all parts of the civilized world, and in all instances pronouced equ<a>l, and by many, better than in other countries. Thus far, it had been the work of women. After applying to the Territorial Legislature for means, which was generously granted, we purchased a sett of Machinery; we then applied to the authorities of the Church, and in response to our request, a meeting was called—a new organization formed, with Mr. William Jennings Prest., and other gentlemen associated. I held the position of Vice Pres. for some length of time, and resigned in favor of another lady with fewer responsibilities than myself.[61]

Although two Hospitals, St. Marks and St. Mary's had been established in Salt Lake by their respective religious denominations, the Latter-day-Saints felt the need of one of their own where the sick and maimed, who desired, could have the sacred ordinances of anointing with oil and laying on of hands administered without being exposed to the contempt and ridicule of of those who ignored them. But the means, labors, and attention of our people being necessarily directed in so many channels, that in cases in which Hospital appliances were indispensably requisite for the alleviation of suffering humanity, we patronized those in operation.

Leading "Mormon" women have, from time to time, suggested that we make a move in the direction of a Hospital of our own, but without location, building, and without funds, to start out in an enterprise of such magnitude seemed preposterous even to the most sanguine. At one time, President Young proposed to me, if I would take charge, and preside over the Institution, he would donate a cer-

tain Lot, on which was a moderately sized house, for the commencement of a Hospital, of which he would give a warrantee deed for that
purpose. But at that time my labors and responsibilities were such as
rendered it an utter impossibility for one to accept the proposal,
and, as he declined entrusting it to another, the generous offer
passed from our reach; but the want of a Hospital of our own grew
more apparent year by year until the winter of 1881–2, when in the
minds of several "Mormon" women it was settled as a <u>necessity</u>, and
<the idea was> coincided in by some of the leading men.

In the Spring following, the "Catholic Sisters," who for seven years
had conducted St. Mary's Hospital on premises which they rented,
were going to vacate them, which suggested an opportunity for us to
obtain the place by paying rent as they had done. After consulting
the First Presidency and other prominent brethren <with regard to
the feasibility of the undertaking,> and receiving encouragement respecting means for that purpose; it was decided for the L. D. Saint
women to inaugurate a Hospital. Accordingly an organization was
formed, entitled "<u>Deseret Hospital Association</u>"—consisting of a
Board of Directors—House Surgeon—Matron—<u>etc</u>. <u>etc</u>., and I was
required to preside, which, although acknowleding the honor con-
ferred, I accepted with the greatest reluctance—reluctance that approached nearly to obstinacy. I saw at once that we were grasping a
Mammoth—that as we had to commence at the bed-rock—build ad-
ditions—make repairs in the building, and fit up in every department, much thought, labor, and time must be devoted in that direction. I realized the great need, and the importance of the movement,
and did not feel to shrink from any labor or responsibility but when
my time was all occupied, as it truly was at that time; for me to involve
myself in other and untried duties, seemed nothing short of sub-
scribing to neglect of those already resting upon me; but I obtained a
promise that after the Hospital was in good running order, I <might
resign.>

In connexion with the "Board of Directors," which consisted of
ten ladies, I spent very much time—calling, and attending Board
meetings—consulting <u>etc</u>. <u>etc</u>, and succeeded beyond our most sanguine anticipations. Although many of our patients were unable to
pay expenses for treatment, by liberal donations we were enabled to
fit up the building, supply each department, and pay our work-
hands, nurses, <u>etc</u>. But <u>our</u> remuneration consisted in the conscious-
ness of doing our duty, and in the sweet enjoyment which follows extending relief to suffering humanity—not one of us received one

cent for our services—we were not hirelings—dollars and cents, with us personally, were out of the question.

I retained the position of President nearly two years, when I resigned, and Bishop H. B. Clawson succeeded me, retaining the original Board. And here I must say, that my associations with the members of that Board, in the struggles, labors, trials, and success, in starting out in a new direction, have very strongly endeared them to me, I trust never to be severed from my affections.[62]

Since my resignation as Pres. of the "Hospital Association," I have had no time to be idle. Visiting Associations, organizing <u>etc.</u>—officiating in sacred ordinances in the "House of the Lord"—administering to the sick—writing for publication—proof-reading, in connexion with an extensive correspondence and other etceteras, keep me fully employed. And, at this period of my life, to be able to perform the many duties, and labors of love required of me, is certainly worthy of a higher tribute of gratitude to God, the Giver of all good, than I am capable of expressing.

Thus closes "Sketch of my Life"
E. R. Snow Smith—[63]

<u>Yes, I would be a Saint.</u>[64]

My heart is fix'd—I know in whom I trust.
'Twas not for wealth—'twas not to gather heaps
Of perishable things—'twas not to twine
Around my brow, a transitory wreath—
A garland deck'd with gems of mortal praise,
That I forsook the home of childhood: that
I left the lap of ease—the halo rife
With friendship's richest, deep, and mellow tones—
Affections' fond caresses, and the cup
O'erflowing with the sweets of social life,
With high refinement's golden pearls enriched.

Ah, no! a holier purpose fired my soul—
A nobler object prompted my pursuit;
Eternal prospects opened to my view,
And Hope Celestial in my bosom glow'd.

God, who commanded Abraham to leave
His native country, and to offer up
On the lone altar, where no eye beheld
But that which never sleeps, his fav'rite son,

Is still the same; and thousands who have made
A covenant with Him by sacrifice,
Are bearing witness to the sacred truth,
Jehovah speaking has reveal'd His will.
    The proclamation sounded in my ear—
It reached my heart—I listen'd to the sound—
Counted the cost, and laid my earthly all
Upon the altar, and with purpose fix'd
Unalterably, while the spirit of
Elijah's God within my bosom reigns,
Embraced the Everlasting Covenant.

* * * *

    It is no trifling thing to be a Saint
In very deed—to stand upright, nor bow,
Nor bend beneath the heavy pressure of
Oppressiveness—to stand unscathed amid
The bellowing thunders and the raging storm
Of persecution, when the hostile powers
Of darkness stimulate the hearts of men
To warfare—to besiege, assault, and with
The heavy thunderbolts of satan, aim
To overthrow the kingdom God has rear'd,
To stand unmoved upon the withering rack
Of vile apostacy, when men depart
From the pure principles of righteousness—
Those principles requiring man to live
By every word proceeding from the mouth
Of God—to stand unwavering, undismay'd
And unseduced, when the base hypocrite
Whose deeds take hold on hell, whose face is garbed
With saintly looks drawn out by sacrilege,
From the profession, but assumed and thrown
Around him for a mantle, to enclose
The black corruption of a putrid heart—
To stand on virtue's lofty pinnacle,
Clad in the robes of heavenly innocence,
Amid that worse than every other blast,
The blast that strikes at moral character,
With floods of falsehood foaming with abuse—
To stand with nerve and sinew firmly steeled,

When, in the trying scale of rapid change,
Thrown face to face, and side by side to that
Foul hearted spirit, blacker than the soul
Of midnight's darkest shade, the traitor, the
Vile wretch that feeds his sordid selfishness
Upon the peace and blood of innocence;
The faithless, rotten-hearted wretch, whose tongue
Speaks words of trust and fond fidelity,
While treachery, like a viper, coils behind
The smile that dances in his evil eye—
To pass the fiery ordeal, and to have
The heart laid open, all its contents strewed
Before the bar of strictest scrutiny;
To feel the <finest> heart-strings drawn unto
Their utmost tension, and their texture proved.

And yet, although <u>to be a Saint</u> requires
A noble sacrifice, an arduous toil,
A persevering aim; the great reward
Awaiting the grand consummation, will
Repay the price, however costly; and
The pathway of the Saint, the safest path
Will prove, though perilous; for 'tis decreed
All things that <u>can</u> be shaken, God will shake:
Kingdoms and Governments and Institutes,
Both civil and religious, must be tried—
Tried to the core, and sounded to the depth.

Then let me be a Saint, and be prepared
For the approaching day, which like a snare
Will soon surprise the hypocrite—expose
The rottenness of human schemes—shake off
Oppressive fetters—break the gorgeous reins
Usurpers hold, and lay the pride of man—
The pride of nations, low in dust!

<u>Bury Me Quietly When I Die</u>.[65]

On the "iron rod" I have laid my hold;
If I "keep the faith," and like Paul of old,
Shall have "fought the good fight," and Christ, the Lord
Has a crown in store, with a full reward
Of the Holy Priesthood in fulness, rife

With the gifts and the powers of an endless life,
And a glorious mansion for me on high;
 Bury me quietly when I die.

I am aiming to earn a celestial crown—
To merit a heavenly, approv'd renown;
And whether in grave or in tomb I am laid
Beneath the tall oak or the cypress shade;
Whether at home with dear friends around,
Or in distant lands upon stranger ground—
Under wintry clouds or a summer sky;
 Bury me quietly when I die.

When my spirit ascends to the world above
To unite with the choirs in celestial love;
Let the finger of silence control the bell,
To restrain the chime of a funeral knell—
Let no mourning strain—not a sound be heard
By which a sad pulse of the heart is stirr'd—
No note of sorrow to prompt a sigh;
 Bury me quietly when I die.

What avail the parade and the splendor here,
To a legal heir to a heavenly sphere?
To the heirs of salvation, what is the worth,
In their perishing state, the frail things of earth?
What is death, to the good, but an entrance gate,
That is placed on the verge of a rich estate,
Where commissioned escorts are waiting by?
 Bury me quietly when I die.

Like a beacon that rises o'er ocean's wave,
There's a light—there's a life beyond the grave:
The future is bright, and it bec<k>ons me on
Where the noble and pure and the brave have gone,
Who have battled for truth with their mind and might,
With their garments clean and their armor bright:
They are dwelling with God, in a world on high:
 Bury me quietly when I die.

Salt Lake City, Utah.
April 13, 1885   Eliza R. Snow Smith—

"A Day of Much Interest"
The Nauvoo Journal
and Notebook

OF THE ELIZA R. SNOW DIARIES extant, the first written, the Nauvoo journal, was the last to come to light. Before its discovery, scholarly curiosity had posited stories of her Nauvoo years: her separation from her family, her responsibility in the first Relief Society, her secret marriage to Joseph Smith, her involvement in the endowment work of the temple. Her nephew LeRoi C. Snow, son of Lorenzo Snow's later years, told interested visitors to the Church Historian's Office in Salt Lake City, where he worked as curator of photographs, of her liaison with the Prophet Joseph, leading many to believe he had a diary from the Nauvoo years. But at his death it was the two little trail diaries which his wife Burma sold to the Huntington Library; there was no Nauvoo journal among his papers to confirm his oft-repeated story of Eliza's presumed altercation with Emma Smith, who was supposed in a fit of jealousy to have thrown Eliza down a flight of stairs, or threatened her with a broom, or caused her to have a miscarriage. Eliza *must*, people agreed, have written the story *somewhere*.[1] Somewhere there had to be a Nauvoo journal of Eliza R. Snow.

Its unheralded appearance in the vault of the Relief Society presidency in Salt Lake City is not unusual for such documents. The story of its provenance, now pieced together with the help of James Kimball, Oma Wilcox, Inez Thomas, and Sonoma Snow Wilson, is as follows:

Eliza Snow's brother Lorenzo lived in Brigham City, some seventy miles north of Eliza's Salt Lake City home. He regularly called on her in Brigham Young's Lion House on his visits to the city, and she would occasionally pass through Brigham City on her tours of the Relief Societies in the northern settlements. When, in the early 1870s, rails joined the two locations, Eliza often rode "the cars" of the Bamberger Railroad to visit Lorenzo and his families there. Most of the Snows were still living in Brigham City at the time of her death in 1887.

Lucius Snow, one of the oldest sons of Lorenzo Snow, was married to Elizabeth Wilson and lived with her on a farm north of Brigham City. Elizabeth, the last survivor of the first family, and known as "Grandma Snow" to the younger family members, eventually moved from the farm to a small house in town at 332 North Main. There, stored away in the attic, she kept some family memorabilia.

At the time of Elizabeth's death in 1943, Clifford Forrest, Elizabeth's "ward teacher," appointed by her bishop to see to her needs, came to help clear the house for sale. A neighbor remembered that a bonfire in the backyard was consuming household discards. Forrest climbed into the attic and discovered, hidden back under the eaves, a corrugated cardboard box containing Snow family papers—"old letters, tithing receipts, and the like."[2] Among them was a large bound volume partly filled with handwriting and inscribed on its inside cover to Eliza R. Snow by Sarah M. Kimball. Guessing that his wife Helen would find them interesting, Forrest took the book and the box of papers home. Helen and her sister, Inez Thomas, read the volume "a couple of times," wondering the while what might be their responsibility towards it.

In 1949 the Forrests moved to Layton, Utah, taking the book with them. At this point, the story as told by Inez Thomas ends. In Layton, among the Forrests' neighbors were Elias and Fidelia Dawson, who in 1965 visited Nauvoo and became enthusiastic about LDS Church-sponsored restorations there. Mrs. Forrest, widowed now and aging, entrusted the book into the care of the Dawsons, who in 1966 presented it to LeRoy Kimball, then director of Nauvoo Restoration, Inc.

Making two photocopies of the volume, one for the use of Nauvoo Restoration researchers and one for the LDS Church Archives, Kimball then presented the original notebook to Belle S. Spafford in her office as general president of the Relief Society. With her kind permission, I first published its diary entries in *Brigham Young University Studies*.[3] In the meantime, President Spafford ordered the book repaired, its weakened bindings reinforced. Unfortunately some yellow sheets of research notes, undoubtedly those of the Nauvoo Restoration staff, were bound into the restored book, there to remain to puzzle future researchers.

The first typescript of the present text was made by Edyth Romney from the LDS Church Archives photocopy. I appreciate the assistance of Barbara S. Smith, successor to President Spafford, and Mayola Miltonberger, general secretary, in making the original book available to me later for checking and photographing. The volume now rests in the vault of the LDS Church Archives.

The Nauvoo journal, at last available, did not directly answer the anxious speculations of historians. The founding of the Relief Society preceded the first entry by two months; there is only one reference to its activities in the diary. There is no overt mention of a sealing between Eliza Snow and Joseph Smith, and there is no description of a scene with Emma Smith on the stairs. No explanation is given of Eliza's parents' removal from Nauvoo and their disaffection from Mormonism. Also, the martyrdom of Joseph Smith and the dedication of the Nauvoo Temple both occurred after the last of the dated entries.

But to one schooled not so much in history as in literature, the text speaks covertly to most of those themes. The book has an intimate connection, for instance, to the Relief Society. "Politely presented" to Eliza by Sarah Kimball, it is dated on its inscription page "March 1842," suggesting that the young Sister Kimball, at whose behest and in whose home the preorganization meeting had taken place, had intended the volume to be used by Eliza, secretary of the new society, as a minute book. Willard Richards, who had taken minutes of the organizational meeting until the appointment of Sister Snow as secretary, provided Eliza with another book for that purpose, however, so Sarah Kimball's volume, intimidating in its size and suggested import, remained tantalizingly empty for two months.

It took an event of heroic dimensions to entice the modest Eliza to begin making personal entries in a volume so unlike the tiny ladies' diaries in use at the time. Such an incident was her secret marriage to Joseph Smith on 29 June 1842. The event could not be related openly: Eliza's recording of it is indirect, oblique, obscure. As women often do when they wish to remember an incident but intend to keep it hidden from others, Eliza wrote this first entry in half-truths, in unconnected details, in metaphor. But the deviation from her usually clear, objective prose gives the game away: that and the research which unearthed the fact that this first entry marked Eliza's sealing as a plural wife to the charismatic prophet.

"This is a day of much interest to my feelings," she begins engagingly. "Reflecting on past occurrences," she continues in obscure generalities, "a variety of thoughts have presented themselves to my mind with regard to events which have chas'd each other in rapid succession in the scenery of human life." "Change" is personified and capitalized "in reference to present circumstances and future prospects," and the specific circumstance of her own continued stay in Nauvoo in spite of her family's move is imbued, by its very mystery, with extraordinary significance.

The event itself could not be mentioned. In proposing marriage to the thirty-eight-year-old spinster, Joseph Smith had placed her in an emotional, spiritual, intellectual, and social bind akin to that put upon the ancient Abraham when he was commanded to sacrifice his son. In accepting Joseph's proposal, Eliza had to bend to the breaking point her sense of moral accountability, her convictions about the social order, her adherence to biblical injunction, her family values, and her judgment of herself as a righteous, God-loving Christian.

Eliza's admiration of the man Joseph Smith had roots reaching back to Mantua, Ohio, where she had watched him from a corner of the family parlor and judged his to be "an honest face." Her devotion to Joseph as a prophet flourished in Kirtland, where she admired his "affectionate . . . temperament," his "expansive grasp of the great plan of salvation," his "God-like intuition." Now, in requiring her to accept not just mentally but spiritually, emotionally, and physically a proposition her contemporaries were condemning as licentious "spiritual wifery," Joseph was forcing her to redefine the requirements put upon her by the God she had long worshiped. No language, especially that which must conceal its content, could convey the intensity of the deliberations that had brought her to this point. "Though I rejoice in the blessing of the society of the saints," she wrote, "and the approbation of God; a lonely feeling will steal over me before I am aware, while I am contemplating the present state of society—the pow'rs of darkness, and the prejudices of the human mind, which stand array'd like an impregnable barrier against the work of God." Of course "a lonely feeling!"—to whom could she vouchsafe her secret? Of her women friends, only Sarah Cleveland knew, having witnessed the ceremony. And could Eliza really be sure of "the approbation of God"? Is one ever really sure of such a witness? "Powers of darkness" she could ascribe to the adversary, but the "prejudices of the human mind" were her own.

Only in metaphor could Eliza represent the intensity of the moment: "While these thoughts were revolving in my mind, the heavens became shadowed with clouds and a heavy shower of rain and hail ensued, and I exclaim'd 'O God, is it not enough that we have the prepossessions of mankind—their prejudices and their hatred <to contend with;> but must we also stand amid the rage of elements?' " Like a rainbow after the storm, solace comes: "The grace of God is sufficient, therefore I will not fear." Whether Eliza actually experienced such confirmation, or, as she often did, was using her own words to convince herself, she seems to have arrived at a point of peace. "As I increased in knowledge concerning the principle and design of Plural Marriage," she reflected thirty years later, "I grew in love with it."[4]

The next entry is dated a full month later. It and most subsequent entries are concise, concrete accounts of events, such as a public chronicler might inscribe. Discreet distance reduces Joseph to his official capacity—"Prest. Smith," or "Prest. S," not unusual in a Victorian lady's diary even in reference to her acknowledged husband. Between the lines, however, and underlying the verses, there lies a barely decipherable layer of the love Eliza holds for Joseph, concealed under such phrases as "society which is dear to me as life," or "circumstances of very peculiar interest," or "Every thing connected with our <u>affections</u> is engraven on the heart, and needs not the perpetuating touch of the sculptor." Not until the 1880s could she acknowledge publicly her feeling for this first husband; but from their earliest meetings Joseph had been to Eliza "the choice of my heart and the crown of my life."[5] The diary ends two months before his death in 1844.

Nauvoo Journal

City of Nauvoo, June 29th 1842.

This is a day of much interest to my feelings. Reflecting on past occurrences, a variety of thoughts have presented themselves to my mind with regard to events which have chas'd each other in rapid succession in the scenery of human life.

As an individual, I have not passed altogether unnoticed by Change, in reference to present circumstances and future prospects. Two weeks and two days have pass'd since an intimation was presented of my duty and privilege of remaining in the city of the saints in case of the removal of my father's family: one week and two days have transpired since the family left, and though I rejoice in the blessing of the society of the saints, and the approbation of God; a lonely feeling will steal over me before I am aware, while I am contemplating the present state of society—the pow'rs of darkness, and the prejudices of the human mind, which stand array'd like an impregnable barrier against the work of God.

While these thoughts were revolving in my mind, the heavens became shadowed with clouds and a heavy shower of rain and hail ensued, and I exclaim'd "O God, is it not enough that we have the prepossessions of mankind—their prejudices and their hatred <to contend with;> but must we also stand amid the rage of elements?" I concluded within myself that the period might not be far distant, that will require faith to do so; but the grace of God is sufficient, therefore I will not fear. I will put my trust in Him who is mighty to save; rejoicing in his goodness and determin'd to live by every word that preceedeth out of his mouth.

Thursday July, 29th, Just return'd from Quincy, where I visited the Governor in company with Mrs. Emma Smith who presented him a Petition from the Female Relief Society. The Gov. received us with cordiality, and as much affability and politeness as his Excellency is master of, assuring us of his protection, by saying that the laws and Constitution of our country shall be his polar star in case of any difficulty. He manifested much friendship, and it remains for time and circumstance to prove the sincerity of his professions.[1]

Wednesday, August 3, Day before yesterday I rode to the burial of bishop Knights—from there to Prest. Smith's house, from which place I have just returned to my excellent friend, Mrs. C[leveland].

Tuesday, 9th. Prest. S. and P. R. taken for the attempt to assassinate Boggs.— Prest. S. left in the care of the City Marshal while those who took him return to Quincy to ascertain whither they must submit him to a City trial.[2]

> O God, thou God that rules on high
>   Bow down thy ear to me:
> Listen, O listen to my cry
>   And hear my fervent plea.
>
> Rebuke the heartless, wicked clan
>   That wish thy servant harm:
> Protect him from the pow'r of man,
>   By thy Almighty arm.
>
> Let unseen watchmen wait around
>   To shield thy servant's head—
> Let all his enemies be found
>   Caught in the net they spread.
>
> Thy grace, like prairie dews distil'd
>   To all his need, apply;
> And let his upright heart be fill'd
>   With spirit from on high.
>
> The work is thine—thy promise sure
>   Though earth and hell oppose
> Roll, roll it onward, but secure
>   Thy prophet from his foes.
>
> O, hide him in thy secret hold

> When on his path they tread
> Safe, as Elijah, who of old
> Was by the ravens fed.

> Bring our accusers' deeds to light
> And give thy people rest—
> Eternal God! gird on thy might
> And succor the opprest.[3]

Sunday 14th, Yesterday Mrs. Smith sent for me, having previously given me the offer of a home in her house, by Miss A. Coles, who call'd on me, on the 12th. Mrs. Cleveland having come to the determination of moving on to her lot; my former expectations were frustrated, but the Lord has open'd the path to my feet, and I feel dispos'd to acknowledge his hand in all things. This sudden, unexpected change in my location, I trust is for good; it seem'd to come in answer to my petitions to God to direct me in the path of duty according to his will.

King, the deputy Sheriff and Pitman from Quincy, with the Sheriff and his associate from Mo.; are yet watching about the City, for Prest. S. who had absented himself while they were on their return to Quincy.

Esqr. Powers, Prest. S's attorney from Keokuck called this evening— thinks the prospect flattering with respect to the excitement abroad.[4]

Thursday 18, Monday evening I return'd to my former residence in order to adjust my things for a removal, and return'd with them last evening to Prest Smith's.

As near as I can ascertain, the Quincy Sheriff and Constable left the place monday afternoon, and yesterday Wilson, the Sheriff from Carthage came in disguise, and has taken lodgings at Daviss' tavern. This evening Esqr. Warren arriv'd—said he concluded from the fact that the Gov. said all was quiet, that they were proceeding to get a new Writ.

Monday, 22 Last night, six men came in, suppos'd to have a new Writ.

Yesterday Prest. Rigdon spoke on the stand in the grove; giving a narration of Eliza's sickness and the very singular manner in which she address'd the family after having been as he express'd it dead three times. He declar'd his confidence in the work of God—said it had been reported of him that he had call'd Prest S. a fallen prophet—but he denied having said it, &c. How it would rejoice my heart to see him once more standing firmly in the dignity of his station and strengthening the hands of those who are struggling against every kind of opposition for the cause of God![5]

Thurs. 25th. It has been satisfactorily ascertained that those men who came sunday evening, were not authoriz'd to take Prest. S. but that there is ~~one~~ a now Writ issued and on its way

Esqr. Powers call'd today

This evening Prest S. said he had some good, news, viz. that George W. Robinson had declar'd his determination to forsake his evil deeds and return to the church. If he <u>does</u> return, I hope it may be for his soul's salvation; not to act the part of Hinkle and betray the innocent, in the time of danger.[6]

I had a rich treat yesterday in perusing the Book of the Lord—was much gratified with the spirit breath'd in the letters of Maj. Gen. L[aw].—[7] felt myself rather reprov'd for having distrusted his integrity and devotion to the cause. In such critical times, much is depending on the fidelity of those who fill the higher offices.

Sunday, 28th. Last evening Prest. S. was at home and met in the large drawing room with a respectable number of those considered trustworthy—counsel'd them to go out forthwith to proclaim the principles of truth. I was busied the forepart of this day in needlework to prepare br. Derby for his mission.[8]

Sunday Sept. 4th. Surely we know not what a day may bring forth. The little season of quietfude with which we have been bless'd for a few days, has gone by, and our City is again infested with some eighteen or twenty men, who are lying in wait, for the blood of the innocent!

Yesterday, Pitman from Quincy and Ford from Mo. with another stranger arrived about one o'clock at the house of Prest. Smith, who having a moment's notice, left the dinner table, where he was seated and made his escape. Pitman enquired for him and ask'd permission to search the house. Mrs. S. said she had no objection if he had the proper authority. Pitman said he had <u>no authority</u> but with her consent he proceeded to search, preceded by John Boynton and D. Huntington, whom Mrs. S. requested to show them into the rooms.

After sundown, King, the Deputy Sheriff and his associate came in King seem'd in an unpleasant humor—after enquiring for Prest. Smith spoke about searching the house, Mrs. S. mention'd authority—he said he had authority at any rate he said his <u>will was good</u>

<u>enough</u>. Mrs. S. said she thought he could have no objections to telling what he wanted Mr. S. for. He said in a surly tone that it would be time enough to tell <u>that</u> afterwards.[9]

Sunday Sep. 11th. Returned from Lima, where I had a very pleasant visit with Sister L[eonora].[10] After a short time at the Conference on sat. evening, where Elders G. Smith & A. Lyman, who rode down in our carriage met Prest. Young, already started on his mission.[11]

Sun. 18th. Went to meeting in the forenoon & heard elder G. J. Adams who arriv'd here last Monday; deliver an eloquent discourse from the 15th of 1st Cor. commencing with the 12th verse, "Now if Christ be preached that he rose from the dead" &c, on the subject of the resurrection of the dead.
    Yesterday I wrote the following

Conjugal,
To Jonathan & Elvira.[12]

Like two streams, whose gentle forces
    Mingling, in one current blend—
Like two waves, whose onward courses
    To the ocean's bosom tend—

Like two rays that kiss each other
    In the presence of the sun—
Like two drops that run together
    And forever are but one,

May your mutual vows be plighted—
    May your hearts, no longer twain
And your spirits be united
    In an everlasting chain.

Friday 23d—Last evening spent at sister Knights—On my way, call'd at the Post-Office, and found a letter from Eli & Amanda, announcing their expectation of moving to this country.[13] Their intention of settling near father & mother is a subject of much gratification to my feelings, hoping it may add much to the comfort of the aged; in this age of disappointment and sacrifice. But the mind must be fix'd on God, that the cheering influence of his spirit may elevate our hopes above the power of changing circumstance; then will the aged rejoice, and the young be encouraged, even amid scenes of difficulty and peril.

To stand still and see the salvation of God seems to be the only alternative for the present. While reflecting on the present, and its connexion with the future; my thoughts mov'd in the following strain:

O, how shall I compose a thought
　　Where nothing is compos'd?
How form ideas, as I ought
　　On subjects not disclos'd?

If we are wise enough to know
　　To whom we should give heed—
Thro' whom intelligence must flow
　　The church of God to lead,

We have <u>one</u> grand position gain'd—
　　<u>One</u> point, if well possess'd—
If well established—well maintain'd,
　　On which the mind may rest.

<u>This principle</u> will bear us up—
　　It should our faith sustain,
E'en when from "trouble"'s reckless cup
　　The dregs, we have to drain.

What boots it then, tho' tempests howl
　　In thunders round our feet—
Tho' human rage, and nature's scowl
　　By turns, we have to meet.

What though tradition's haughty mood
　　Deals out corroding wrongs;
And superstition's jealous brood
　　Stirs up the strife of tongues.[14]

Sunday October, 9th, Last night Prest. S. left home in consequence of intelligence that King & Pitman were on the way in search for him. It was a sorrowful time. Sister Emma had been sick eleven days,— still confined to her bed—but he must go or be expos'd to the fury of the merciless! Gov. Carlin has offered 200, and Reynolds 300, for his apprehension.[15]

Wed. 12th—Having heard of the safe arrival of Prest. S. at the place of his destination, I wrote as follows and sent to him

Prest. Smith,

Sir, for your consolation permit me to tell
That your Emma is <u>better</u>—she soon will be <u>well</u>;
Mrs. Durfee stands by her, night & day like a friend
And is prompt every call—every wish to attend;
Then pray for your Emma, but indulge not a fear
For the God of our forefathers, smiles on us here.

Thou hast found a seclusion—a lone solitude
Where thy foes cannot find thee—where friends can't in-
   trude;
In its beauty and wildness, by nature design'd
As a retreat from the tumult of all human kind,
And estrang'd from society: How do you fare?
May the God of our forefathers, comfort you there.

It is hard to be exil'd! but be of good cheer
Thou art destin'd to triumph: then like a chas'd deer
Hide yourself in the ravine, secure from the blast
Awhile, till the storm of their fury is past;
For your foes are pursuing and hunting you still—
May the God of our fore-fathers screen you from ill.[16]

November 16th

An Apostrophe to Death

What art thou Death? I've seen thy visage and
have heard thy sound—the deep, low murm'ring sound
That rises on thy tread!
      Thy land is call'd
A land of shadows, and thy path, a path
Of blind contingence, gloominess and fear—
Thy form comprising all that's terrible;
For all the terrors that have cross'd the earth
Or crept into its lowest depths, have been
Associated with the thoughts of Death.

   The tales of old bear record of thy deeds,
For thou hast been in ev'ry rank and grade—
In every circumstance—in every place

A visitor. Unceremoniously
Thou'st strode into the mansions of the great,
And rous'd a strain of agonizing grief
Above the rich embroider'd carpetings
That decorate the splendid citadels
Where pomp and fashion reign; where bolts & bars
To each intruding form; all but thyself
Preclude admittance; Thou hast added oft
To the abode of wretched poverty
A larger, deeper draught of wretchedness!
The rich and poor, the little and the great
Have shared thy bitterness—have seen thy hand!

    But thou art chang'd—the terror of thy looks—
The darkness that encompass'd thee, is gone
There is no frightfulness about thee now.
    Intelligence, the everlasting lamp
Of truth, of truth eternal, lighted from
The world on high, has pour'd its brilliant flame
Abroad, to scatter darkness, and to chase
The horrors that attended thy approach.
And thou art chang'd—for since the glorious light
Of revelation shown upon thy path
Thou seem'st no more a hideous monster, arm'd
With jav'lins, arrows, shafts and iron barbs
To fix in everlasting hopelessness
The noblest prospect and the purest hope.
Beyond thy presence and beyond thy reach
Beyond the precincts of thy dread domain
Beyond the mansions where in silence lie
The scatter'd relics of thy ghastly pow'r—
High on eternity's projecting coast;
A glorious beacon rears its lofty disk,
And the bright beams of immortality
By revelation's bold reflection giv'n,
Have fall'n upon thee, and roll'd back the shades
Which superstition, ignorance and doubt
Had heap'd like ocean's mountain waves upon
Thy lone, unsocial, hourly trodden path.
    Hope, the bright luminary of the heart,
In coursing round thee, and her orbit's breadth

Extends beyond the utmost of thy shades
And points her radius to celestial spheres.
    The mesh that hung in troubled folds around
Thy pulseless bosom has been torn aside.
Seen as thou art, by inspiration's light
Thou hast no look the righteous need to fear.
With all thy ghastliness—amid the grief
Thy presence brings, I hear a thrilling tone
Of music sweet as seraph notes that ride
Upon the balmy breath of summer eve.
    Art thou a tyrant holding the black reins
Of destiny that binds the future course
Of man's existence? No! thou art, O Death!
A haggard porter, charg'd to wait before
The Grave, life's portal to the worlds on high.[17]

The noblest, proudest joys that this
    World's favor can dispense
Are far inferior to the bliss
    Of conscieous innocence.

~~The finer which~~
<The peace which>
That joy that in the bosom flows
    No circumstance can bind—
It is a happiness that knows
    No province but the mind;
It makes the righteous soul rejoice
    With weight of ills opprest

~~feel~~
To hear <feel> the soothing still small voice
    Low whisp'ring in the breast.
The favor of eternal God—
    The favor of his Son—
The holy Spirit shed abroad—
    The hope of life to come;
Are higher honors, richer worth
    Surpassing all reward

Than kings and princes of the earth
 Have taken or confer'd.
And when in Christ the Spirit finds
 That sweet—that promis'd rest
In spite of ev'ry pow'r that binds
 We feel that we are blest.
Though vile reproach its volumes swell
 And friends withdraw their love
[*One the side.*] If conscience whispers "all is well"
 And God and heav'n approves;
We'll triumph over ev'ry ill
 And hold our treasure fast;
And stand at length on Zion's Hill
 Secure from ev'ry blast.[18]

[*Added later.*] Saturday Evening Thoughts
(published in the Times & Seasons)

"My heart is fix'd"—I know in whom I trust.
'Twas not for wealth—'twas not to gather heaps
Of perishable things—'twas not to twine
Around my brow a transitory wreath,
A garland deck'd with gems of mortal praise
That I forsook the home of childhood: that
I left the lap of ease—the halo rife
With friendship's richest, soft and mellow tones—
Affection's fond caresses, and the cup
O'erflowing with the sweets of social life
With high refinement's genial pearls enrich'd.
 Ah! no; a holier purpose fir'd my soul—
A nobler object prompted my pursuit
Eternal prospects open'd to my view
And hope celestial in my bosom burn'd.

 God, who commanded Abraham to leave
His native country, and to offer up
On the lone alter, where no eye beheld
But that which never sleeps, an only son;
Is still the same, and thousands who have made
A covenant with him by sacrifice—
Are bearing witness to ~~the~~ its sacred truth.

Jehovah speaking has proclaim'd his will,
   The proclamation sounded in my ear—
It touch'd my heart—I listen'd to the sound,
Counted the cost and laid my earthly all
Upon the alter, and with purpose fix'd
Unalterably while the spirit of
Elijah's God within my bosom reigns,
Embrac'd the "Everlasting" Covenant,
And am determin'd now to be a saint
And number'd with the tried & faithful ones
Whose race is measur'd by their life—whose prize
Is everlasting, and whose happiness
Is God's approval, and to whom 'tis more
Than meat and drink, to do his righteous will.

It is no trifling thing to be a saint
In very deed. To stand upright, nor bow
Nor bend beneath the heavy pressure of
Oppresiveness—to stand unscath'd amid
The bellowing thunders and the raging storm
Of persecution when the hostile pow'rs
Of darkness stimulate the hearts of men
To warfare; to besiege, assault, and with
The heavy thunderbolts of satan, aim
To overthrow the kingdom God has rear'd.
To stand unmov'd upon the with'ring rack
Of vile apostacy, when men depart
From the pure principles of righteousness,
Those principles requiring man to live
By every word proceeding from the mouth
Of God. To stand unwav'ring, undismay'd
And unseduc'd, when the base hypocrite,
Whose deeds take hold on hell, whose face is garb'd
With saintly looks, drawn out by sacrilege
From the profession, but assum'd and thrown
Around him for a mantle to enclose
The black corruption of a putrid heart—
To stand on virtue's lofty pinnacle,
Clad in the heav'nly robes of innocence,
Amid that worse than every other blast—
The blast that strikes at moral character

With floods of falsehood, foaming with abuse—
    To stand with nerve and sinew firmly steel'd,
When in the trying scale of rapid change,
Thrown side by side and face to face to that
Foul-hearted spirit, blacker than the soul
Of midnight's darkest shade, the traitor,
The vile wretch that feeds his sordid selfishness
Upon the peace and blood of innocence;
The faithless rotten-hearted wretch, whose tongue
Speaks words of trust and fond fidelity
While treachery, like a viper, coils behind
The smile that dances in his evil eye—
To pass the fiery ordeal and to have
The heart laid open—all its contents ~~searched~~ <proved>
Before the bar of strictist scrutiny—
To have the finest heartstrings stretch'd unto
Their utmost length—to try their texture—to
Abide with principle unchang'd, the rack
Of cruel, torturing circumstances, which
Ride forth on revolution's blust'ring gale.

    But yet, altho' <u>to be a saint</u> requires
A noble sacrifice—an arduous toil—
A persevering will <aim>; the great reward
Awaiting the grand consummation, will
Repay the price, however enormous; and
The pathway of the saint, the safest path
Will prove, tho' perilous; for 'tis foretold
All things that can be shaken, God will shake:
Kingdoms and governments and Institutes
Both civil and religious must be tried—
Tried to the core and sounded to the depth.
    Then let me be a saint and be prepar'd
For the approaching day, which like a snare
Will soon surprise the hypocrite—expose
The rottenness of human schemes—shake off
Oppressive fetters—break the gorgeous reins
Usurpers hold, and lay the pride of man—
[*Half page empty*] The pride of nations level in the dust![19]

* * *

Retirement

O how sweet is retirement! how precious these hours
They are dearer to me than midsummer's gay flow'rs
Their soft stillness and silence awaken the Muse—
'Tis a time—'tis a place that the minstrel should choose
While so sweetly the moments in silence pass by
When there's nobody here but Eliza and I.

This is truly a moment peculiarly fraught
With unbound meditation and freedom of thought!
Such rich hallowed seasons are wont to inspire
With the breath of Parnassus, the languishing lyre
For sweet silence is dancing in Solitude's eye
When there's nobody here but Eliza and I.

O thou fav'rite retirement! palladium of joys
Remov'd from the bustle of nonsense and noise
Where mind strengthens its empire—enlarges its sphere
While it soars like the eagle or roams like the deer
O these still, sober moments, how swiftly they fly
While there's nobody here but Eliza and I.

November, Wed. 30th. [*No entry*]

Dec. 12th This day commenced school-teaching in the Masonic Hall[20]—the weather very cold and I shall never forget the kindness of Bishop Whitney, who opened the school by prayer after having assisted in preparing the room—

In undertaking the arduous business with my delicate constitution, at this inclement season of the year I was entirely governed by the wishes of Prest. and Mrs. Smith; trusting in God for strength to fulfil, and acknowledging his hand in this as well as in every other circumstance of my life; I believe he has a purpose to accomplish which will be for my good ultimately, inasmuch as I desire and aim to be submissive to the requirements of those whom he has plac'd in authority over me.[21]

Feb. 11th, 1843. Took board and had my lodging removed to the residence of br. J. Holmes.[22]

Lines written by request of Elder [*unfinished title*][23]

If we're faithful and live by each forth-coming word
    And abide by the prophet's dictation
And with constant humility trust in the Lord
    We, ere long, shall behold the salvation
Of God, coming forth in his glory and pow'r
    In a time of his wisdom's own choosing:
It will suddenly come—it will come in an hour
    When the many are foolishly dozing.

What boots it tho' darkness encompass us round,
    And tradition's shrill thunderbolts ringing
If we in obedience to Jesus are found
    And are still to the iron-rod clinging?
If we are submissive and willing to be
    Like clay in the potter's hand moulded;
Our hearts will be glad and rejoice when we see
    God's purposes fully unfolded.

Though I'm ever determin'd to watch unto pray'r
    I'm so human—so subject to feeling
I, oft on a sudden, before I'm aware
    Find unhallow'd thoughts over me stealing
And a dark featur'd spirit, foreboding no good
    O'er my feelings insensibly creeping,
And twining around me a sorrowful mood
    That with grace cannot be in good keeping;

But I hastily bid all such spirits depart—
    My <u>detector</u> pronounces them evil;
They should never be suffer'd to rankle the heart—
    Let them go, whence they came, to the devil:
In whom I have trusted I verily know;
    I'll confide in his goodness forever—
I'll obey him—eternity's records will show
    If my heart from his precepts can sever.

God knows his own purpose—he'll finish it too
    Unassisted by human advisings—
He's abundance of means, and he'll carry it thro'
    Tho' vain man should be proudly despising
'Twas the faithful in Israel who bow'd down to drink
    Like a dog, and they scorn'd not to lap it:

Ev'ry proud fashion'd scheme will to nothingness shrink
   For the pow'r of the Priesthood will sap it.

When we act for eternity shall we regard
   The ills of the present? No: never:
But heedless of consequence trust in the Lord
   And abide in his precepts forever,
And forever rejoice in his favor and love,
   Giving heed to the voice of his spirit
Until we arrive at the mansions above
   And the glory celestial inherit.

March 17th 1843. This day clos'd my school much to my <u>own</u> satisfaction; having the pleasure of the presence of Prest. J. Smith, his lady, Mrs. Allred, Mrs. Durfee and others. After reading in the hearing of the school several beautiful parting pieces, addressed to myself by the scholars I read a farewell address which I had prepared for the occasion—and after singing the following parting hymn; Prest. S. closed the school by prayer.

                    The Parting Hymn.

How sacred is the tie that binds
In lasting bonds congenial minds?
What sacred feelings swell the heart
When friends from friends are call'd to part—
When fond endearment twines a spell
Around the parting word, "<u>Farewell</u>"?

The hours have glided swift away
While we have met from day to day
To echo studies in the Hall—
Those hours we never can recall
For now their dying numbers tell
That we must bid the Hall "<u>Farewell</u>."

Long, mem'ry's vision will hold dear
The season spent together here—
And <u>long</u> [*added later*] <will> recollection chime
Its music to far distant time,

And oft in thrilling numbers tell
The time—the hour we bade "Farewell."

O God! thy guardian care extend—
Be thou our father and our friend—
Let each within thy presence share
Thy favor, thy protecting care;
And may thy smile the shades dispel
That gather round the word "Farewell."

Thy spirit and thy pow'r impart
To guide aright each youthful heart;
And all our feet securely guide
Where thy salvation's streamlets glide;
That we may in they presence dwell
When we to time, shall bid "Farewell."

The following is a copy of the address.

My dear Pupils,

The Time has arrived which is to dissolve the tie of relationship with which we are connected to each other, as Instructor and the instructed.

While I feel myself about to be liberated from the <duties, and relieved from the> great weight of responsibility which have ~~rested~~ devolved upon me, the thought of a separation from you, impresses my mind with feelings which I cannot describe.

Altho' most of you were strangers to me at the commencement of the school; the endearing association has created in my bosom, an attachment which cannot easily be eradicated; and the deep interest I feel in your present & future welfare, must be my apology, if any is thought requisite, for my offering you an address on the present occasion. Be assured, the earnest desire which I have felt and which I still feel for your welfare, will not cease with the termination of my scholastic services.

The business in which I have been officiating is an arduous one—a calling which awakens into exercise every faculty of the mind; and with all fidelity to my patrons, I have endeavored to discharge its duties with uprightness and impartiality, in the fear of God.

Amid all the variety of habits, manners, and understandings—amid all the dissimilarity of views & feelings that are huddled to-

gether in a large promiscuous school like <u>this</u>, where children are as
differently govern'd at home, as the subjects of opposing nations; for
a teacher to give universal satisfaction, would be almost an anomaly
in literary practice. Of this, I have ever been so well apprized, previous to engaging in the arduous employment, as to fortify my mind in
such a manner, as, after having conscientiously officiated according
to the best of my ability; to be satisfied with an approving conscience
and the sanction of heaven, regardless of human praise or censure.

I take the liberty on this occasion to express my satisfaction and
approbation of your conduct in general, while under my charge, and
you will please accept my thanks for the respectful attention which,
with very few exceptions, you have paid to my instructions.

The progress you have made in your several studies while under
my tuition, is very gratifying to me, and does honor to yourselves.
Before relinquishing my care, I wish again to impress your minds
with the importance of scholastic pursuits. Altho' they may appear of
little consequence in themselves; they form the laws of civilization,
literature and refinement; therefore let them occupy a due share of
your youthful attention—let not your time run to waste—let not your
early life be trifled away on nonsensical objects; but in all your pursuits, have a wise reference to the future, ever bearing in mind that
the manner in which you improve the present period, will have a
bearing <upon> on your conditions and character hereafter, and let
the attention and the improvement of your minds and manners engage much of your present attention in order to prepare you for the
relations you will be call'd to sustain in the busy scenes of life which
are lying before you. You live in a very important age, an age teeming
with events, and if your lives are spared, you will each have a part to
act in the grand scenery which precedes and is to prepare the way for
the second [coming] of the Messiah. You should endeavor to realize
the consequence of the period, and to act accordingly. Let your
thoughts be elevated—let them rise superior to the superficial
glare—the pompous nothingness of the fashion of this world which
ever passes away, and study to make yourselves useful. By early habit
you will accustom yourselves to blend the useful with the agreeable
in such a manner as that the every-day duties of life will be pleasur-
able; and that course of life which proposes the most usefulness, will
conduce most to your individual happiness by contributing most to
the happiness of others. How much better—how much nobler the
principle of habituating yourselves to derive pleasure by contributing

to the happiness of those around you, than to seek it in the indulgence of that little selfishness of feeling which extends no farther, and has no other object than mere personal gratification?

Endeavor to cultivate sufficient independence of mind, that you will <u>dare to do right</u>—that will inspire you with moral courage enough to stem the tide of evil example, realizing that the eyes of the great God are <continually> upon you, and let his approbation be esteemed the richest reward, regardless of the frowns and the smiles of the vain & unprincipled, who would fain lead you from the paths of rectitude.

Situated as you are in the "City of the Saints"—the place destined for the gathering of people from every nation, kindred, tongue and people; you must expect to associate with people of widely different dispositions and understandings, and whose habits and manners have been formed under every variety of circumstances. With these expectations it will be peculiarly necessary for you, if you wish either to be happy yourselves or promote the happiness of those around you, to cultivate feelings of philanthropy and consanguinity: accustom yourselves to view the conduct of others in the most favorable light; and always be more ready to find a redeeming apology for inadvertences and failings, than to indulge in severe censures and criticisms; remembering that so long as people are differently educated and the customs of different places are so very unlike; no individual judgment will be acknowledged as a criterion of propriety; therefore it is better to be indulgent and forbearing especially in all cases which are merely matters of taste, and allow to others every privilege which you wish to enjoy yourselves. After all your utmost exertions in welldoing, do not be discouraged when you learn by sad experience that the world does not appreciate your doings in a manner to meet the expectation of youthful anticipation.

Do not overestimate the merit of your own actions, and console your feelings with the idea that the eyes of Him who judgeth righteously are upon you—that the time will come when all will be rewarded according to their works—when the secrets of all hearts will be made known; and endeavor to hold sufficient command over your feelings to be satisfied with the approval of the great God, and patiently await the decision of his tribunal, regardless of the praise and censure, smiles and frowns of those persons who are guided by the preconceived notions of contracted, silly, and selfish minds

The human mind possesses an adhesive quality—it is apt to adhere to, and contract a likeness to that with which it comes most in contact, or with which it is most conversant; therefore it is all important that you should be wise in the choice of your particular associates—Let the good—the honest and the upright constitute the society in which you familiarize your thoughts and feelings, at the same time, be courteous and affable to all. That kind of haughtiness of manner which many mistake for dignity, which by its repulsiveness is calculated to hold every body at a distance, is a stranger to the amiability which flows from a philanthropic disposition, and genuine goodness of heart.

Court the society of the aged who have trod the path of life before you—those who have accumulated wisdom by length of years and practical experience. Listen respectfully to their instructions, and profit by their counsels. Never treat them with that arrogance and insolence which too much characterizes the manners of the present age. Honor them as they honor God—look up to them with reverence and treat them with kindness and affection; reflecting that, should you arrive to their years, how gratifying it will be to yourselves to see the children and youth, look up to you with respectful attention, and leaning upon you as the guardians of their virtues, and the protectors and supporters of their morals, like the tender twig sheltering itself beneath the spreading umbrage of the sturdy and inflexible oak

Many of you now are in that season of life when fascinating charms of ~~youth~~ <the> world seem most attractive to the human heart, and when its ten-thousand snares are most liable to attract the unsuspecting and inexperienced feet aside from the paths of virtue, religion and piety; and as many if not all of you are members of the Church of Jesus Christ, let me say to you, remember now your Creator in the days of your youth and serve him with a perfect heart and a willing mind—set your faces as flint to keep the commandments of God, and to live by every word that proceedeth out of his mouth. Turn your backs upon the vanities and follies of the world, and hold them in comparative contempt. Be steadfast without bigotry. If you are faithful and true to the profession you have made, you are to become the companions of angels.

How awkward you would feel to be introduced into the society of beings filled with intelligence and surrounded with glory, if entirely unprepared for such society? Life itself might seem too short for such a preparation. Then diligently seek wisdom and knowledge. Study attentively the revelations which God has given heretofore, and receive & treasure up whatever shall proceed from his mouth from time to time; for we live in a day when he is speaking to his people and to the inhabitants of the earth, through the prophet whom he has raised up for that purpose. If you calculate to live by every word that proceeds from the mouth of God, you must be <u>determined</u>—you must not be afraid to be <u>singular</u>: for though you are privileged above all the world with regard to society by being associated with the Latter-day saints; remember that all are not Israel that are of Israel—that the kingdom of heaven is like a net cast into the sea which gathers of every kind, and even *here* are some who would entice you from the pure principles of the religion of Jesus. I pray that God will enlighten your minds by his spirit continually, to enable you to judge correctly and distinguish between the false honor of the world, and the honor that comes from God—between those things that are highly esteem'd among men but which are of short duration; and those things that will abide the changes of time and endure eternally, when earthly things shall have measured their sublimary existence and numbered the fleeting moments that defined their being—that you may have wisdom to know the will of God, and integrity and courage sufficient to perform it—that you may be truly the sons & daughters of Zion—that you may be ornaments to the church—patterns of piety and virtue, and prepared for a glorious state of existence, to share in the triumphs over death and the grave when this mortal shall have put on immortality—when the first resurrection shall bring forth the righteous, and thro' the merits of Jesus give them an eternal victory, and place them on high, above the ruins of divisible and combustible matter.

With the most earnest desires for your present & eternal welfare, praying God in the name of Jesus Christ that you may be blest with the richest of heaven's blessings—that you may be preserved from the evils that are in the world, and be of that number who, having the harps of God, shall sing the song of Moses and the Lamb and inherit the glory of the celestial kingdom, I bid you all, an affectionate <u>farewell</u>!

A number of farewell addresses were presented me by the scholars among which were the following:

> And has the hour arrived
>   That we must bid adieu
> To you, our pleasant mates and friends—
>   Our kind instructor too!

Yes—but in love we part
   And every friendly tie
Shall still be cherished when away
   As memr'y brings it nigh.

And while from heart to heart
   There thrills the tender pain
As thought of saying "farewell" friends,
   Yet hope will love sustain.

For kind remembrance yet
   Shall still those hours retrace
Where we together sought the gem
   Of knowledge to possess.

And dear Instructress! say:
   Will you not further deign
Some future day to aid our minds
   And lead us forth again?

This hope would cheer our hearts
   And chase the shade away
Which "gathers round the word farewell"
   And gild the parting day.
      (signed) Fanny Decker

To My Teacher.

The time has now arrived when it falls to my lot to bid you farewell as a teacher; it is with feelings of regret that I do so. I would still wish to continue under the guidance of one who I feel is possess'd of every qualification necessary to instruct the useful mind in all the branches of useful knowledge. I am not insensible to the interest you have manifested in my behalf, but have witnessed it with pleasure, and my desire is, that I may have as great an interest for myself and endeavor as far as possible to profit from the instructions given me. Receive my heartfelt gratitude for every kindness bestowed upon me; and may the time not be far distant when I shall again sit under the sound of your voice and listen to all the good advice and every instruction which you may deem proper to give me. Excuse all imperfections and receive these lines as a token of that high regard which I feel for a kind and affectionate teacher.

      (signed) Sophia Roundy.

To Miss E. R. Snow

Fair thee well my dear Teacher, the time is at hand
When we must be parted from this friendly band
The hours have flown quickly tho' sweetly away
And I wish O, dear Teacher you could still with us stay.

I thank thee dear Teacher for the lessons thou'st taught
They will oft be the theme of my happiest thought
And if far from each other, we chance to remove
I will ever remember thy kindness and love.

It is true the dear hours we can never recall
That we've spent here together, in this pleasant hall
And my bosom's warm feelings hereafter will swell
When I think of the time that I bade you "Farewell."
                    (signed) Eliza A. Allred.

To my Teacher

With pleasure now I take my pen, to write these humble
    lines
In token of respect for one, whose heart with wisdom
    shines
Whose words of admonition given, have caused me to re-
    joice
And pray that I, like <u>thee</u> might make intelligence my
    choice.

I feel that nobleness of mind, is what the Lord admires,
And from thy pen effusions flow, which oft my heart in-
    spires;
I feel an anxious wish arise that I like thee might be
In time the favor'd one of heaven, to write sweet poetry.

I now return my thanks sincere, for kind attention giv'n
And pray that thy reward may be, rich blessings sent from
    heav'n;
May all thy future days be crown'd with peace and happi-
    ness
Thy works obtain for <u>thee</u> at last, a robe of righteousness.
                    (signed) Samantha Roundy.

Sunday April 9th, Conference closed yesterday—it has been a very
interesting season to those present, but from ill health I have been

deprived attending except one half day. With mingled emotions of pain and pleasure I perused a letter written by P. P. Pratt, with which I was this evening favored by the politeness of elder Woodruff. The joyful intelligence of the arrival of my brother with a company of 230, in St. Louis was accompanied with the announcement of the death of br. L. Barnes, the first elder in the church of Latter-day Saints, who has laid his bones upon a foreign soil.

> Ah! has he gone! And did he die upon
> A stranger land? Yes, far away from home
> He'd gone across the proud Atlantic's waves
> And left behind his kindred and the friends,
> Bound by association's strongest spell,
> Wrought in the sceneries of early youth.
>   Why did he go? The gospel was his theme,
> And with salvation's tidings on his tongue,
> And with its genial influence in his heart
> He cross'd the ocean to extend the light
> Of heav'nly vision, which the servants of
> The Lord, by recent revelation as
> In ancient days, had borne to distant climes.
>   A transatlantic bard has sung his name
> In sweetest strains; but yet a tribute waits
> His mem'ry here—here in his native land
> Where friends by long acquaintance prov'd his worth
> To be like gems of neverfading hue
> That deck the wreath where friendship has his name
> And character indelibly inscrib'd—
> Where thousands that have known him will respond,
> His is a mem'ry that will never die.[24]

Wednesday 12th. This day I have the inexpressible happiness of once again embracing a brother who had been absent nearly three years. I cannot describe the feelings which fill'd my bosom when I saw the steam-boat Amaranth moving majestically up the Mississippi, and thought perhaps Lorenzo was on board: my heart overflowed with gratitude when, after the landing of the boat, I heard Prest. Hiram Smith say to me "your brother has actually arrived." It is a time of mutual rejoicing which I never shall forget.

Sat. 15th. Spent a very interesting and agreeable afternoon at Mr. Lyon's present L., Mrs. Scovill, Miss Frost, &c.

Tues, May 9th Had a delightful excursion up the river to Burlington

Thurs. May 11th. Accompanied L. to Lima—very pleasant ride.

Monday 15th. Returned to Nauvoo after a very pleasant visit and an interesting Conference at [which] were present Prest. J. Smith, W. Woodruff, & George A. S.[25]

Friday—Visited at Prest. Marks in company with Sophie Robinson, O. Frost, Miss Mitchell &c.—Sat. visited at Mr. Harris.

Tues. 23d. Last night L. and myself staid at New Lancaster & this evening arrived at our father's residence in Walnut Grove; where we found sister A., and all in tolerable health and pleasantly situated in a beautiful country; for which I feel very thankful; The care and anxiety which I have experienc'd for the difficulties to which my parents have been subject since our expulsion from our home in Mo. ~~has~~ have been a source of much bitterness of feeling; and that bitterness has been aggravated by the reflection that they did not in their trials draw out from the springs of consolation which the gospel presents that support which was their privilege, and which would have enabled them to rejoice in the midst of tribulation & disappointment.

Thurs. June 1st. My brother & I returned again to our beloved City after visiting my aunt & cousins at Spring-Creek 12 miles south-east from La-Harpe. A severe storm occur'd this day week—much injury done in Monmouth.

Sun. 4th. Yesterday & last night I spent alone except L.s company for a few hours; the people having gone on a pleasure excursion to Quincy.

Friday 9th. The melanch<ol>y news of the sudden death of Elias Higbee Esqr. who died yester<day> morning has spread a feeling of deep sorrow over the City. How truly it may be said that "in the midst of life we are in death." It is to us a mysterious providence at this time, when every talent and exertion are peculiarly needed for the

erection of the Temple; that one of the Committee should be so suddenly call'd from time to eternity.[26]

Today Lorenzo leaves for Ohio—may the Lord prosper his way
and return him soon to my society

Tues. 13th Last sunday I had the privilege of attending meeting and
in the forenoon listening to a very interesting discourse by Prest. J.
Smith He took for his subject the words of the Savior to wit. "O
Jerusalem thou that killest the prophets and stonest them that are
sent unto you! How oft would I have gathered you as a hen gathereth
her chickens under her wings and you would not!" He beautifully
and in a most powerful manner illustrated the necessity of the gathering and the building of the Temple that those ordinances may be
administered which are necessary preparations for the world to
come: he exhorted the people in impressive terms to be diligent—to
be up and doing lest the tabernacle pass over to another people and
we lose the blessings.[27]

Sunday 18th. Last tues. Prest S. & family started for a visit to her relatives.[28] Friday, spent the night very pleasantly at bishop Whitney's after attending a very interesting meeting of the Relief Society in the
afternoon. This morning sister Mills left us for the eternal world.

I spent the day at home—wrote a letter for Mother Smith. several
brothers & sisters call'd on me in the evening—inform'd me that
brother L. did not leave at the time we expected—probably did not
go till monday morning.

Tues. 20th. Last evening heard the unpleasant intelligence that the
Gov. of Missouri has issued another Writ for the arrest of Prest.
Smith. How long will the hand of persecution retain its iron nerve!
How long must the innocent be harrass'd and perplexed! Word that
a messenger arrived from Springfield, sent by Judge Adams, saturday
night to apprize Prest. S. of the expected arrival of the officers.
Visited at elder Taylor's

Friday 23d. Judge Adams arrived this morning from Springfield. I
call'd to see him—he confirm'd previous intelligence respecting the
Writ being issued, but nothing as yet is heard of the officers—

Yesterday I was presented with the following lines, which had been
sent to press without my knowledge, & of which I had retaine'd not
copy.

For the Wasp.
<u>To who needs Consolation</u>.

O can a gen'rous spirit brook
   With feelings of content
To see an age, distrustful look
   On <u>thee</u> with <u>dark intent</u>!

I feel thy woes—my bosom shares
   Thy spirit's agony:—
How can I love a heart that dares
   Suspect <u>thy</u> purity?

I'll smile on all that smile on <u>thee</u>
   As angels do above—
All who in pure sincerity
   Will love <u>thee</u>, I will love.

Believe me, thou hast noble friends
   Who feel and share thy grief;
And many a fervent pray'r ascends
   To heav'n, for thy relief.[29]

Sunday June 25th This afternoon, while the people were assembled for service in the Grove, Br. Clayton who had been sent with br. Markham to Lee Co. to notify Prest. Smith of the issue of the Writ for his arrest; returned which occasioned considerable excitement. He announced the capture of Prest. S. with his request that a number of the Militia should be sent to his assistance if needed. It was truly gratifying to see the spirit manifested on the occasion, not only by brethren but also by many persons not members of the church. All seem'd desirous of proving their patriotism in the cause of the persecuted prophet. The City literally swarmed with men who ran together from every quarter to volunteer their services. A selection of about eighty horsemen started about dusk, while fifty others were chosen to go by water, who went on board the "Maid of Iowa" to go down the Mississippi and up the Illinois to Ottawa, expecting that Prest. S. would be taken there for trial.

Tues. 27th. Mrs. S. arrived—I went to see her, and learned more particulars concerning the manner in which her husband was taken by J. H. Reynolds, Sheriff of Jackson Co. Mo. and Willson a constable of Hancock Co. Ill. who came to Dixon on Rock river professing to be Mormon elders & enquired for Joseph Smith who they were informed was 12 miles distant at a place called Palestine Grove. They proceeded there & took him a savage manner & brought him to Dixon, intending the same evening which was friday the 23d, to take him into Mo. but thro' the providential interference of the patriotic citizens of the place he was rescued & reserved for a more lawful proceeding.

Thurs. 29th. Took a ride to br. Lot's[30] in company with Mrs. Whitney, Mrs Durfee & Mrs. Holmes. Before we returned, it was announced that a messenger had arrived bringing the joyful intelligence that the prophet would arrive in a few hours.

Sat. 30th A very interesting day. A military Escort accompanied by the Band and a number of ladies on horseback & a vast multitude of citizens in carriages left the City at 11 o'clock A.M. and returned at 2, to the house of Prest. S. with the Prest., where I witness'd a scene of mingled joy & sorrow, which language cannot describe; for who can paint the emotions of the heart—the burst of parental and filial affection amid scenes of deepest anguish and the highest joy? The affectionate manner in which he introduced his family to those worse than savage officers, and the very hospitable treatment they received, was a lesson that should have made an impression on every heart, not to be eradicated.

Lines written on the arrest or rather kidnapping of Prest. S.

> Like bloodhounds fiercely prowling
>   With pistols ready drawn—
> With oaths like tempests howling
>   Those kidnappers came on.
>
> He bared his breast before them
>   But as they hurried near
> A fearfulness came o'er them—
>   It was the cowards fear.
>
> Well might their dark souls wither
>   When he their courage dared—
> Their pity fled—O whither?
>   When he his bosom bared!

"Death has to me no terror"
 He said, "I hate a life
So subject to the horror
 Of your ungodly strife.

What means your savage conduct?
 Have you a lawful Writ?
To any legal process
 I cheerfully submit."

"Here" said the lawless ruffians
 "I[s] our authority"
And drew their pistols nearer
 In rude ferocity.

With more than savage wildness
 Like hungry beasts of prey
They bore in all his mildness
 The man of God away.

With brutish haste they tore him
 From <u>her</u> he loves so well.
And far away they bore him
 With scarce the word <u>farewell</u>!

Their hearts are seats where blindness
 O'er foul corruption reigns—
The milk of human kindness
 Flows not within their veins.

Their conduct was unworthy
 The meanest race of men—
'Twould better fit the tiger
 Emerging from its den.

Missouri! O Missouri!
 You but prolong your shame
By sending such as Reynolds
 Abroad to bear your name.

Could Jackson County furnish
 No <u>tamer</u> shrub than he?
Must legal office burnish
 Such wild barbarity?

Go search your fields and forests—
The panther and the bear
As well would grace your suffrage—
As well deserve a share.

Then might the heartless Wilson—
Thy shame O Illinois!
Become confed'rate with them
And teach them to destroy.

So much ferocious nature
Should join the brutal clan,
And not disgrace the feature
That claims to be a man.

But hear it O Missouri!
Once more "the prophet's free":
Your ill-directed fury
Brought forth a "Jubilee."[31]

July 20th. Sister [*blank*] called to see me. Her appearance very plainly manifested the perturbation of her mind. How strangely is the human countenance changed when the powers of darkness reign over the empire of the heart! Scarcely, if ever, in my life had I ~~ever~~ come in contact with such forbidding and angry looks; yet I felt as calm as the summer eve, and received her as smilingly as the playful infant; and my heart as sweetly reposed upon the bosom of conscious innocence, as infancy reposes in the arms of paternal tenderness & love. It is better to suffer than do wrong, and it is sometimes better to submit to injustice rather than contend; it is certainly bet-ter to wait the retribution of Jehovah, than to contend where effort will be unavailable.[32]

[*eight lines left blank*]

July 21st, In company with br. Allen left Nauvoo for the residence of sister Leavitt in the Morley Settlement. We rode most of the way in the night in consequence of the annoyance of the Prairie flies. It was the season for contemplation, and while gazing on the glitt'ring expanse above, which splendidly contrasted with the shades hat surrounded me; my mind, as if touched by the spirit of inspiration, retraced the <u>past</u> and glanced at the <u>future</u>, serving me a mental treat spiced with the variety of changes subsequent to the present state of mutable existence.

The likeness and unlikeness of disposition & character with which we come in contact, is a fruitful theme of thought; and the <u>very few</u>, who have strength of mind, reason & stability; to act from <u>principle</u>; is truly astonishing, and yet <u>only such</u>, are persons <u>worthy</u> of <u>trust</u>.

July 30th

> Some Good Things. (Inscribed to Mrs. [*blank*])
> When from injustice' bitter cup
> We're forc'd to drink the portion up
> And wait in silence, heav'n's reward,
> 'Tis <u>good</u> to lean upon the Lord.
>
> When haplessly we're plac'd among
> The venom of the lying tongue,
> 'Tis <u>good</u> to feel our sins forgiv'n
> And know our names inscrib'd in heav'n.
>
> 'Tis <u>good</u>—'tis soothing to the mind
> If friends we cherish, prove unkind
> And meet us in an angry mood;
> To know we've <u>always done them good</u>.
>
> When pale-fac'd envy seeks to fling
> Along our path, its pois'nous sting;
> 'Tis <u>good</u> to know we never aim'd
> To draw the prizes, others claim'd.
>
> When by unmerited demand,
> We bow beneath oppression's hand;
> 'Tis <u>good</u> within ourselves to know,
> The tides of fortune <u>ebb</u> and <u>flow</u>.
>
> When persecution aims to blind
> The judgment and pervert the mind;
> 'Tis <u>good</u> to know the path we've trod
> Is sanction'd and approv'd of God.
>
> When superstition's meagre form
> Goes forth and wakes the wrathful storm;
> 'Tis <u>good</u> amid the blast to find
> A steadfast, firm, decided mind.

When we are tossing to and fro
Amid the varying scenes below;
'Tis <u>good</u> to hope through Jesus' love
To share his glorious rest above.

'Tis <u>good</u> to live by ev'ry word
Proceeding from the mouth of God—
'Tis <u>good</u> his faithfulness to trust
And freely own his statutes just.

August 28. Last evening was entertained by br. Huelett reading to us from his own manuscript.[33] This morning wrote the following,

Lines addressed to Mr. Huelett.
I always love the pages fraught
With noble truth & native thought
Where mind, unshackled seems at home
Where e'er abroad it wills to roam.
I wonder'd when I heard your lay
Why you should seek to hide away
Your harp, nor let its cheering sound
Move on the gales that flutter round.

Why should you yield to self distrust
And hide your talent in the dust?
Why should you selfishly suppress
A source of mutual happiness
And lavish on your solitude
That which might do your neighbor good—
That which might cheer the toilsome way
Amid the ills of latter-day?

Why so tenacious that your name
Should be unknown? All earthly fame
Will pass away; but Zions' spire
Is destin'd to be rising higher
Until celestial glories blaze
And earth is lighted with the rays—
Till upper Zion shall come down
And be an everlasting crown.

Though fame's a paltry aim, 'tis well
For Zion's chronicles to tell

How, carefully, within the sphere
However small, allotted here;
Her children each with child-like heart
With promptitude perform'd a part;
And each improv'd the talent giv'n
In honor of the law of heav'n.

When young in years—in all a child—
With thought untrain'd, and fancy wild
'Twas my delight to spend an hour
Beneath the Muse's fav'rite bow'r;
While there I fan'd Parnassus' fire
The letter'd pinions ask'd my lyre;
I <u>deeply scorn'd</u> the Poet's fame
And from the world witheld my name.[34]

But when from the eternal throne,
The truth of God around me shone;
Its glories my affections drew
And soon I tun'd my harp anew:
By counsel which I'd fain abide
I laid fictitious names aside:
My <u>duty</u>, not a love of fame
Induc'd me to divulge my name.

It surely is a glorious thing
To mount imagination's wing;
With Inspiration's chart unfurl'd
That bids defiance to the world;
And ride triumphantly abroad
Where the unthinking never trod,
And gain an empire for the mind
That leaves tradition's throne behind.

Aug. 28th. This afternoon had the inexpressible happiness of greeting Lorenzo, just return'd from Ohio.

Sept. 1st. Br. L. left this morning which leaves a great void in our association—it seems like forcing a wide breach in our family circle.[35] The more endearing the reciprocation of friendship—the more implicit the confidence; the more painful is the separation. This we realize in the present instance.

Oct. 5 Lines addressed to Mr. & Mrs. Scott on the death of their son.

> Cease ye fond parents, cease to weep—
>   Let grief no more your bosoms swell,
> For what is death? 'Tis nature's sleep—
>   The trump of God will break its spell;
> For he whose arm is strong to save
> Arose in triumph o'er the grave.
>
> Why should you sorrow? Death is sweet
>   To those that die in Jesus' love;
> Tho' call'd to part, you soon will meet
>   In holier, happier climes above;
> For all the faithful, Christ will save
> And give them vict'ry o'er the grave.
>
> There's consolation in the blow
>   Altho' it crush a tender tie;
> For while it lays its victims low—
>   Death opens to the worlds on high;
> Celestial glories proudly wave
> Above the confines of the grave.
>
> Let heathen nations clothe the tread
>   Of death in faithless, hopeless gloom;
> While vain imaginations spread
>   Terrific forms around the tomb;
> For human science never gave
> A light to shine beyond the grave.
>
> But where the light—the glorious light
>   Of revelation freely flows;
> Let reason, faith, and hope unite
>   To hush our sorrows to repose—
> Through faith in Him who died to save,
> We'll shout hosannas o'er the grave.[36]

Thurs. Oct. 5th. A disposition to conform to circumstances is a blessing for which I feel very grateful. As saints of the Most High subject to all the vicissitudes attendant on an adherence to the principles of the celestial kingdom: in order to render life desirable; we must cultivate feelings of submission, and cherish in our own bosoms, that peace and tranquility which will enable us to rejoice in whatever situation we may be placed.

To <u>rejoice</u>, or even feel <u>calm</u> and <u>contented</u>, when suffering injustice from our fellow creatures; would certainly require an exertion of mind and a firm command of feeling; yet it is an attainment within our reach, or at least proportionably so; inasmuch as we verily believe that God whom we worship to be a God of justice, and that sooner or later a just retribution will follow—

Psalm Third

Thou that created the heavens and the earth, the seas and the fountains of water! Thou art my God.

Thou art the same—thou changest not, therefore I will not fear, for thy word will endure and thy promises will surely be verified.

In thee have I put my trust, and I know in whom I have confided, and I shall not be confounded.

Though difficulties rise before me higher than the Himmaleh mountains, I will go forward for thou, Lord will open the way before me and make straight paths for my feet.

When the billows of change encompass me—when its surges dash furiously, and the foam thereof is nigh unto overwhelming; thy power will sustain me: I will laugh at the rage of the tempest, and ride fearlessly and triumphantly across the boisterous ocean of circumstance.

Thy spirit is better than the juice of the grape—thy approbation is preferable to the smile of earthly princes—thy favor is richer than the finest gold, and thy wisdom transcendeth all human understanding.

Thy power is supreme—thy plans are founded in wisdom—thou wilt perform thy work and accomplish thy purpose; man cannot prevent it.

The principles of the kingdom are principles of truth and truth is everlasting as thyself, therefore thy kingdom will stand and those that abide its laws will come up before thee to dwell in thy presence.

I will adhere to thy statutes—I will maintain the new and everlasting covenant, not counting my life dear unto me.

When the clouds of uncertainty gather upon the horizon darker than the shades of midnight—when distrust is

raising its standard over the broad field of expectation—thy word will dissipate every obstruction, and the
testimony of Jesus will light up a lamp that will guide
my steps thro' the portals of immortality, and communicate to my understanding the glories of the celestial
kingdom.[37]

Oct. 10th Yesterday returned from Nauvoo,— The trials of Prest.
Rigdon occupied that portion of the Conference which I attended.[38]
Some circumstances of very peculiar interest occur'd during my visit
to the City. Every thing connected with our <u>affections</u> is engraven on
the heart, and needs not the perpetuating touch of the sculptor.

[*Inserted later*] 12th Dream'd that my father spoke to me of prospects
nineteen months to come.

Oct. 19th—Wrote the following for Miss Eliza Partridge.[39]

> You know, dear Girl, that God is just—
>   He wields almighty pow'r;
> Fear not his faithfulness to trust
>   In the most trying hour.
>
> Though darkness like the shades of night
>   Should gather round your way;
> The Lord our God will give you light
>   If you his will obey.
>
> In sweet submission humbly wait
>   And see his purpose crown'd
> He then will make the crooked straight
>   And spread salvation round.
>
> Our heav'nly Father knows the best
>   What way we must be tried:
> Stand still and his salvation test—
>   <u>Thou shalt be satisfied.</u>
>
> "Straight is the gate and narrow is the way that leadeth
>   unto life and <u>few</u> there be that find it."
>
> The trials of the present day
> Require the saint to watch and pray

That they may keep the "narrow way"
    To the celestial glory.

For even <u>saints</u> may turn aside
<u>Thro' fear</u> of ills that may betide,
Or else induc'd by worldly pride
    And lose celestial glory.

O'er rugged cliffs and mountains high—
Through sunless vales the path may lie
Our faith and confidence to try
    In the celestial glory.

Why should we fear tho' cowards say
Old Anak's hosts in ambush lay,
Or there's a lion in the way
    To the celestial glory?

Fear not though life should be at stake
But think how Jesus for our sake
Has suffer'd that we might partake
    Of the celestial glory.

We sometimes here may suffer wrong.
But when we join with Enoch's throng
We'll loudly echo vict'ry's song
    In the celestial glory.

What tho' by some who seem devout
Our names as evil are cast out,
If honor clothe us round about
    In the celestial glory.

Be steadfast and with courage hold
Thy key of God's eternal mould
That will the mysteries unfold
    Of the celestial glory.

O let your hearts and hands be pure
And faithful to the end endure
That you the blessing may secure
    Of the celestial glory.

Then let the times and seasons fly
And bring the glorious period nigh

When Zion will be rais'd on high
  In the celestial glory.[40]

<For the Times & Seasons>
  Before leaving London, Elder Lorenzo Snow, presented to Her Majesty, Queen Victoria and His Highness, Prince Albert, thro' the politeness of Sir Henry Wheatley; two neatly bound copies of the Book of Mormon, which had been donated by Pres't. Brigham Young, and left in the care of Elder Snow for that purpose: which circumstance suggested the following lines.

Queen Victoria
Of all the monarchs of the earth
  That wear the robes of royalty,
She has inherited by birth
  The broadest wreath of majesty.

From her wide territorial wing
  The sun does not withdraw its light,
While earth's diurnal motions bring
  To other nations, day and night.

All earthly thrones are tott'ring things
  Where lights and shadows intervene;
And regal honor often brings
  The scaffold or the guillotine.

But still her scepter is approv'd
  All nations deck the wreath she wears;
Yet like the youth whom Jesus lov'd
  One thing is lacking, even there.

But lo! a prize possessing more
  Of worth, than gems with honor rife—
A herald of salvation bore
  To her the words of endless life.

That <u>gift</u>, however fools deride
  Is worthy of her royal care;
She'd better lay her crown aside
  Than spurn the light reflected there.

O would she now her infl'nce bend—
  The influence of royalty;

Messiah's kingdom to extend
  And Zion's "nursing mother" be:

Thus with the glory of her name
  Inscrib'd on Zion's lofty spire
She'd win a wreath of endless fame
  To last when other wreaths expire.

Though over millions call'd to reign—
  Herself a pow'rful nation's boast
'Twould be her everlasting gain
  To serve the King, the Lord of Hosts.

For there are crowns and thrones on high
  And kingdoms there to be confir'd—
There honors wait that never die—
  There fame's immortal trump is heard.

Truth echoes—'tis Jehovah's word;
  Let kings and queens and princes hear,
To distant isles the sound is heard—
  Ye heav'ns rejoice! O earth, give ear!

The time—The time is now at hand
  To give a glorious period birth—
The Son of God will take command
  And rule the nations of the earth.

Dec. 6th Spent the day at Mr. Lindsay's in cutting clothes.

9th. Lorenzo left for Nauvoo

Dec. 19th Tuesday evening L. having return'd, we had the pleasure of the company of Father & Mother Morley: it was an interesting season, in the order of a blessing Meeting, father Morley officiating. The following is a copy of the blessing confer'd on me, as a Patriarchal Blessing.

"Sister Eliza, In the name of Jesus Christ I lay my hands upon thy head, and I confirm all thy former blessings together with the blessings of a Patriarch upon thee. Let thy thoughts, thy mind and thy affections be stay'd upon the mighty God of Jacob.

Thou hast the blessing and gift to know in whom thou hast put thy trust—he is thy friend and thy great Benefactor. He has been mindful of thee and has given thee an intellect capable of receiving & understanding all things necessary, pertaining to thy present and everlasting welfare; and thou hast & shall have the blessing to improve upon every talent and gift that the God of nature has bestow'd upon thee. The powers of thy mind are fix'd as firmly as the pillars of heaven, to comply with the requisitions of thy Creator, and thou shalt never be disappointed in the cause thou hast espous'd. The Lord thy Savior loves thee and has been bountiful in pouring his blessings upon thee; and thou shalt have the blessing to be admired & honor'd by all good men. Thou hast the blessing to speak in wisdom & to counsel in prudence, and thou shalt have the blessing to be honor'd by those who have spoken reproachfully of thee; and thou shalt yet stand in high & holy places, to be honor'd and admired for the integrity of thy heart. Thy fidelity has reach'd the heavens, and thy name is honor'd & admir'd by the heav'nly hosts. Thy steps shall be trac'd in prudence—thy examples are worthy of imitation, and thou mayest ever confide in the friend of thy bosom. Thou mayest open thy mind to thy Creator and thy requests shall be granted because thou hast an advocate even Jesus, & in his name thou art invited to pay thy devotions to the Most High, and in and thro' his name thou mayest ever rejoice in the New & everlasting covenants: Ask, and there shall be given an additional blessing to thee; and thou shalt have influence & power over all those who have sought to injure thee, to do good unto them, and to cause them to become a blessing to thee. Thy influence shall be great—thy examples shall not be excel'd. Thou hast a heart to be enlarg'd, and a mind capable of expansion; and for thy comfort remember in thy retired walks, that yonder sun is typical of a crown of glory that shall be seal'd upon thy head: The stars that twinkle in yonder sky shall show to thy mind the workmanship of thy Creator, and by those glories thou shalt read the destinies of man and be capable with thy pen to communicate, to thy fellow man the blessings & glories of futurity: and thy blessing shall roll and continue to thee until time is lost in eternity: and thy name shall be handed down to posterity from generation to generation: and many songs shall be heard that were dictated by thy pen and from the principles of thy mind, even until the choirs from on high and the earth below, shall join in one universal song of praise to God and the Lamb. —These blessings, together with Eternal life I seal upon thy head in the name of thy Redeemer. Amen."

Recorded in book E. Page 67
A L Morley[41]

Missouri.

What aileth thee Oh Missouri! that thy face should gather blackness, and why are thy features so terribly distorted?

Rottenness has seiz'd upon thy vitals—corruption is preying upon thy inward parts, and the breath of thy lips is full of destructive contagion.

What meaneth thy shaking, and why are thou terrified? Thou has become like the trembling Belshazzar—"<u>Mene, Mene, Tekel Upharsin</u>" is indeed written against thee; but it is the work of thine own hand—the characters upon thy wall, are of thine own inscription, and wherefore dost thou tremble?

Wouldst thou know the interpretation thereof? Hast thou sought for a Daniel to declare it? Verily, one greater than Daniel was in the midst; but thou hast butcher'd the saints, and hast hunted the prophets like Ahab of old!

Thou has extinguished the light of thy own glory—thou hast pluck'd from thy head the crown of honor—thou hast divested thyself of the robe of respectability—thou hast thrust from thy own bosom the veins that flow'd with virtue and integrity.

Thou has violated the laws of our sacred Constitution—thou hast unsheathed the sword against thy dearest national rights, by rising up against thy own citizens and moistening thy soil with the blood of those that legally inherited it

When thou hadst torn from helpless innocence its rightful protectors, thou didst pollute the holy sanctuary of female virtue and barbarously trample upon the most sacred gem of domestic felicity!

Therefore the daughters of Columbia count thee a reproach, and blush with indignation at the mention of thy name.

Thou has become an ignominious stain on the escutcheon of a noble, free and independent Republic—thou art a stink in the nostrils of the Goddess of Liberty.

Thou art fall'd <n>—thou art fall'n beneath the weight of thine own unhallow'd deeds, and thy iniquities press as a heavy load upon thee.

But altho' thy glory has departed—though thou hast gone down like a star that is set forever; thy memory will not be erased—thou wilt be had in remembrance even until the saints of God shall forget that the way to the celestial kingdom is "through great tribulation."

Though thou shouldst be sever'd, like a mortified member from the body of the Union—though the lion from the thicket should devour thee up; thy doings will be perpetuated—mention will be made of them by the generations to come.

Thou art already associated with Herod, Nero, and the "bloody Inquisition"—thy name has become synonomous with oppression, cruelty, treachery and murder.

Thou wilt rank high with the haters of righteousness, and the shedders of innocent blood—the hosts of tyrants are waiting beneath to meet thee at thy coming.

O ye wise Legislators! Ye Advocates of equal rights! Ye Distributors of Justice! Ye Executives of the nation! Arise and redress the wrongs of an innocent people and redeem the cause of insulted Liberty.

Let not the contagious spirit of corruption wither the sacred wreath that encircles you, and spread a cloud of darkness over the glory of your star-spangled banner.

Lest the monarchs of the earth should have you in derision—lest you should be weigh'd in the balance with the heathen nations and should be found wanting.

Lest the arm of the Lord should be reveal'd in judgment against you—lest an arrow of vengeance from the Almighty should pierce the rotten fabric of a once sheltering Constitution, and your boasted Confederacy become like an oak dismember'd of its branches, whose shattered trunk is torn piecemeal by the uprising of the tempest.

For the cries of the widow—and fatherless—the groans of the oppress'd, and the prayers of the suff'ring exile, have come up before the Lord God of Hosts, who brought our pilgrim fathers across the boisterous ocean, & rais'd up a Washington to break the yoke of foreign oppression. [*Half page blank*]

Sunday evening Dec. 31st The year 1843 is just closing upon us with all its eventfulness. While meditating upon the subject, the thought suggested to my mind that brother Lorenzo speak an address before the quiet circle present. I made the motion which was carried and he arose and delivered a very interesting address; beautifully adapted to the occasion. He spoke of the anticipations of the future—the probable eventful scenery of the year about to open before us. He refer'd to the past and said that the individuals present, while standing on the threshhold of the year now closing; <u>did not</u> and <u>could not</u> imagine it possible for the changes to transpire that have transpired, with the reception & understanding, the light & intelligence connected with principles of salvation &c, which will have an important bearing upon our future welfare; and we may also expect that the coming year will be as replete with interesting consequences, & changes of more importance than our minds are capable of comprehending: But from the marvelous dealings of Divine Providence in overruling all things for our good—in bringing us safely thro' difficult scenes, we may look forward without the least anxiety—having everything to hope & nothing to fear. In referring to his own personal experience, he said that one year ago he was in the great City of Birmingham presiding over the Conference of saints in the Metropolis, and standing first Counsellor to the President of all the churches in the British Empire, looking forward with the deepest solicitude, anticipating the difficulties and dangers that awaited him in crossing the boisterous ocean, and leading up to Zion a company of 250 saints; but the Lord has brought him through most triumphantly; and we are here together, enjoying the blessings of social life &c. &c.

He said the year upon which we are soon to enter, will probably release some of us from the difficulties into which the changes of the past ~~have~~ has thrown us, it will open our path & make things clear before us, but we shall then find other things, perhaps, of an unpleasant nature as consequent attendants on those circumstances & that scenery in which we may find ourselves placed.— He enforc'd the utility of suppressing all anxiety with respect to the future by saying, "How illy qualified, were we one year ago, to pass thro' the scenes thro' which we have been led with success, from which let us realize the folly of an over anxiety to pry into scenes that are lying before us, inasmuch as God will prepare us by a gradual process, step by step; leading us forward in a manner that will prove easy as we pass along, but which, if presented to our view at once, would seem insurmountable. He said that inasmuch as we are disposed to do right, we may learn from the past year's experience, that those things that we are call'd to suffer, produce a very different effect upon the mind from what we should anticipate if they were presented before us in prospect; producing pleasure & satisfaction, when we would look for misery. While we look with astonishment on the past, we may be instructed to set our hearts at rest with regard to the future, and also by contrasting the situations of some present, with our situations one year ago, and taking into consideration our present enjoyments; we find it practicable for the mind to rise superior to circumstance—by having cultivated in our bosoms such principles as are calculated to elevate the affections, bring the feelings into subjection and give stability to the mind, thus producing happiness independant of outward contingencies—possessing our happiness within ourselves.

He said in taking a retrospective view of our lives, even from the time we embrac'd the gospel; altho' we had pass'd thro' some scenes of severe trial; God had borne us off victoriously thus far, even to our great astonishment and we may confidently trust in his guidance and protection, for the coming year.

Jan 1st, 1844.

                    The ~~new~~ past Year.
        A year—what is a year? 'Tis but a link
        In the grand chain of time extending from
        The earth's formation, to the period when
        An angel standing in the sun shall swear
        "The chain is finish'd—time shall be no more."
            Then by the pow'r of faith—that pow'r by which
        The great Jehovah spoke and it was done,
        And nature mov'd subservient to his will;
        Earth leaves the orbit where her days & nights
        And years & ages have been measur'd long,
        By revolution's fix'd, unchanging laws;
        And upward journies to her native home
            Where is the Year? Envelop'd in the past
        With all its scenes & all its sceneries
        Upon its bosom laid; the year has gone
        To join in fellowship with all the years
        Before & since the flood; leaving behind
        A train of consequences—those effects
        Which like a fond paternal legacy
        That firmly binds with int'rest kin to kin;
        Unite the future, present & the past.
            The Year is gone! None but Omnipotence
        Can weigh it in the balance & define
        The good and evil mingled in its form.
        None but an Omnipresent eye can view
        The fountains and the springs of joy & grief,
        Of pain & pleasure which within its course
        It open'd and has caus'd to flow thro'out
        The broad variety of human life.
        None else is able to explore the length
        And breadth—to fathom the abysses and
        To pry into the cloister'd avenues

Of this life's sceneries, and testify,
Or count the seeds of bitterness which yield
Pois'nous effluvia, proving, when infus'd
Into society its deadliest curse;
Or number the bright rays of happiness,
Whether in sunbeams written, or defin'd
By those soft-featur'd pencilings of light,
Whose want of dazzl'ing brilliancy, is more
Than compensated by their constance
In every day attendance,—little joys,
Which shed a soothing infl'ence on the heart,
Yet imperceptibly—by habit made to seem
More like appendages that gifts bestow'd—
    But who, with common sense & eye unclos'd—
With sensibility enough to keep
The heart alive—with warmth enough to give
An elasticity to half its strings;
But finds inscrib'd upon that tablet of
The memory, a reminiscence of
The year departed, deeply written there
In characters that stand in bold relief:
And more especially in these last days
When nature, seeming conscious that her time
Of dissolution is approaching; hastes
With all the rude impetuosity
Of the tumultuous hurricane; to close
Her labors. Ev'ry spirit is arous'd
Both good and bad, each at its handy work;
Diffusing in the walks of social life
Their honey & their gall: each heart imbibes
That which is most congenial to its own
Inherent qualities of character,
Of which a full developement is wrought
By the effective hand of circumstance.
    A few more years of hurried scenery
Will tell the tale—the present drama close—
Decide the destiny of multitudes,
And bring this generation to the point
Where time extending to its utmost bound,
Will tread the threshhold of eternity.
[*Added later:*] Nauvoo, Ill.

PSALM SECOND [*Added later*]

Let the Saints lift up their voice—let them not keep silence—let them declare in the ears of this generation, what the Lord has done for his persecuted people.

Let them speak of His mercy and His goodness—let them proclaim His wisdom & His power, in delivering us from the hand of our enemies.

When the authorities of Missouri had risen up against us— when her chief magistrate who had been placed on high, to execute justice and equity, had become the leader of those who sought our destruction—

When we had fallen low beneath the weight of oppression, and had well nigh become a prey to those that thirsted for our blood!

Then the Lord heard our supplications; and the Most High wrought a way for our deliverance: With His strong hand, He stayed the powers of darkness—He provided a path for our feet, and led us forth from the gates of death.

He caused the fetters to be loosed from those that were bound; and the prison doors to be opened, that the unoffending captive might escape.

He brought us into a land of freedom, and planted our feet upon a soil of peace.

He established us in a country of strangers—and in a country of strangers hath He raised up unto us, a multitude of friends.

He opened the hearts of the affluent, to feel for our distress; and their hands, to minister to our necessities. He hath given the tongue of eloquence to the honorable, and they are pleading the cause of innocence, in our behalf.

Verily, the Lord is bringing us "up through great tribulation"—He hath already placed us on high, even above the fear of those that counsel in darkness— whose devices are against the work of the Most High—He hath rolled back the ~~waters~~ waves of persecution—He hath staid the hour of oppression—He hath brought their names into derision, who dealt out to us the cup of affliction.

The Lord hath done it—let His name be exalted—
let His faithfulness be declared in the congregations
of the people— let His statutes be kept in continual
remembrance by all who profess to be His Saints.
Nauvoo, Ill.

Jan. 23rd. In accordance with a communicated request, wrote the
following. To Mrs. M. Pratt on the death of her little Son.[42]

Time with an arrow's speed has gone
　　Since I beheld a blooming flow'r
As fresh as summer morning's dawn
　　Its beauty grac'd the vernal bow'r.

'Twas lovely and its op'ning bloom
　　A joy-inspiring halo spread;
And rich as Eden's first perfume
　　Was the sweet fragrance which it shed.

Such was your little one, and more
　　Than rosy beauty grac'd its air—
A higher charm its features bore—
　　A noble intellect was there.

With fondest hopes, from earliest hour
　　You saw the mind, a royal gem
Expand with reason's genial pow'r
　　To form a future diadem.

But Oh! a frost has nip'd the flow'r,
　　And all its loveliness is gone!
A hand unseen, with ghastly pow'r
　　Has laid full low your little one!

But soon, by nature's annual round
　　That flow'r, beneath the vernal skies
Will bloom:—Ere long the trumpet's sound
　　Will bid your sleeping cherub rise.

How was that lov'd departed one
　　Endear'd by scenes of deep distress!
Missouri's prison walls have known
　　Its infant cry—your fond caress!

When in your arms with tenderness
   You bore it to the wretched cell
That with your presence you might bless
   The heart of him you love so well.

But hush the sorrows of thy breast
   And wait the promise of the Lord
To usher in a day of rest
   When all will be again restor'd.

Altho' a tender branch is torn
   Asunder from the parent tree;
Back to the trunk it whall be borne
   And grafted for eternity.

Feb. 17th. Address'd the following lines to Mrs. [*blank*] Lyons on hearing [of] the death of her beautiful little Daughter.[43]

Earthly happiness is fleeting—
   Earthly prospects quickly fade—
Oft the heart with pleasure beating
   Is to bitterness betray'd!
Ah! methinks I see you bending
   Like a willow o'er the urn;
Yet a heav'nly voice descending
   Sweetly whispers 'do not mourn'.

Scenes of sorrow most distressing—
   Scenes that fill the heart with pain
Often yield the ~~richest~~ <choicest> blessing—
   Present loss is future gain.
In the darkest dispensation
   O remember, <u>God is just</u>;
'Tis the richest consolation
   In his faithfulness to trust.

Let the heart oppress'd with sorrow—
   Let the bosom fill'd with grief—
Let the wounded spirit borrow
   From his promise, sweet relief.
While affection's surge comes o'er you
   Look beyond the dark'ning wave;

See a brighter scene before you—
    Hail the triumph o'er the grave.

Though your lovely child is taken
    From your bosom to the urn;
Soon the sleeping dust will waken
    And its spirit will return.
Yes, again you will behold it
    Fairer than the morning ray—
In your arms, you will enfold it
    Where all tears are wip'd away.

Thurs. 20th. Spent last evening much to my satisfaction, entertainment and instruction, at a Blessing meeting at br. Beeby's in Lima. It was quite a treat to my mind—one of the bright spots on the page of my life, never to be forgotten.

April 14th. On the fifth I came to the City to attend the Conference Spent the time very pleasantly in the affectionate family of Bishop Whitney in company with my sister. Having received counsel to remain in the City, after spending a few days at elder Sherwood's & br. Joshua Smith's; I took up my residence at the house of Col. S. Markham being invited to do so; and I feel truly thankful that I am again permitted to enjoy society which is dear to me as life. I find Sister M. an agreeable, noble, independent minded woman; willing to sacrifice for the truth.[44]

Pac. Mss. F 57.

Sketch of my Life.

I was born in Becket, Berkshire Co., Mass. Jan. 21, 1804.
My parents were of English descent — their ancestors were among the earliest settlers of New England. My father, Oliver Snow, a ~~native of M——~~ — my mother, Rosetta L. Pettibone, of Connecticut.

In my early childhood, my parents moved to that section of the State of Ohio bordering on Lake Erie on the North, and the State of Pennsylvania on the East, known as the "Connecticut Western Reserve," where they purchased land, and settled in Mantua, Portage County.

I am the second of seven children — four daughters and seven sons: all of whom were strictly disciplined to habits of temperance, honesty, and industry; and our parents extended to us the best educational facilities attainable at that time, without preference to either sex.

Although a farmer by occupation, my father performed much public business — officiating in several responsible positions; and, as I was ten years the senior of my eldest brother, so soon as I was competent, he employed me as Secretary in his Office. This experience has proved of great benefit to myself and to others, at different periods of my variegated life.

Whether my mother anticipated or originated the wise policy of Queen Victoria, concerning the training of girls, does not matter — at all events, my mother considered a practical knowledge of house-keeping the best, and most efficient foundation on which to build a magnificent structure of womanly accomplishments — that useful knowledge was the most reliable basis of independence. Hence her daughters were early trained to the kitchen and house-keeping in general; then

On lined foolscap paper Eliza R. Snow copied for Hubert Howe Bancroft her "Sketch of My Life" in 1884–85. The first of forty-three pages is shown here. The dark stroke covers the words "a native of Massachussetts," easily read in the original. Reproduction approximately 70 percent of original size. Courtesy Bancroft Library, University of California, Berkeley.

To the "Sketch of My Life" Eliza Snow appended to the text two poems, "Yes, I would be a Saint," written in her journal in November 1842 and published in the *Times and Seasons*, 2 January 1843 as "Evening Thoughts"; and "Bury me quietly when I die," published in the *Woman's Exponent*, 1 December 1881. The photograph is of the last two stanzas of the latter poem, concluding with the poet's signature. Reproduction 70 percent of original. Courtesy Bancroft Library, University of California, Berkeley.

A portion of the first page of Eliza Snow's Nauvoo diary and notebook, indicating that it was a gift to her from Sarah M. Kimball, who later became her close friend and associate. Reproduction approximately 70 percent of original. Courtesy Relief Society and Historical Department, Church of Jesus Christ of Latter-day Saints.

The first entry in Eliza R. Snow's Nauvoo diary: it is dated 29 June 1842, the day she later identified as the date of her secret plural marriage to Joseph Smith. Reproduction approximately 60 percent of original. Courtesy Relief Society and Historical Department, Church of Jesus Christ of Latter-day Saints.

The second entry in Eliza Snow's Nauvoo journal reports her 29 July 1842 visit as companion of Emma Hale Smith to Quincy where they petitioned Governor Thomas Carlin for protection for Joseph Smith and the Saints. Reproduction approximately 60 percent of original. Courtesy Relief Society and Historical Department, Church of Jesus Christ of Latter-day Saints.

Eliza R. Snow's trail diaries, located at the Huntington Library. The larger, tan colored, saddle-stitched notebook, February 1846–May 1847, is 3 5/8" wide, 5 1/4" tall, and 1/4" thick. The smaller, black leather diary, June 1847–October 1849, is 2 1/4" wide, 4" high, and 1/2" thick. Photograph is full size of original. Courtesy Henry E. Huntington Library, San Marino, California.

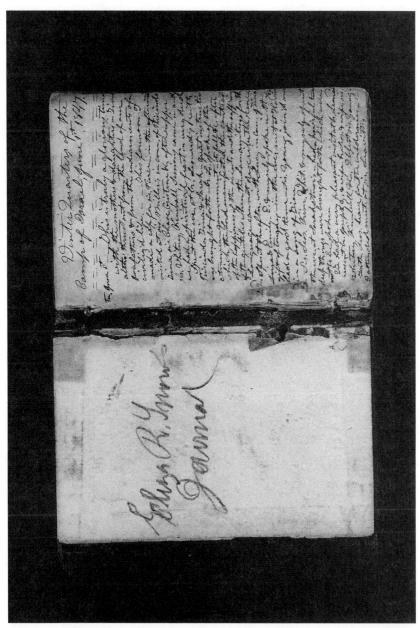

The tiny black leather diary, opened to its first page. The verso inscription is presumably the handwriting of a curator or of LeRoi C. Snow, who had possession of the volume. His widow, Burma C. Snow, sold both volumes to the Huntington Library on 8 October 1963. Photograph is full size, turned 90 degrees. Courtesy Henry E. Huntington Library, San Marino, California.

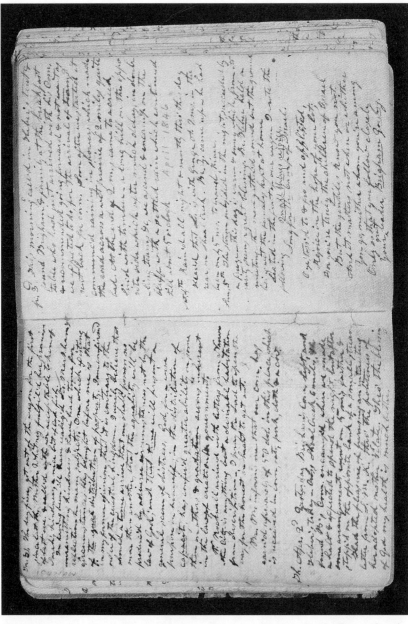

Eliza Snow kept her first trail diary in a tan, leather-backed notebook, here opened to entries of 31 March and 2 April 1846. Two leaves have fallen from the center of the saddle-stitched book. Fortunately, however, before the book was sold to the Huntington Library it had been microfilmed in Salt Lake City. The missing eight pages are printed here. Photograph is 87 percent of full size, turned 90 degrees.

Chapter 3

"A Growling, Grumbling, Devilish, Sickly Time"

The Trail Diary, February 1846–May 1847

THE LAST ENTRY of Eliza Snow's Nauvoo journal was written when she was in the care of Stephen Markham, colonel in the Nauvoo Legion and defender of Joseph Smith, and Stephen's wife, Hannah. In her pristine room in their attic Eliza would mourn alone the death of Joseph, her secret husband and public prophet. There she would write her public eulogy to the martyrs; "Lines on the Assassination of Generals Joseph Smith and Hyrum Smith, . . . " published in the *Times and Seasons* dated four days after the martyrdom, has the ring of epic grief, and speaks for all the Saints.[1]

No one was near to understand her private grief. Her parents, ninety miles away in Walnut Grove, did not know of her relationship to Joseph Smith; her sister Leonora, who must have known, was in Lima, thirty miles south; and Lorenzo, in whom she could have found solace, was in Ohio on a mission. Her "dear friend" Sarah Cleveland, who had witnessed her marriage, had long since left Nauvoo, and young Sarah Kimball, with whom she shared most things precious to her, was not sympathetic to the new doctrine.

Eliza essentially felt like an orphan child. In the Markhams' attic room, in October 1845, she would compose under the title "Invocation, or the Eternal Father and Mother" the poem for which she is most remembered. An impersonal reading of the familiar "O My Father" reveals poignantly outlined the core Mormon doctrine of the continuing existence of man. Consideration of the poet in her time and place, however, uncovers the anguish of "a stranger here" and her wish to return to her timeless home. "With your mutual approbation,/ Let me come and dwell with you," she pleads of the eternal Parents.[2]

Even when in October 1844 Brigham Young took her as a plural wife, as he did others of Joseph's widows, there was no accompanying sense of belonging for Eliza. As leader of the church during those turbulent times, Young was relieved to leave Eliza in the circumstances in which Joseph had placed her, at the Markhams' home. In Hannah Markham Eliza found camaraderie for a time; but as the trail diary unfolds, her life with the Markhams became intolerable—"with *family discord,* which I think proper to call *hell,* reigning around me," she wrote in September 1846. The explosive incident on the Iowa trail, momentous enough for Eliza to record it in detail, is a microcosm of the failure of Eliza's almost frantic search for her "proper" family in the new covenant, a place of true belonging.

Many who must have shared her sense of isolation, of alienation, found comfort in applying to themselves the image of the tribes of Israel through their wanderings in this American Sinai. Brigham Young, their Moses, organized them in family groups of various sorts. There were sealings in plural marriage to a capable patriarch; "adoption" of whole families to a high priesthood figure; organization into wagon companies with sub-groupings of messes, smaller groups which would share meals.[3] The Markhams, whose mess frequently changed personnel, were part of Heber C. Kimball's large company. On one occasion Eliza, requiring more than organizational connectedness, demanded of Kimball, in whose company the Markhams traveled, the assurance of fatherly interest:

> Elder Kimball was passing my "study" to day when after the usual compliments, I told him as I was number'd among his children, I wished to know if he would acknowledge me as one. He said he would & I told him that I should claim a <u>father's blessing</u>. He said he would give me one. I asked when? to which he replied "<u>now</u>" I told him I was ready; he said to me then, "<u>A father's blessing shall rest upon you from this time forth.</u>" From this time I call him <u>father</u>.

The ploy was not entirely successful; Kimball seemed incapable of the kind of familial fondness Eliza craved.

"It is a growling, grumbling, devilish, sickly time with us now," Eliza mourned as her camp settled in for a time at Mount Pisgah, halfway across Iowa to what would become Winter Quarters on the Missouri River. Lorenzo was near by, but was deathly sick for several weeks; and Leonora, coming along with the Morley family, returned to Illinois to care for her siblings there. Eliza was sick at heart as well as in body.

Occasionally in all of this she found solace in the friendly concern of several of the women, named in her diary as "sister" this or that: "Sis. Whitney—Sis. Kimball, Sis. Young, Sis. Lott, Sis. Holmes & Sis. Taylor. Without whose attentions I must have suffer'd much more," she acknowledged. The list is significant: all of these women were participants in plural marriages. Since their crossing of the Mississippi River, which took them away from their critics and the threat such information had presented, the women had begun to share information about their secret alliances. Zina D. H. Young, another of Brigham Young's wives, remembered that it was at Sugar Creek, the first camp west of Nauvoo, that "we first saw who were the brave, the good, the self-sacrificing. Here we had now openly the first examples of noble-minded, virtuous women, bravely commencing to live in the newly-revealed order of celestial marriage."[4]

Louisa Beaman, Clara Decker, and Sarah Lawrence, the first three to call on Eliza after they left Illinois, were participants in the new order—Sarah having been sealed to Joseph in 1843, Clara to Brigham in 1844, and Louisa, like Eliza, having been married sequentially to both. They knew of Eliza's liaisons, and could mutually congratulate or commiserate.

As the trek, and the diary, continued, these wives in the covenant became increasingly the family Eliza sought. Brigham visited Eliza's tent only rarely, and then merely for quick greetings and occasional assurances, each one duly noted. Eliza and his other wives understood and accepted his minimal attentions to them.

Christmas 1846 brought Eliza a joyous homecoming with her sister wives in Brigham Young's family as they waited out the winter halfway to Zion. With "the girls," a euphemism for the plural wives, Eliza found not only a community of caring, but the means and occasions to summon evidences of divine approval. Exercising together the pentecostal gifts became daily practice for many of the women at Winter Quarters.

It is not easy for observers of contemporary Mormon practicality to appreciate the less sedate experiences of their nineteenth-century forebears. Such "enthusiasm," a term rooted in the Greek *enthous,* to be possessed or inspired by a god, is often a characteristic of newly formed religions, Christian as well as others. From the words of St. Paul to the Corinthians, early Latter-day Saints, women as well as men, assumed permission to receive and to honor gifts of the spirit, not only the dignified "wisdom," "knowledge," and "faith" but also the more sensational manifestations of "healing," "the working of miracles," "prophecy," "discerning of spirits," "divers kinds of tongues," and "the interpretation of tongues."[5]

Revelation and prophecy by the gift of faith were Joseph Smith's first claims; his miraculous healing of Elsa Johnson's arm called further attention to his spiritual potency. Brigham Young spoke in tongues shortly after his baptism. Men and women alike participated in glossolalia during the Kirtland period, sometimes creating such disorder among the believers that in 1839 Joseph Smith publicly discouraged use of the gifts of tongues and interpretation.[6] In Nauvoo the pentecostal gifts arose among the women in their newly organized Relief Society. Eliza Snow herself pronounced a blessing in tongues at the organization's second meeting, and a Sister Durfee was healed by the administration of the female presidency, to the consternation of the more staid among the Saints.[7] Joseph Smith commended the women's actions, however, and from then on the sisters felt themselves at least justified if not encouraged in their spiritual exercises.

When Brigham Young and the majority of the church's male leaders were about to leave Winter Quarters for the final segment of the move west, the women returned again to the spiritual practices which confirmed their faith but required no priesthood leadership. The gifts provided comfort, closeness, excitement, and the assurance of divine favor.

It is not surprising, then, given the many bonds which their religion created—sisterhood, sister-wifehood, shared spirituality, as well as the interdependency imposed by physical necessity—that the women encircled themselves in a protective web of their own weaving. So supported, Eliza found her "growling, grumbling, devilish, sickly" season that is reflected in this diary transformed into "a glorious time with the mothers & daughters in Zion" with which the next volume begins.

Trail Diary,
February 1846–May 1847

Feb. 12th 1846. We left our home and went as far as br. Hiram Kimball's where we spent the night and thro' the generosity of sister K. [Sarah M. Kimball] & mother [Lydia] Granger, made some additional preparations for our journey.[1]

13th Cross'd the Missisippi and join'd the Camp—found my br. L.[Lorenzo] & br. [David] Yearsley's families tented side by side; we lodg'd in br. Y.'s tent which before morning was covered with snow.[2]

14th After breakfast I went into the buggy and did not leave till the next day. Sis. M.[Markham] and I did some needlework tho' the melting snow dripp[ed] thro' our cover

15th Sunday. Had a very pleasant visit with Sarah Lawrence

17th Visited Sis. [Vilate] Kimball who had just arrived[3] Mov'd our tents to the upper end of the encampment. The day fine

18th The weather fine—received a visit from Loisa B.[Beaman] C.[Clara] Decker & S. Lawrence. Last night very cold

19th Snow storm commenced in the night and continued thro' the day—it was so disagreeable out that I did not leave the buggy. Suffered considerably from a severe cold—Amused myself by writing the following

The Camp of Israel.

A Song for the Pioneers: [*Added later:*] No. 1.

Altho' in woods and tents we dwell
  Shout, shout, O Camp of Israel
No <u>christian mobs</u> on earth can bind
    Our thoughts, or steal our peace of mind
      Chorus.
    Tho' we fly from vile aggression
    We'll maintain our pure profession—
Seek a peaceable possession
<u>Far from Gentiles and oppression</u>.
    We better live in tents and smoke
    Than wear the cursed gentile yoke—
    We better from our country fly
    Than by mobocracy to die.
      Chorus. Tho' we fly &c.
    We've left the City of Nauvoo
    And our beloved Temple too,
    And to the wilderness we'll go
    Amid the winter frosts and snow.
      Chorus. Tho' we fly &c.
    Our homes were dear—we lov'd them well
    Beneath our roofs we hop'd to dwell,
    And honor the great God's commands
    By mutual rights of christian lands,
      Chorus. Tho' we fly &c
Our persecutors will not cease
Their murd'rous spoiling of our peace
    And have decreed that we must go
    To wilds where reeds & rushes grow.
      Chorus. Tho' we fly &c.
The Camp—the Camp—its numbers swell
    Shout, shout O Camp of Israel!
    The King the Lord of hosts is near
    His armies guard our front & rear
      Chorus. Tho' we fly &c.[4]

Sat. 28th For several days past the weather has been extremely cold—
people visiting us from the City think the weather as severe as has
been thro' the winter. This morning, that portion of the Camp to

which we were attach'd was to start out. Bishop [George] Miller's company left, several days before,[5] but the intense cold prevented, the body of the Camp from following soon as was anticipated.

We travelled but 4 miles and encamp'd in a low, truly romantic valley just large enough for our tents, wagons, &c. We arrived a little before sunset, and the prospect for the night seem'd dubious enough. The ground was covered with snow, shoe deep, but our industrious men with hoes, soon prepared places and pitch'd the tents, built wood-piles in front of them, and but a few minutes, with many hands transform'd the rude valley into a thriving town. [*Added later:*] On indian Creek

Sund. Mar. 1st. The weather considerably moderated in the eve. the remainder of the Camp from sugar Creek arrived with the Twelve, the Band &c. and tented on the bluff which surrounded us.[6]
[*In margin:*] wrote to Sis. S.M.K.

> Song for the Pioneers. No 2.
> The Camp of Israel.

Lo! a mighty <num'rous> host of ~~Jacob~~ people
  Tented on the western shore
Of the noble Missisippi
  <They> ~~Which they had been~~ <for weeks were> cross-
        ing o'er.
At the last day's dawn of winter,
  Bound with frost & wrapt in snow,
Hark! the sound is onward, onward!
  <u>Camp of Israel</u>! rise & go.

All at once is life in motion—
  Trunks and beds & baggage fly;
Oxen yok'd & horses harness'd—
  Tents roll'd up, are passing by.
Soon the carriage wheels are rolling—
  Onward to a woodland dell,
Where at sunset all are quarter'd—
  <u>Camp of Israel</u>! all is well.

Thickly round, the tents are cluster'd
  Neighb'ring smokes together blend—
Supper serv'd—the hymns are chanted—

> And the evening pray'rs ascend.
> Last of all the guards are station'd—
> Heav'ns! must guards be serving here?
> Who would harm the houseless exiles?
> <u>Camp of Israel</u>! never fear.
>
> Where is freedom? where is justice?
> Both have from this nation fled;
> And the blood of martyr'd prophets
> Must be answer'd on its head!
> Therefore to your tents, O Jacob!
> Like our father Abra'm dwell—
> God will execute his purpose—
> <u>Camp of Israel</u>! all is well.[7]

Mon. 2d According to the order of the preceding night, the whole Camp <except some appointed to do a job of work> move forward as early as practicable, and the weather having moderated considerably, after starting on frozen ground & ice, the travelling in the afternoon was in mud & water. Journey'd 12 m. & encamp'd in a field where piles of small wood were scattered very conveniently for our fires as if prepare'd for the purpose, but they had been heap'd by the owner and left either thro' hurry or neglect. The last of the way being very bad, the last of the com. only arrived in time for the next mor. start

The country was timber land and quite broken, with high bluffs rising loftily over low valleys, and but little cultivated.

tu 3d, Camp mov'd in a body 8 miles which was on the bank of the Des Moine. the travelling much better than the previous day—the weather fine—pass'd thro' the town of Farmington where the inhabitants manifested great curiosity and more levity than sympathy for our houseless situation—We join'd Bishop Miller's com. where he halted to perform a job of chopping & fencing [*Added later:*] on Reed's Creek—

Our encampment this night may truly be recorded by this generation as a miracle A City rear'd in a few hours, and every thing in operation that <u>living</u> required, & many additional things which if not <u>extravagances</u>, were in fact <u>conveniences</u>

This eve. was very agreeably surpriz'd by sis. [Elizabeth Ann] Whitney's appearance in front of the buggy where I was seated eating my supper. I rejoiced much to learn that her family had arrived & were tented close by us—having before this time been separated from all old associates

Just before entering Farmington, finished the cakes which Sis. M. made at Sis. K.s—

W. 4th This morning was usher'd in with the music of the Band which was delightfully sublime

Stop'd this day to organize—Bishop M.s company went on, others were appointed to finish the work he had commenc'd.

I spent some time with Sis. W. and Sarah A.[Sarah Ann Whitney Kimball]. Last night dream'd of being in elder K.s mess thought myself quite awkwardly situated. Just at night Sis. Whitney came to our tent expressing much joy in her countenance & said we are all to go together in br. Kimball's com. the Camp being divided into different companys under the Twelve, for the convenience of travelling.

Col. Markham exchang'd the Buggy in which Sis M. & myself rode, & which serv'd me as sitting room & dormitory, for a lumber wagon. Great numbers of the inhabitants of the country were to be seen walking in companys this day, up and down the nameless streets of our magnificent & novel City.

Sis. M. and I took a walk this eve. lost our way—call'd at A.[Amasa] Lyman's tent—after a little chat with E.[Eliza Partridge Lyman] br. L. conducted us toward home until we came in sight of it, which we could hardly have found without a pilot.

Th. 5th—Our newly constructed City is razed and the inhabitants thereof take up their line of march—return to the bank of the Desmoine which we had left at a half mile distance, for our encampment. Sis. M. and I are nicely seated in an ox wagon, on a chest with a brass kettle and a soap box for our foot stools, thankful that we are as well off.—The day fine we travelled 2 miles on the bank of the river & cross'd at a little place called Bonaparte. I slung a tin cup on a string and drew some water which was a very refreshing draught. After crossing the river the road was thro' timber & intolerably muddy the banks on this side rising almost perpendicularly the teams had hard work to draw the loads, as we ascended hill after hill. Our com. consisting of Pioneers, br. Markham's & br. Yearsley's families all of whom were attach'd to elder K. com. of fifty were only able to go 3 miles after crossing, when we came upon a prairie & encamp'd.[8] The present division of our com. was rather awkward. The little boys had gone on with the cows, we knew not where, but afterwards learn'd they were 8 miles ahead with br. L. where most of the Camp had gone. Elder K. was ¾ of a mile beyond us and bishop W. 1½ miles in the rear

fr. 6th We cross'd the prairie & join'd the other encampment, on a small creek & uncomfortably muddy, but in good com. being directly in the neighborhood of the fifty to which we belong'd.

Sat. 7th Left the timber—road very bad for a mile or more—the weather warm & the ox-teams seem'd almost exhausted. I got out of the wagon & walk'd for the first time on the journey. The face of the country quite broken for the first 5 or 6 miles; the timber principally oak, contrasting very much with the beautiful sugar groves on the Desmoine. After a few miles travel in small openings interspers'd with strips of timber land, we pass'd thro' several miles of rolling prairie, under better cultivation than any we had seen since leaving Montrose. Arrived at the place of our encampment after dark, tho' not in the dark for the moon shone brilliantly upon our path. 10 or 12 miles this day.

Sun. 8th The day warm & fine. Heard this mor. of the birth of Sarah Ann's son.[9] Bishop W. did not come up last night and the word was for the camp to remain thro' the day. Call'd on Loisa [Beaman] Emily [Dow Partridge Young] &c. went to meeting, but when br. [Jedediah] Grant commenc'd discourse I understood the citizens had requested the meeting—concluded it would be for their benefit & not so interesting to us, L. and myself went to elder [John] Taylor's tent & spent 2 or 3 hours very pleasantly with sis. [Leonora] T. [Taylor] who was laboring under a rheumatic affiction & felt quite disheartened. I told her she must not be discourag'd—could not feel that she would be long infirm—may God heal her.

    We went to Col. [Albert P.] Rockwood's tent—father [Isaac] Chase quite sick & Clarissa looking disconsolate.

mon. 9th Our <u>town</u> of yesterday morning has grown to a <u>City</u>, laid out in the form of a half hollow square, fronting east & south, on a beautiful level, with an almost perpendicular, on one side and on the other, a gradual descent to a deep ravine on the west & north.[10] At nine this mor. I notic'd but a few rods from our tent, a black-smith's shop in operation, and every thing indicated real life; not a cooking utensil was idle. Sis. M. baked a batch of eleven loaves but the washing business was necessarily omitted for the want of water, an inconvenience the present location suffers more than any previous one. Had the pleasure of the first interview with Prest [Brigham] Y. [Young] since we left the City. Call'd on Sis W. and Sarah with her fine boy.

Tu. 10th Rainy all day

Wed. 11th Rain'd all day—This mor. elder [Henry G.] Sherwood ascertain'd from observations, our geometrical distance from Nauvoo, to be 55 and ¼ miles.

From the dampness of my lodging or some other cause—did not rest much & feel rather indispos'd—took no breakfast, but for my dinner my good friend Sis. M. brought me a slice of beautiful, white light bread and butter, that would have done honor to a more convenient bakery, than an out-of-door fire in the wilderness.

Th. 12th Rainy yest—intolerably muddy

Fri. 13th Rain'd some in the night but colder before morning—quite windy—our tent blew down & with other accidents upset a pail of potatoe soup which was intended for breakfast, but instead thereof we had coffee, fried jole and "jonny cake."[11] This mor. the subject of the fare of the pioneers of our fifty was call'd in question. H.C.K. said a distribution must be made and inasmuch as they did most of the labor they should have while any thing remain'd. L. [Lorenzo] Y. [Young] said they must eat as he did which was a few slices of dried beef boiled & a quart or two of milk added, in which he ate his bread they said they would do so, but had neither the meat or the milk. Meat was furnished by some of the com. our mess had divided with them at the large encampment on the other side the DesMoine among those who remain'd behind to finish Br Miller's job who are said to remain there yet not having means to come on—the rest that have been left at work having all come up including those who stopped about 6 miles back to do a job at rail splitting of which I had not made mention. Sis. M. and I made mother W. and Sarah A. a call in the eve—heard the melancholy news of the death of the amiable & much belov'd Mrs. Caroline C. Spencer[12]

Also thro' the medium of letters receiv'd from Nauvoo, that Wm. Smith & G. [George] J. Adams were gathering on one side, & John E. Page in conjunction with [James] Strang, on the other, while Orson Hyde advocates the cause of truth in favor of the Church—has baptized Luke Johnson, who has gone east for his family intending to join the <u>Camp of Israel</u>[13]

Sat. 14th Cold & windy—Sis. M. Harriet, Elizabeth & myself go to the Creek about a half mile distant, to wash, while Sis. Y. [Yearsley] & Catharine [Markham] stay to attend to the cooking department the result of which we receiv'd some tokens before night, to wit. Catharine sent us some nice sweet biscuits for dinner, & when B. came with the buggy for us at night, Sis. Y. sent us a supper of rich pot-pie made of wild game, rabbits pheasants, quails, &c. which is the <u>fourth</u> dish of the kind on which we have feasted since we left the City, being 4 weeks yesterday—our hunters have been very fortunate. I think few have fared as well in this respect as our family which now numbers 22, elder Sherwood being with us

Before we left the <u>washing vale</u> it commenc'd raining—turn'd windy before morning & I was heartily glad to see the moon shining on the wagon cover a few inches above my head.

This eve. 2 of the ten pioneers left at the incampment on the other side the DesMoine came up with their knapsacks on their backs—The brethren get corn for 12 & 15 cents pr. bushel which is the highest they have given except in one instance when they gave 20.

Sun. 15th So intolerably windy, the men fail in their efforts to keep the tent upright—I did not leave the wagon till night—Sis. [Patty] Sessions made us a visit in the afternoon. Sis. M. making the wagon comfortable with coals. The subject of <u>brotherly oppression</u> was forcibly presented to my view, & I was led to inquire "How long O Lord?" Is there no reward for patient submission? Will the insolent oppressor always go unpunished? How long shall some feast while others famish?

mon. 17th [16] The day fine—took coffee with Sarah A. & went to bro A. Lyman's tent—found a little child of Sydney Tanner at the point of death.[14]

tu. 18th [17] Rainy & windy

wed. 19th [18] Warm & pleasant. Had expected to leave the encampment but are detain'd by the death of br. [Edwin] Little, a
nephew of Prest. B. Young.[15] A very busy day with us in overhauling
and arranging wagons, baking &c. Prest. Y. shook hands with us

th. 20th [19] Left the encampment—the day very cold & windy The
country mostly prairie, broken with strips of timber, mostly oak—
sufficiently rolling for farming—not much cultivated, but decorated
with many new beginnings which promise beautiful homes with a few
years improvement—saw a few fine young peach-orchards. Our Mess
with the pioneers were belated & after travelling 8 or 10 m. put up
for the night—the body of the Camp being a mile & a half in advance—The road was good most of the way—a few mud-holes to ford
by star-light.
[*In margin:*] wrote to Sis. L. [Leonora Leavitt] & Mrs. K.

fr. 20th The cold more intense insomuch that we were obliged to
close the front of the wagon. Traveled 8 or 9 m. & stopped on the
bank of a creek with a pole bridge, call'd Fox river our com. still
ahead—much difficulty in getting feed for the teams. Saw Harriet &
Sarah [Snow].

Sat. 21st The going very bad for 3 or 4 m.s after crossing the river,
half of the distance timber'd land—we met Prest. Y. who had return'd from his encampment to see to the repairing of one of the
wagons. The day fine & the remainder of the road beautiful, over a
prairie 15 miles & encamp'd in the edge of the timber that skirts the
Chariton, 4 m.s [miles] from the stream. Having overtaken the
Camp, in the morning.

Sun. 22d After passing the timber <land> which was very rugged—
came to a bottom of 3 miles on which I counted upward of 80 wagons
before me at one view.[16] Cross'd the Chariton which at this place is a
muddy looking stream perhaps 2 rods in width with steep banks. The
pioneers assisted the teams with ropes. Pass'd on about ¼ m. and encamp'd on a beautiful ridge, where the tents were arranged on each
side the road. Saw Sis. [Sarah DeArmon Pea] Rich for the first time,
encamp'd on the river, one of the girls sick with the measles.
    Br. L. [Lorenzo] came up just before night—had not seen him be-
fore since crossing the Des Moine

Song for the Pioneers of The Camp of Israel No. 3
Dedicated to Prest. B. Young & Elder H.C. Kimball.

Let us go.

Let us go—let us go to the ends of the earth—
Let us go far away from the land of our birth;
For the banner of "freedom" no longer will wave
O'er the patriot's tomb—o'er the dust of the brave.

Let us go—let us go from a country of strife—
From a land where the wicked are seeking our life
From a country where justice no longer remains—
From which virtue is fled & iniquity reigns.

Let us go—let us go from a government where
Our just right of protection we never can share—
Where the soil we have purchas'd we cannot enjoy
Till the time when "the waster goes forth to destroy."

Let us go—let us go to the wilds for a home
Where the wolf and the roe and the buffalo roam
Where the life-inspir'd "eagle" in "liberty" flies—
Where the mountains of Israel in majesty rise.

Let us go—let us go to a country whose soil
Can be made to produce wine, milk, honey & oil—
Where beneath our own vines we may sit & enjoy
The rich fruit of our labors with none to annoy.

Let us go—let us go where our rights are secure—
Where the waters are clear & the atmosphere pure—
Where the hand of oppression has never been felt—
Where the blood of the prophets has never been spilt.

Let us go—let us go where the kingdom of God
Will be seen in its order extending abroad—
Where the Priesthood again will exhibit its worth
In the regeneration of ~~heaven~~ <man> and <of> earth.

Let us go—let us go to the far western shore
Where the blood-thirsty "christians" will hunt us no more;
Where the waves of the ocean will echo the sound
And the <u>shout of salvation be heard the world round</u>.[17]

Mon. 23d Commenc'd raining last evening—rain'd thro the night and this day.

Wed. 25th Commenc'd snowing Mon. night & snow'd with little intermission till this afternoon—the oak ridge on which we are encamped being of a clay soil, the mud of our street & about our fires, in our tents &c. is indescribable. Thro' the unremitting kindness of Mrs. Markham, I donot leave the wagon & this evening we supped together thro' the kindness of Catharine on jonny-cake & milk, the product of "old whity" the family cow. Having had a calf a few days ago, she affords us a fine treat

We are now in Daviess Co. having cross'd the line of VanBuren about 4 miles this side the 11 days encampment which is 4 m's from Keosauque, the county town.

It is impossible to obtain grain here for the teams which live mostly on browse. 25 men of our "fifty" took a job of making rails, for which they got 10 bush. of corn, which was distributed tues. night. They also got 100 [pounds?] of bacon for the pioneers, 100 more paid for. Thus the Lord opens the way for his poor saints, thru patience & industry to obtain the necessaries of life, as they journey towards the western wilderness.

The Chariton is now up so as not fordable—those who [can] go to work, & ford on the crossing in a flat-boat

Th 26th The sun, which had not appear'd since last sat. except a few minutes before setting last night, arose this mor. clear and beautiful, which was hail'd with much pleasure by our wayward-deep-in-the-mud sojourners to be sure, altho' it is accompanied with a cool, north breeze, snow'd some before night. I spent an hour or two very agreeably in sis. Yearsley's carriage, not having left the wagon before since sun. eve. partly thro' ill health & partly on account of the mud.

fr. 27th Bishop M. & the Pratts [Parley P. and Orson] who are encamp'd some miles ahead, are recall'd to attend a court & answer to the charge of disregarding counsel &c.[18] I was very ill last night—a little better today

Sat. 28th The Twelve & others go six miles forward to attend to the organization of the Camp—which is divided in hundreds, fifty's, <&> tens—with presidents & captains over each fifty and captains over tens, & 1 travelling commissary to each hundred—

Sun. 29th. <u>Very cold</u> & windy—Elder Sherwood left our tent to act as Commissary in Brigham's fif[fifty] in conjunction with br. Yearsley who is appointed for Heber's. Br. Y. came to the wagon this eve. & said in the name of the Lord I should get my health.

Mon. 30. Sis. M. H. & E. go to the stream to wash. Sis. Y. gave a treat of apple pies, which the rest enjoy'd much but my health is to ill, tho' improving. The day very fine

Tu 31. The day fine, got out of the wagon for the first [time] since last Th. Mother Whitney fulfil'd her promise of last eve. & call'd with an acceptable token of Sarah's kindness, a nice bit of cod-fish.

In having been ill have realiz'd Sis. Markhams unremitting kindness & have had time for reflection on many subjects. One which existing circumstances has brought before me is that of <u>the equal distribution</u> of <u>property</u>. I am confirm'd in my former opinion that it is contrary to the order of the celestial kingdom. I verily believe that should a <u>time</u> arrive that one shall possess no more than another, that the <u>equality</u> will be produc'd by adverse circumstances, not by the law of God; and that <u>time</u> will present a general scene of distress. God, for a wise purpose in himself; in the distribution of <u>capacity</u>, has confer'd greater ability on some than on others & <u>gradation</u> seems inherent in the law of creation for government.

P. [Porter] Rockwell arrived with letters from Nauvoo the City is any thing but a desirable habitation from description—I pray the Lord to open the way for the honest in heart to get out.

Br. M. informs me that our com. has earn'd upwards of 50 dol. in this place, which is received in corn, oats, pork, cloth & a cow.

Th. Apr. 2d Yesterday Brigham's Com. left, and Heber's today—Cross Shoal Creek 6 miles, & found B's Com. encamp'd, where we made a halt & expected to spend the night, but after some arrangements, went on 5 m.'s farther & stopp'd on the opposite bank of a small stream

Had the pleasure of perusing an interesting letter from S. M. K. thru' the politeness of her adopted mother <u>Vilate</u>.[19] Thro' the blessing of God my health is much better.

fr. 3d. This morning call'd in Heber's tent & found Brigham & family at the breakfast table who had just arrived with his Com. & recommended going forward & not wait as we expected to do, for the arrival of teams sent back for corn. Soon after we started it commenc'd raining in showers which made the road across a wet prairie of 2 miles quite bad. At the end of 2 m.s came to a creek lin'd with timber—a long hill on the opposite side which after much delay, in doubling teams &c, we ascend & encamp on the bluff with a settled rain which continued till about 5 o'clock

sat. 4th Rain'd all night & mostly thro' the day Heard that L. is with George A. [Smith] 7 ms. in the rear on Shoal Creek. Br. Y. came up— he had been on 45 ms. to Grand River.

Sun 5th The storm subsided in the night, succeeded by a freeze—this day is warm & suny which, from its rarity seems a great blessing. Br. <u>Heber</u> held a meeting—the men gather'd round but the ground being wet the females kept at home
  Seated in the front of our wagon I wrote the following

<u>In all things rejoice</u> [*Added later*]
<u>Song for The Camp of Israel.</u>

O ye! toss'd to & fro and afflicted
  Rejoice in the hope of your lot;
For you're truly the children of Israel
  But the gentiles know you not.
And it matters not when or whither
  You go, neither whom you're among
Only so that you follow closely
  Your <great> leader, <u>Brigham Young</u>.

Let the spirit of peace & union,
  And the practice of righteousness
Be your prominent characteristics
  As you go to the wilderness.
And the blessings of heaven will attend you
  Both in time & eternity
If you strictly adhere to the counsel
  Of <u>Brigham</u> & <u>Heber C</u>.

The spirit and pow'r of Jehovah
  Will be guiding your feet along:
For the Lords & the Gods <are> with you,
  They are number'd in Israel's throng
In the sunshine, in storms & in tempests—
  In all changes console yourselves
That your sharers in sorrow & joy are
  <u>Brigham</u>, <u>Heber</u> & all the <u>Twelve</u>.[20]

At 4. o'clock, according to the instruction that each <u>Ten</u> should meet together in their several divisions and partake of the sacrament, we attended to the ordinance for the first time since we left the City. My heart was made to rejoice in the privilege of once more commemorating the death of him whom I desire to behold. Roll on ye wheels of time! hasten thou long anticipated period when he shall again stand upon the earth.

In consequence of some disaffected feelings, Br. Markham's & br. Yearsley's families this mor. separate their table, br. Barney wishing to board with br. M. remains with us. <Br. M. had the misfortune to cut his foot by the fall of an axe from the front of his wagon.>

Mon. 6th Commenc'd raining soon after day light—rain'd all day with little intermission. Soon after we had retired to rest, the wind rose with a perfect gale attended with a heavy shower of rain—several of our habitations were level'd & the roofs of our wagons barely escap'd the wreck of elements. With the storm, the weather became extremely cold

tu. 7th Very cold & windy, moderated a little before night

Wed. 8th The ground froze quite hard this mor.—the wind changed to the south and west. Elder K. thought best to move forward this mor. early & go as far as practicable, rather than wait here for the road to dry, while the teams are losing more than when at work; but the men who started Mon. to go 12 ms. for corn did not return last night as was expected & we must wait for them

Elder Kimball was passing my "study" to day when after the usual compliments, I told him as I was number'd among his children, I wished to know if he would acknowledge me as one. He said he would & I told him that I should claim a <u>father's blessing</u>. He said he would give me one. I asked when? to which he replied "<u>now</u>" I told him I was ready; he said to me then, "<u>A father's blessing shall rest upon you from this time forth</u>." From this time I call him <u>father</u>.

th. 9th Started early as practicable, but before we left Sis. Markham did her 2d churning of butter in the wagon—the road was almost impassable, being low prairie, & to render it worse it commenc'd raining about noon & with the greatest exertion we went but 7 m.s and put up in the open prairie where we had not sufficient wood to keep warm and the teams were let loose without feed, to shirk[21] for themselves. There we pass'd a dreary night of wind & rain.

fr. 10th The cattle & horses had stray'd in the night & it was noon before we left our <u>miry</u> habitation, and when we went it was by doubling teams, leaving some wagons behind—a little after night we arrived at the place of destination where father K. & many others were once more on "Terra Firma" before us with plenty of wood, & fires blazing, & browse for the beasts together with the blessing of an unburnt sod for our carpet which was very delightful

Sat. 11th A council held a few rods from our wagons with most of the Twelve in attendance, to consult the interests of the <u>Camp of Israel</u> & the kingdom of God. It was thought best to change the course of our journey & go more to the north, which would bring us into the later <u>purchase</u>, we being now on the <u>disputed ground</u> between Mo. & Iowa—to travel about 50 m.s & stop to put in crops, build houses, &c. & that the poor in the City be written to immediately to reach the proposed plantation soon as possible—teams were sent back for those of our com. who did not come up

Sun. 12th The Sacrament was administered to those that could assemble in the open air which was very chill—tho' the day was fine. Father K. presided and gave us excellent instruction, reminding us of the goodness of God which had been greatly manifested on our way—altho' it seem'd to us that we had experience'd the worst of weather we should not have thought anything about it had we been at home. He strongly impress'd the necessity of union of feeling & action—said "his feelings were wounded by reflections made by some respecting sending their teams back for others, particularly br. L. Young—said that those who were selfish about helping others would find their teams weakening & dying," &c, &c.

It was a refreshing season to me & while I partook of the elements in remembrance of the death of our Savior, my prayer was O Jesus let me soon behold thy face"

Mother Whitney call'd at our wagon just as the word went forth for meeting, & I remark'd to her that my mind had been impress'd with the idea of going to the land of Palestine & I felt to prophesy that we should yet walk hand [in hand] upon the mountains of Judah even the land of our inheritance & pick rich clusters of grapes which were "dropping down new wines" upon the sides of the mountains while sitting at the meeting I felt a strong confirmation of the above, yet the very feeble state of my health seems to forbid the expectation, but with God all things are possible.[22]

Mon. 13th Sis. M. & myself spent most of the day in Sarah Anns wagon dined with Sis. W. & S; Sarah assisting to prepare tea for the first time since the birth of her <u>promising son</u>.

Tu. 14th The weather continues fine, and father K.s com. according to previous arrangement leave our very beautiful <u>woodland dell</u> to join Brigham's Camp about 3 m.s ahead—while starting some of the teams, father K. pass'd where I was sitting, saying to the brethren that "<u>each one should have a care for all—that if others would have no care for him he should take care of himself & others might take care of themselves</u>"—he said that I might write it, for it was a <u>correct principle</u>.

   After about 3 m.s travel over a rough road, tho' more tolerable than the last, we join'd Brigham's camp on the edge of a high sandy prairie, with gen. [Charles C.] Rich's com. about half m. in the front & bishop Miller's in the rear; on the opposite of a stream call'd Big Locust thickly skirted with timber, over which the Pioneers had made a bridge. Here I think the whole Camp of Israel once more come together with perhaps the exception of br. Spencer's Com. Charles Decker arrived in 4 days from Nauvoo altho' it is nearly 9 weeks since we cross'd the river; our journey bearing some little resemblance to that of the Camp of Israel in former days. David [Markham] brought me a package this eve. which prov'd to be another token from S. M. Kimball, a roll of neat <u>gimp</u>, yet I had to regret that the envelop contain'd only her <u>signature</u> & her <u>love</u>.[23]   .

Wed. 15th Saw with much pleasure br. L. [Lorenzo] whom I had not seen since he left the Camp on the Chariton, sorry to hear that Sarah is sick with the ague.[24]

   A Com. of [*space*] of the pioneers with br. Yearsley are sent out to get work in the country. Several of the companies move on. B.s & H.s remain.

th. 16, We move 6 m.s, encamp on the prairie in separate companies—our situation is fine—The 50 wagons being arrang'd in double file, with the appearance of a public square between. The prairie begins to look green—the rattlesnakes make their appearance much to the annoyance of our horses & cattle, several of them having been bit in trying to allay their hungry appetites

fr. 17th Mov'd 8 m.s—came up with Parley's com. encamp'd on a beautiful timber'd ridge—but our com. getting divided, we broke up again, cross'd the stream [*space*] and located on the prairie with B.s com. in front, Miller's on the left; but before we started, I sent for L. & told him I thought best for him to come with us—br. M. spoke to father K. who said it would be perfectly right for him to take the place he previously occupied. I found that some disorder & apparently much dissatisfaction was existing throughout P.s com.—A. Lyman one days journey in the rear.

Sat. 18th The brethren having met in Council, the word is for a com. immediately to prepare for the mountains—those that have means are to go & the rest are to make a farming establishment on the Grand river & furnish themselves from time to time as Com.s will be going. A report of the means of each fam. is to be made by the capt. of <u>tens</u>, which is to be submitted to the Coun. on mon. where a decision will be made &c.

Sun. 19th A meeting in the forepart of the day at B.s encampment—in the eve. between ours & elder Taylor's—elder T. spoke of our trials &c. which he thought very small—rejoic'd much—spoke of the importance of our mission, said those about him were to act an important part in political affairs—they were going to raise the standard of liberty around which the nations of the earth will yet assemble—Father K. spoke of the lavish manner in which prov. [provisions] had been used by many, that to pursue that course would bring destruction upon the Camp & we should be scatter'd to the four winds. Said it was impossible to take all over the Mt.s—that each one must help himself—he should divide no longer[25]—the com. voted to sustain him, or rather to sanction the measures adopted by the Coun.—He spoke of the great blessings of the Lord upon the Camp—that he never saw so little sickness among so many—that the feeble should become healthy—that sis. E. Snow should be able to walk 20 m.s before we get ~~to~~ <over> the Mt.s. While at meet. saw P. Rockwell ride up and after sup. had the treat of a letter from S. M. Kimball.
[*In bottom margin:*] (B.m call'd at our tent door)

Mon. 20th Col. M.s family commence weighing their flour according to Heber's advice last eve. which is a half lb. pr. day to each person.—wrote to S.M.K.

tu 21st L. came to our place, said P. was unwilling for him to leave—thought he would wind up his business after a short time—brought a letter from A.L.L.[26]

Col. M.s and L. Young's Ten's move 8 or 9 miles Heber not being ready the rest of the Com. remain Brigham's Com. encamp a little ahead of us—Miller between—but fire breaking out he moves beyond B.s our people fire the grass around their wagons to prevent its spread.

Wd. 22d. Taylor's Com. encamp'd in our rear, towards night we saw fire coming towards us with furious rapidity—our men immediately set fires to burn a broader space around our encampment, the wind being so strong that it would have swept across almost instantaniously. After getting ourselves secured we gaz'd with admiration & astonishment at the terrific & majestic spread of the devouring element—the flames rising at times to the incredible height of 30 & 40 feet. I had often listen'd to and read descriptions of "Prairies on fire" & thought them too highly painted, but can now say that the reality "beggars all description." weather fine.

th. 23d Last night we had some heavy showers—Col. M.s Ten remain by ourselves—Several Com.s are moving on—the feed is so that cattle get a good living on the streams—& low swails—we had a pot-pie of turkey yest.—our rations with the milk & butter we have would be an abundance were they of <u>fine flour</u>—do very well with <u>shorts</u> which is all we have since commenc'd weight[27]—I find that ½ rations would be quite sufficient for me as my appetite has been for several weeks—

fr. 24th Heber & the rest of the com. come up but can go no farther today in consequence of his carriage horses having stray'd—hear of them in the afternoon—several animals snake-bit.[28] Myself very ill.

Sat. 25th—Wrote the following

To Mrs. Vilate Kimball

Thou much belov'd in Zion!
    Remember life is made
A double-sided picture,
    Contrasting light and shade.

Our Father means to prove us—
    And here we're fully tried.
He will reverse the drawing
    And show the <u>better</u> side

And then we'll be astonish'd
   That ignorance could throw
Such dismal shades of darkness,
   Where light and beauty glow.

The mists that hide the future
   Are round our vision thrown;
But when, as <u>seen</u>, <u>we're seeing</u>,
   And <u>know as we are known</u>,

Whatever seems forbidding,
   And tending to annoy;
Will, like dull shadows vanish,
   Or <u>turn</u> to <u>crowns</u> of <u>joy</u>.[29]

Left our incampment with some of the wagons, not having sufficient teams; and went about ten m.s encamp'd on a beautiful green prairie lawn by the side of a small, timber'd stream.—My health so ill that I was oblig'd to ride on my bed.

Sun. 26th Went five m.s—came up with the general Camp on the head waters of the Grand river, the place selected for the first farming establishment[30]

   After the meetings of the day, where it was suggested that only <u>men</u> go over the Mt.s, the brethren met in council to deliberate on measures &c.

   By abstaining from milk & substituting tea my health is improving.[31] Our location is a beautiful, undulating grove, which apparently may become a garden of fruits in a short time. <u>But my spirit rests not here</u>.

Mon. 27th Commenc'd raining very early in mor.

fr. May 1st Rain'd every day this week. Warren & Whiting [Markham] go out with the Pioneers to work—Lorenzo arrived this eve.

Sun. May 3d. Meeting at B.s Camp in the mor.—a powerful rain the eve. Br. Thomas died last night.—Br. [Lewis] Barney left for N. [Nauvoo] yester

tu 5th. Yesterday & today the first days without rain since we stop'd here. The brethren exhibit their good disposition in obeying the instructions of last sunday, which were that all should go to work to start this plantation &c.—Yesterday sent a letter to N. to be mail'd for Walnut Grove.[32]

Wed. 6th Got a promise from H. of being present at the first wed[?] . . . among the [*space for two words*] A heavy storm of wind, rain & hail—some slight injury done in consequence of the falling of limbs from trees.

    Forgot to mention the circumstance of last Mon. Sis. Whitney presented me a bowl & did us the honor of drinking tea in it at our tent Col. M's family having tented with Br. Dalton since separating from bro Yearsley—

th. 7th. Sis. Green buried today by the side of br. T.—she died out in the country where the Pioneers are at work[33]—Sis. D. [Desdemona] Gleason commences boarding with us

fr 8th The day fine—spent it at L.s

sat. 9th [*Space*] passing, step'd in. Call'd into Sarah's found Sis. W. quite ill with her lame wrist & in a discourag'd state of mind. she was administer'd to by father [John] Smith, [Newel K.] Whitney & Kimball—

Sun. 10 Preaching in the forenoon—sacrament in the afternoon— Pass'd that this establishment be the property of those that go on, & be for a resting place for those behind. Father [Samuel] Bent, br. [Ezra T.] Benson & br. [Daniel] Fulmer appointed to preside here.
    The day fine. I was not able to attend meeting—tho'

Mon. 11th Parley's com. leave with the expectation of going to the big Platt to commence a farm. George A. arrived to day with his ten. A. Lyman came up. E. called on us. Whiting return'd.

tu 12th The Camp wish to move forward—George Boyd starts for Grand river to notify those of our Com. who are there with teams. I visited B.'s Camp found Eliza had a few minutes interview with Sis. Young—they wish to go out, but one of the girls being sick—doubtful—I told him much oblig'd for leaving us, said should not leave me—confirm'd the promise of my health. Heber, or father Chase & family leave to cross the Creek.

Wed. 13th. Bm's Com. leave this morning—Amus'd myself by reading one of W. Scott's poems entitled "Rokeby"[34] My health much improv'd—I think by using a tea made by Cranesbill for a few days past.[35] Last eve. the clouds threaten'd a heavy shower, but pass'd off with little rain. rain'd little today but at night a heavy storm came on.

I saw the funeral train following to its <u>wilderness grave</u> a little child of br. [Theodore] Turley[36.] It was a lonely sight—my feelings truly sympathize with those who are call'd to leave their dear relatives by the way.

Br [Peter] Haws[37] having had considerable difficulty—his Com. is broken up.

th. 14th Last night a very heavy rain

fr 15th Bishop W. & family leave us this mor.—every departure makes us more & more lonely—it seems almost like the days of Peleg when the earth was divided but we hope to follow soon—may be the pleasure of meeting compensates for the parting.[38]

Sun. 17th The meeting held at Taylor's camp which has not mov'd—Yesterday I enjoy'd the novel scenery of a quilting out-of-doors, after which with much conviviality & agreeable sociability the party took tea with sister Dalton, the mistress of the quilting. present Sis. Markham, Yearsley, Gleason, Harriet, & Catherine. Our treat was serv'd in the tent, around a table of bark, spread on bars, supported by four crotches drove into the ground; and consisted of light biscuits & butter, dutch cheese, peach sauce, custard pie & tea.

This eve. Warren return'd—had but little success in the country—Yearsley not expected for several days—looks rather discouraging but we are not at all discourag'd, tho we hear that the Camp is 30 ms. ahead & still going

mon. 18th Capt. Smith & Lyman [&] Whitney leave us quite masters of the field—Altho' so much alone, I feel no despondency—my health is daily improving & my spirits buoyant—I feel that the blessings of the Lord & the blessings of many who have gone on, attend me. Surely happiness is not altogether the product of circumstances—our father who watches over his children's welfare will order all things for good if we will put our trust in him, we need not fear.

But I find from every day's experience that while we are thrown into the midst of all sorts of spirits, it is my lot to have one about me that is a constant annoyance, one with whom I <u>cannot</u> & <u>will</u> <not> hold fellowship—thro' whose instrumentality much disquietude has been occasioned![39]

tu. 19th This morning a circumstance occur'd which renew'd my reflections on the subject of family government. Without <u>order</u> all is confusion. & without mutual action in the head (& mutual feeling & mutual understanding must produce mutual action) there can be no order. One parent must support the claims to respect for the other & this can never be done while either exposes the faults of the other in the presence of the children

In the eve. we took leave of our transient place of residence—cross'd the Creek over which the brethren had built a bridge & went perhaps 3 m.s, leaving Sis Yearsley in waiting for her husband not yet return'd from the country. Our encampment consisting of 3 waggons, to wit. Col. M's, Warren's & Capt. Dalton's

Wed. 20th Rain'd all day—did not leave

Th. Rain'd in the forenoon—did not leave—br Dany came up.

fr. 22d Travel'd 5 ms. came up with Turley & Smith

Sat. 23d. Travel'd 1 2 ms. over a rolling prairie. Horace Whitney & King came up with us last night, who had gone with teams to assist Col. Markham. br. Yearsley &c to the next location. We overtook Gen. Rich—met [Joseph] Kingsbury & L.W. going out to trade—pass'd a guide board &c.[40]

Sun. 24th Travel'd 10 or 11 ms.—

Mon. 25th Rain'd heavily last night streams overflow the bridges & render them almost impassable. After crossing one where the men carried the women over (br. W. Cahoon liberally contributing his services as ferry-boat) we ascended a hill on which we had the novel pleasure of viewing a huge pile of stones We arriv'd at the Camp, situated in a small grove with a beautiful prospect; happy once more to meet with home & friends. On the middle fork of the Grand River.[41]

Bishop Miller had started out before our arrival

tu. 26th Spent the day at Lorenzo's. Call'd at prest Y's. Hard show'r last night.

Sat 30th Spent the day with Sis. W. & Kimball at Sarah's—the br. rode out for Council. Had a pleasant interview with Sis Young & spoke with [*unfinished*]

Sun. 31st Conference today interrupted with rain. Harriet call'd in the eve. said L. is quite sick—sent him some aloy.[42] Br. N[oah] Rogers died

June 1st The month commences with a volley of natures tears quite cold. D. Gleason & I are in the wagon with a kettle of coals Last night I dream'd that sis. M.—came to me much animated & said that the calculation for us to stop here was revers'd and we were to go on— which she this mor. fulfil'd in part—not exactly.

I do not know why some are called to more self denial than others—I pray that I may live to see the time when patience & submission will be rewarded in righteousness.

Inasmuch as I have plead the cause of the oppress'd at the risk of life (for my life has been openly threaten'd in consequence of it)— inasmuch as I have ever plead the cause of liberty, I think God would approbate & sanction as a just right for me to be present when the saints shall rear the <u>standard</u> to the nations of the earth; at all events I prefer stopping behind for the present that every possible means may be appropriated to liberate the ~~oppres~~ Twelve from the oppression of selfish ones who never have made sacrifices for the truth's sake—yet I find a trial to my feelings in being separated from those with whom I have ever been associated in the church

B-m's com. cross the river today—Sis. Sessions brought me the "Hancock Eagle" from sis. [Sylvia] Lyon & bade "<u>good bye</u>"[43]

Tues. 2 Those of Heber's com. who are ready leave today with a mingled sensation of pleasure & regret I bade sis. K. & those connected, "<u>farewell</u>" she made me a little present which I prize much for her sake. A. Fielding arriv'd.

Wed. 3d Bish. W. & fam. leave this mor. Sis. W. came to our wagon & sang me a beautiful song of Zion, which I rejoic'd in as a parting blessing—it is a season not to be forgotten.[44] Whiting goes to drive team for Heber

About noon Harriet came & helping me to a horse I rode home with her—found L. very sick altho' the med. I sent on sun. eve. had a good effect I pray the Lord to restore him to health—I feel the worth of his unremitting kindness to myself & others.—Walk'd home at night.

Th. 4th. Br. Dalton left—Wrote a letter to S.M.K. expecting br. M. to start for Nauvoo but he did not get off. Mov'd into a house built of logs some peeled & some with the bark on, laid up cob fashion from 3 to 8 inches apart—the roof formed by stretching the tent cloth over the ridge pole & fastening at the bottom on the outside, which, which carpetting, blankets &c. fasten'd up at the north end to prevent the wind which is almost cold as winter, we find ourselves very comfortably & commodiously situated.

Heard that one of the br.n. sent to B-m for a yoke of cattle which he had appropriated—I not only feel <u>reconciled</u>, but rejoice that we stop'd, that others may have the means, br. M. having given up all his cattle & one wagon for the benefit of the cause.

fr. 5th Col. M. Left for Nauvoo.[45] S. Smith, Adaline Aunt G. & H arrive.

Sun. 7th Yes. I was sent for to visit Lorenzo, found him worse—Orson Pratt crossed the river to day after meeting—Orson Hyde arriv'd yes. or the day before yes. saw Leonora & the girls—but the pleasure of our meeting was lessened by our brother's severe illness

Wed. 10 Smith & Calvin start for Fox river

Th. 11th L. seems considerably better: in the eve. I return'd to br. M's—The last few days have pass'd in much anxiety—I feel great reason for thankfulness that the Lord has given me strength to administer to L.[46]

Time passes almost imperceptibly yet every day brings the arrival of saints from the City—and the departure of saints from Mount Pisgah. A. Lyman crosses the riv. today—parted with Cornelia &c.

Sat. 13th Sent for to visit L. again—found him worse staid till sun. eve.—propos'd that Porter make a garden

Mon. 15th Harriet came to let me know that L. is very raving I walk'd over & found him in a distress'd condition father H. [Huntington] & Gen. R. [Rich] soon came, they administer'd to him & leaving him in the care of br. Hoyt, said they would go & clothe & pray for him in the order of the Priesthood[47]—he soon became calm—had a short return of the paroxysm in the eve. I sat by him all night—he rested quietly—P.'s making garden at father M's camp.

Tu. 16th Elder Woodruff call'd to see us—had a very pleasant interview—he administer'd to L.[48]

Wed. 17th L. was baptiz'd[49]—I return'd to Col. M's in the eve.

Th. 18 rain'd very little our people finish planting garden

Sat. 20. Yes. a letter was receiv'd from B-m's Camp which is 125 ms. from here where they propose stopping to replenish their provisions, build boats &c. Br. Benson returns who left a week ago to visit the Camp.—Br. & sis. Smoot call'd on us.

Wed. 24—It has been very cold & windy for several days—commenc'd raining in the night, rain'd all day Monday eve. a meet. was call'd & a letter read from Head Quarters calling for 100 men, baggage wag. &c.
   Reported that Boggs is ahead of the Camp with troops—[50]
   —My health improving—Yest. sis. Gleason sewed a hat of my braid[51]—O Lord my God I pray for health that I may be useful

fr. 26th Amos Rogers died last night

Sat. 27th Heard that a messenger pass'd thro here on thursday eve bringing word that Cols Backenstos & Markham were at the head of a Com. of troops last sunday to defeat Williams who was at Golden's point with 500 mob &c. L. had his wagon driven to our tent & I could not dissuade him from his purpose but I must go with him to fath. Morley's settlement about a mile up the river, where Porter has made a garden. Forgot to mention that four Government Officers were here on friday trying to raise volunteers for the Mexican war.[52]

Tu. 30th A very heavy rain last eve. fath. Morley & fam. leave this afternoon for the west. I wrote to sis. W. & K. The last word from the Camp is for all to come on who can

July 1st wed. P. P. Pratt arriv'd from the Camp in two days or a little more—a meeting call'd—Benson who with father Huntington & Gen. Rich, form'd the presidency here, is appointed to take the place of J. E. Page in the quorum of Twelve. I. Morley is to be sent for to return & fill his place as Coun. to f. H.—A Com. of 500 without families are call'd for to go with the Twelve over the mts.
   I have been quite sick since I left Mt. Pisgah—am some better—[53]

th. 2d L. walk'd from the wag. to the garden—seems getting well The weather is extremely hot

Sun. 5th Br. Little, who is appointed to preside over the eastern churches, at meeting today—is on his way to the Twelve with business from Washington.[54]

tu. 7th. Brigham & Heber arriv'd last eve. a general meeting call'd to-day—Volunteers call'd for to go to California in the U.S. service—the same business br. Little was commission'd with, who return'd with B. & H.

th. 9th Yesterday we had the honor of a visit from B, H, Dr. Richards & W. Markham—all in good health & spirits—said L. must get out of this place soon as possible—must come on to G. Island L. ask'd what he should do for provisions when he gets there. B. said, do as I shall tell you after you get there—they administer'd to Porter, who has been quite sick for several days, but now appears to be on the mend. I told B. I wanted his promise that we shall come—he said we shall if we obey counsel.—Weather extremely hot

fr. 10th Br. Smith return'd with a supply of meal, flour, & meat—he has taken a job near Bonaparte where Calvin is at work—expects to get an outfit of provisions for the Mts. & be here to start for G. Island about the 1st of Sep. according to present calculations

S. 12th Busy at work preparing Porter to go with Smith who starts back tomorrow—The hand-mill is now dismiss'd—it has supplied us with bread for some time—

tu. 14th Return'd to br. Markham's—found David sick—Sis. M. gone after hat-timber[55]—Charlotte & I took dinner with sis. Page

Wed. 15th Sis. P. starts this mor. for the Bluffs leaving Sis. M. W. C. D. & myself sole occupants of the habitation & almost of the soil, most of the brethren having left—I commence to braid

Sun. 19th David quite sick with the ague which he has had for three days—is administer'd to—I have braided for one hat pr. day since I return'd

tu. 21st Sis. Gleason return'd—had been for some time over the river

Th. 23. Sis Ally & E. P. call'd on us—both sick with the ague—David has got quite smart—we are looking for br. M.

24th Finish'd the braid for 60 hats since br. M. went away—braided for 11 myself—

tu. 28th Harriet & Sarah spend the day with us—Cath. better of the ague.

August 3d Lorenzo rode over to see us—

mon. 3rd. Last night br. Mark [Mack?]—arriv'd in the night—left his teams 6 m.s back—they arriv'd in the forenoon—Sis. M. quite ill. prospects unpromising—more folks than means—br. G. arriv'd

tu. 5th [4] Sis M. worse—Sis Geen call'd on us—br. & sis. Gleason cross the river with the prospect of going on with sis. Geen

Sat. 9th [8]. Wrote 3 letters, one for br. M. one for sis. Fairchild & one for Cath.

Sun 10th [9] Yesterd. Br. Benson was here—administer'd to Sis. M. Warren & Cath—they are all better today—Olive arriv'd yest. Albert Dimick having gone for her 4 days ago to the lower farm—sis. Fairchild commenc'd living by herself—it is a growling, grumbling, devilish, sickly time with us now[56]—I hope never to see another week like the past one—yet I have great reason to be thankful that it is as well with me—my health is good for this hot weather—G. Gleason & wife left last friday started on yest. with sis Geen.

—Have been a little at loss how to do, but conclude to see the game thro', & enjoy the scenery—The fam. now consisting of br. M. & wife, W. & wife—David, Olive, Margaret and myself—& I had forgotten to mention Olive's son Chancey—

Mon. 11th [10] Sis. M. was worse last night, still growing worse. commenc'd giving her nervine & pepper.[57] W. & C. a little better

tu. 12th [11th] Sis. M's symptoms favorable—continue the nervine & p. with Martien's anti-bilious pills. happening to go in front of my bed in the back end of the wagon, my indignation was arous'd by seeing br. M. & Margaret lying on it side by side—after a moments reflection thought best to suppress my feelings—but return'd to make certain that I was not mistaken—I feel myself in the midst of unclean spirits. O Lord give me wisdom & prudence that I may conduct properly.

Wed. 13th [12] This mor. had the pleasure of perusing a letter from S. M. Kimball—by the hand of Porter Rockwell who arriv'd day before yest.—Wrote 2 letters to send by him to the upper Camp—one to H.C. Kimball & 1 to sis. L.

Mon 18th [17] Last eve. I rode to L.s on horseback—found them well—his health comfortable—staid over night. We expected to have started this mor. but br. M's oxen stray'd & we were only able to go 3 m.s across the river.—It is indeed a time of trial—most of the people at Mt. Pisgah are sick—heard of the death of father Bent—he was a good man—his loss will be felt in Zion—

tu. 19th [18] When we cross'd the river yes. found br. Cummings whom br. Markham expected for company, had gone in the morning—& we were left with only his own family in a forbidding situation for a journey in consequence of sickness & lameness—Sis. Fairchild stops for br. M. to send back for her, & the fam. consists of br. & sis. M. W. & his wife, David, myself, Margaret, Olive & her little boy of about 3 years & Albert Dimick. We have 3 wagons, 4 yoke of oxen & seven cows & heifers & one calf. They talk'd of taking Alma Fairchild to drive one of the teams, but for the purpose of lessening care, lodging &c. Sis. M. propos'd that she & I drive the wagon in which we ride, Olive & Margaret occupying one wagon & W. & C. the other accordingly A. & M. who came to assist on the start, rode back to Mt. Pisgah with P. P. Pratt who met us last night at our encampment on his way to England.

From exertion & too much exercise Sis. M. is quite sick & unable to sit up—I drive of course the boys assisting over bad places. br. M. drives the wagon for O. & M. Albert & David by turns driving Warren's, & the other driving the loose cows. W. not able to sit up, C. some better br. M's hand lame, Olive very delicate & I am so nearly tired out by exerting myself to assist the sick, particularly sis. M. that I can do little but sit in the wagon & drive: but withal we get along first rate travelling about 18 ms. on a good road, stop'd late at night about ½ m. from the road.

Wed. 20th [19] —Rain'd last night—cloudy all day. Sis. M. very sick. W. & C. some better camp'd at night on the 3d branch of the Grand river, where we found br. Cummings <with 5 wagons>. I drive our wagon all day without any trouble; to night are 40 ms. from Mt. Pisgah.

Th. 21st [20] Our sick are better, before noon br. M. made an arrangement to drive his cows with br. C.s and David drive our team—a little before night Whiting met us; he took A.s place in driving Warren's wagon, leaving A. & D. for us by turns. at noon cross'd the 4th branch of G. river.

Fr. 22d [21]. The weather is very cool & fine for travelling—We go on as usual, D. driving for us in the morn. chang'd with A. about 10 o'clock, who was assisting to drive the loose cattle, he was overtaken with a chill—sick all day. I drove till we stop'd for nooning after which D. drove. About 5 in the eve, we came in sight of an Indian Settlement of about 100 wigwams of the Pottawattamie tribe—When in about a mile of the first huts, we were amus'd to see them riding at full speed to meet us—bringing sacks of corn & beans which they were very anxious to sell for money or "swap" for meat baskets &c. They were all pretty well cloth'd & well decorated—talk english some—appear happy & very friendly. Their improvements are small but neatly cultivated—being done by the females—the business of the men being hunting.

We cross'd 2 branches of the Nationa Botana[58] or the Sleeping rock, about 3/4 mile distant from each other—it being quite late we were oblig'd to encamp on the bluff of the western branch in the vicinity of the Indians, they were about our wagons till after dark, and we were fearful of their thievish skill being exhibited at our expense during the night, but suffer'd no annoyance whatever travel'd 12 or 16 ms.

Sat. 23d [22]. Br. M. taken with a chill in the morning sick all day; in the afternoon sat up some—travel'd about 12 ms. & encamp'd on the prairie

Sun. 24th [23]. Started before breakfast for the want of wood & water. Leave Cummings com.—A. & D. drove the cows in the mor. Whiting drove for us a little while when he took Warren's team & I drove the rest of the day. Br. M. able to drive his—about the middle of the forenoon A. came to our wagon with a chill—We travel'd about 5 ms. came to a creek where we overtook br. Carns[?]—took a luncheon & went on perhaps 4 ms.—came to another branch of the Nationa Botana. Here we found the bridge in a dilapidated state in consequence of the flood-woods having been wash'd away; but we cross'd without any accident & encamped in the shade of a fine grove of timber which skirts this stream on both sides.

Br. Cum. came up before night—they went to work to repair the bridge & did not cross. Sis. M. better—

Mon. 25th [24] The cattle stray'd & we were detain'd till after noon, when we started & went 5 or 6 ms. & encamp'd on a small stream. I drove our wagon—David drove for his father who had a chill A. left the calf behind which made late business for night

Tu. 26th [25] A. very sick. About noon we came to where a settlement was commenc'd on a considerable prairie stream—I cannot describe the feelings which occupied me while passing this place; it seem'd like a desolation & the wasting of the house of Israel; yet I almost doubted if any real Israelite would stop in such a place: Here we overtook br. Cum's Com. again also br. Coon's. Saw a grave digging & a rudely constructed coffin the sides of plank & cover'd with bark; prepar'd for interment. Sis. M. was just able to wait on A. while I drove thro' the day. Encamp'd on Cag. [Keg] Creek br. M. last night & night before took lodgings in the wagon he drove.

Wed. 27th [26] —About noon we arrived at the celebrated "Council Bluffs" presenting a scene that is truly wildly beautiful, we drove on to the flat which is call'd [*word omitted*] about 8 ms. wide cover'd with a luxuriant growth of grass, & stop'd to bait the cattle. While stopping here Brigham, Heber, father Morley, W. K. & P. Rockwell drove up in a carriage. B. engag'd a boy to drive our team & I rode with them to fath. M.s at Council Point.[59] While riding down, it was motion'd & carried that fath. M. move to the headquarter encampment

This mor. br. M. manifested a mean jealousy which I need not describe.

Th. 28th [27]. Rode on horseback from Council Point to br. M's encampment 2 or 3 ms. down the river. Had an opportunity of viewing the bank of the stream which in many places was wash'd out to a considerable depth leaving only the turf which seem'd ready to break off & precipitate in the river whatever should be so unfortunate as to venture upon it. The opposite bluffs rudely scallop'd with sh<r>ubbery presented a scene that might well be call'd wildly beautiful.

Before we reach'd the ferry we pass'd a village with perhaps 50 huts or houses. inhabited by French & Ind. &c. &c. we cross'd & went 4 ms. to the cold spring where we found sis. Geen, br. Carns & quite a com.

Aug. 2 [*obliterated*] On our way to the camp we saw before us a com. of Ind. br. M. was driving the front team & thinking they were holding a council, he turn'd off the road that we might not interrupt them. They soon made signs for us to return to the road which we did, when they refus'd to let us proceed. They form'd a circle in our front and commenc'd a war dance, after which they wanted something to eat: Our people contributed crackers, bread meat &c. then they said we might go on—they accompanied us some 3 or 4 ms. much to the annoyance of our teams; the cattle which I was driving became so furious thro' fear, that Whiting had to leave his father's wagon who was sick, & drive for us. When the Ind met the Com. returning from the Camp who had been up to attend Council with the brethren, they turn'd & left us. We saw more than 200 in all 75 or 80 of whom were returning from Council. They were of several tribes, to wit, Omahaws [Omahas], Mohaws [Mohawks], Otas [Otoes]

We arriv'd at the Camp 14 ms. from the Spring 2 or 3 hours before sun-set but instead of joining our old associates as we anticipated, our location was ½ ml. distant on an opposite hill which was name'd Hunter's ridge. Here we have a fine view of the general Camp which presents a curious appearance of grandeur & rusticity—the tents & wagons being arrang'd so as to form hollow circles nearly on the summit of the ridge, the western side of which is cover'd with yards for the cattle & horses made with round poles, & at times teeming with living animals.[60] Saw sis. Whit. Sarah, sis. Lott & Elvira &c.

Sat. ~~30~~29th [*in the margin:* mistake in date Sat. 29th] Margaret quite sick having been threaten'd with the chills for several days. Sis. M. hear'd by the by that br. M. recommended for M. & O. to commence cooking by themselves this mor.

Our encampment receives much addition, by wagons coming up. Sis. Hunter with 2 of their wagons arrive, he remaining at the Bluffs, all sick.

Sister M. better—I go to my trade—make pr. pants for David

Bish. Whit—& E. Wool—left for St Louis on the 1st of Sept.

W. Kim. started for Nauvoo in one week afterwards. Cornelia wrote for me to S. M. Kim— on business—Sis. Whitney & Sis. Kim— replied to the last she wrote. [*Remainder of page is blank.*]

[*Undated; circa mid-September, 1846*] I was taken sick on the last day of Aug. of a fever, which run nearly 40 days and terminated in the chills & fever. During this time, while suffering much in body, & lying as it were

at the gate of death; with <u>family discord</u>, which I think proper to call
<u>hell</u>, reigning around me; I had the satisfacion of experiencing kind-
ness from many of my friends, which is indelibly inscrib'd upon my
memory: Particularly Cornelia C. L.—Sis. Whitney—Sis. Kimball, Sis.
Young, Sis. Lott, Sis. Holmes & Sis. Taylor. Without whose attentions I
must have suffer'd much more, as I was the last in the fam. taken sick
& nobody able to wait on or administer to me as I needed. I cannot recollect dates but not long after the commencement of my sickness a
heavy rain came on & the bed where I lay was wet almost from head to
foot, but the Lord preserv'd my life & while I live I will speak of his
goodness.

About this time a circumstance occur'd which I would forbear to
mention; but having omitted some of a similar nature to which I have
at times wish'd to refer, I will take notice of it.

Without attempting to describe the cause, one night, probably after many of the Camp had retired—tho' it could not have been late
in the eve. for sis. M. was very feeble at the time, which circumstance
would have prevented an untimely exposure to the night air) a conversation took place between Col. M. & his wife of a most disgraceful
nature; and the loud & fervent tones in which it was uttered must
have made it quite public thro'out the Camp. Revenge & retaliation
seem'd the ruling spirits of each, & the pow'rs of darkness seem'd
holding a jubilee around us.

About the 8th of Sept. br. M. mov'd his & Warren's wagons some
40 or 50 rods to a creek leaving Margaret & Olive with the camp.

Here B—m call'd to see [me *or* us] for the second time since our
arrival. My health continued very ill with little improvement

Sep. 20th An alarm was given thro'out the Camp in consequence of a
rumor that a mob was crossing the river to molest us during the night.

22d We mov'd near the river, it having been counsel'd for the Camp
to be in more compact order for the general safety—which place being appointed for our winter quarters

Our place in Heber's Division.[61]

Oct. About the 22d of this month Sis. M. invited Heber & wife—sis. W.
& father & mother Smith to sup on a splendid pot-pie made of veal
&c. when father S. reminded me of an old promise to write for him. I
was not able to write, but thro' the blessing of God in a few days after I
wrote the following

<u>To the Patriarch, father John Smith.</u>

Great glory awaits thee, thou father in Israel
    To reward all thy toils & thy labor of love:
The angels that guard thee—that watch o'er thy pathway
    Are proud to report thee in councils above.
The pathway that leads to the mansions of glory
    Where freedom & justice eternally reign:
The Lord God of Jacob has chose for thy footsteps,
    To bring thee to dwell in His presence again.

Thou art greatly belov'd by the saints that surround thee
    They have tasted thy blessings & greatly rejoice.—
The pow'r of the Priesthood is felt thro' thy presence—
    The weak become strong at the sound of thy voice.
Thou art greatly belov'd in the councils of heaven
    Where once thou wast seated, & where still thy name
Is spoken with honor & held in remembrance
    Till thou shalt return to their sittings again.

I have oft felt the pow'r of thy blessing upon me—
    And my heart feels to bless thee, thou servant of God
And say thou'lt be hid in the chambers of Israel
    While the great indignation is raging abroad;
For He that appointeth the times, & the seasons
    Allotted thy calling & work on the earth;
And here in His sight will thy life be held precious
    Till thou hast fulfil'd the design of thy birth.

When thou shalt have finish'd thy toils & thy trials,
    Thou'lt rest for awhile for thy present reward—
Thou wilt join with the spirits of just men made perfect
    And enter with triumph the joy of thy Lord:
And then in the morn of the first resurrection
    Thou'lt come forth to reign with the Savior on earth
Made holy & pure thro' the regeneration,
    The Gods will rejoice in thy glorious birth.[62]

Oct. 28th A com. of 15 start with teams for St. Joseph after the goods which bish. W. & E. Wooley brought up from St. Louis. Whiting being one to go, we were under the necessity of going from the wagon that he might take it. The day was very cold & blustering—the house into which we mov'd was partly chink'd & only mudded on one side & only covered on one side the other having the tent thrown over it—& no chimney

[*Half page blank*]

Nov. 20th Whiting return'd

Nov. 22 My health quite ill. The day very fine.

Mon. 23d This mor. W<arren> getting quite irritated at his father, threw out an insinuation that I had been talking to elder Kimball against his wife which is as false as hell. He call'd no names but said "it is one that we have been supporting all the while, & one in the family.

Is such the greatful returns which I am to receive for sharing the disgrace, & for all my exertions in upholding the reputation of this unfortunate family.

They are & have been as kind to me as their circumstances would admit, but the Lord knows I have done them more good than ~~har~~ all the trouble I have made them, be it ever so much.

I am reminded of the feelings of Job when he exclaim'd "Young men have risen up against me whose fathers I would have disdain'd to have eat with the dogs of my flock. Yesterday the father & son separated so that W. is to have his living charg'd by weight & measure until he can provide his own.[63]

25th Yesterday br. M. topp'd the chimney as high as the roof & finish'd chinking the house which prov'd very fortunate for our comfort as the weather which had been very comfortable & fine for this season of the year became very cold and blustering towards night & is piercingly cold today, yet sunny & otherwise pleasant except the wind.

I will here make honorable mention of Sis. Geen, whose kindnesses to me from time to time since my sickness shall never be forgotten. May the blessing of the Lord rest upon her; yea, she and her family shall never want for friends to sympathize in trouble & to administer in time of need. Some 4 or 5 weeks since I presented her the following lines

To Mrs. Hester Ann Geen on the death of her husband, Elder William Geen.

Mourn not for him—he's gone to rest
His spirit mingles with the blest;
Freed from the cares, the toils & strife
Attendant on this present life:

Mourn not for him—he's gone to join
With noble ones of Abra'm's line—
For he is one of noble race
And shares a royal resting place.

Mourn not for him—he was belov'd
By those whom God the most approv'd
For he was upright, good & just
And faithful to each sacred trust

Mourn not for him—for tho' he's gone
His works will still continue on—
Until he shall again come forth
To reign in peace upon the earth.

Mourn not for him, altho' your heart
Should seem to say 'tis hard to part—
Be still—the trial yet will tend
To your best int'rest in the end.

Mourn not—rejoice, for you shall prove
An honor unto him you love;
And glorious will be your reward
With him, your faithful, loving Lord[64]

Nov. To Mrs. Geen's daughters,

Anna & Amanda

Ye lovely young Misses, seem happy together
You shall always be lov'd while you love one another

[*Unfinished; space left 1 1/2 inches*]

Mother Chase Sylvia & Sis. Geen visited us—we had an interesting
time. [*1/2 page left blank*]

Th. Nov. 26th The atmosphere a little modified Warren coming into the room I could scarcely avoid fastening my eyes upon him since the time of his insulting me on monday—he inquired why I look'd as though I would look him thro'. Understanding the spirit which prompted him I thought wisdom to keep silence. He said it was an imposition for me to look at him so & also he understood that I had accused him of accusing me of talking to Elder K. &c. which he said was a lie as he call'd no names. Poor foolish young man I wish he might be better cultivated When he first was so impudent, his parents both sat silent, but this time his father reprov'd him.

Loisa & Clarissa visit me <with kindnesses>. The day very fine

Sun. 29th Yester. & to day I have renewed tokens of sis. Leavitt's kindnesses which have been many since her arrival. The Lord bless her & all others who have administer'd to me in sickness. Br. Benson arriv'd on friday.

Last eve. br. M. ask'd me what I had written in my journal that W. was scolding about so much. I gave him the journal to read after which he said it was truth. Br. M. said he did not think of W. meaning me at the time. I told him I thought strange that he was silent—that I never was so abus'd in my life—had alway treated W. as a br. & what he said was without the least provocation—that I always held myself above <such> insolence, & should never condescent to contradict it—that whoever insulted me was planting thorns for their future path.

After making the before mentioned insertion, I let sis. M. read it, after which she said, "Do you think you have been disgrac'd by living in the family? I should not think the Lord would require you to live where you would <u>disgrace yourself</u>. If W. has insinuated any thing that you are not guilty of I think he will make it right <u>if you should make him know it</u>

I saw she had a wrong spirit, & made no reply to whatever she said—and indeed I have not polluted my lips with the silly subject except what I said to br. M. last eve.

W. Dec. 9th Last night the Omahaw Indian Chief, who had been living in a tent in our City for a week or two. He was in bed when some Indians came up—fired 5 or 6 guns, shot the Chief twice in the head—shot off 1 of his thumbs and shot three other Indians, one of whom, a squaw has an arm amputated today.[65]

th. 10th The ground has not been covered with snow. On the 4th or 5th a very little hail was perceptible & a few flakes of snow have fallen from time to time since, but scarcely to be notic'd.

m. Dec. 14th The day warm & sunny and the thin sheet of snow which fell in the night for the first time to cover the ground is melted wherever the sun shines.

A com. goes up the river to look out a location for the Indians of the Omahaw tribe who have become quite an annoyance

Last thurs. this ward held its first meeting which is to be attended weekly, an order being establish'd for each man to give every tenth day or a half cord of wood for the benefit of the poor & widows the town having been divided into wards for that purpose.

Yester. Cath. gave birth to a daughter

Sis. Leavitt inform'd me of the death of Eliza P.'s child. O Lord, comfort the heart of the mother in this sudden bereavement

It died on the 12th inst.

> Belov'd Eliza, do not weep
> Your baby sleeps a quiet sleep;
> Altho' in dust its body lies
> Its spirit soars above the skies.
>
> No more upon your throbbing breast
> It lays its little head to rest—
> From all the pains of nature freed,
> Your fond caress it does not need.
>
> Sweet was its visit but its stay
> On earth was short—'twas call'd away
> By kindred spirits to fulfil
> Its calling & Jehovah's will.
>
> Then soothe your feeling—do not mourn,
> Your noble offspring will return,
> With all its loveliness again
> And with its friends on earth remain.[66]

The Omahaw Interpreter who had gone up to the hunting ground on an express to ascertain the truth of a report concerning the massacre of several of that tribe by the Sioux; return'd with the report that he counted 73 dead bodies.[67]

W. 16th [*No entry*]

Th. 17th —Last eve. after getting asleep in bed, I was awaken'd by an unpleasant conversation (if it might be so call'd) between br. M. & wife which was preceded by one of the same nature last sat. morning.

Before they ended, he propos'd "burying the hatchet & being better natur'd to each other"—said she might live with him or not, only so as to be more pleasant

su. 20th The weather very fine. Yest. I walk'd with sis. Leavitt to Bish. Whitney's which is the 3d time I have walk'd out.

Luke Johnson & br. Pierce call'd on me yest mor.

tu. 22d. Br. M. & Whiting start for Mo.

Heard of the death of my Mother in which I feel a sweet consolation inasmuch as she is freed from the ills of the present life—having liv'd to a good old age, & been useful all her days—She sleeps in peace & her grave & father's, who died a year ago the 18th of last Oct., are side by side.

> They are gone—they are gone to a kingdom of rest—
> They are gone—they are gone to the home of the blest
> Far away from the ills of this lower abode—
> They have gone to reside in a mansion of God
>
> They are gone—they are gone to a residence where
> Noble spirits rejoice in their presence to share
> Who, thro' all their long absence desir'd them to come
> And with shouts of hosanna they welcom'd them home.
>
> They are gone—they are gone back again to pursue
> And accomplish the work there appointed to do;
> Crown'd with blessing & honor they yet will return
> And rejoice with the friends they have left here to
>   mourn.[68]

[*Remaining ¾ page blank*]

th. 24th The day delightful—Sis. Geen sent for me—spent the evening very interestingly with sis. Chase, Sessions & Markham.[69]

fr. 25th Spent the afternoon at br. Wooley's with the same com. as yesterday.

sun. 27th Yest. spent at Sis. Sessions—came to Prest. Y.'s in the eve.—enjoy'd this eve. the pleasure of supping on a bak'd turkey in com. with B. Young, J. Young, br. Benson, f. & m. Chase &c. &c.—after having a chill of the ague in the forenoon.

W. 30th Yest. Had another chill—spent this afternoon very agreeably at br. Pierce's in com. with Prest. B.Y. & lady & Loisa br. P. conducted L. & myself home very politely.

fr. Jan. 1st 1847. This mor. take leave of the <u>female family</u> & visit sis. Sessions with Loisa & Zina very pleasantly. Last eve. we had a very interesting time to close my five day visit with the girls; for whom my love seem'd to increase with every day's aquaintance To describe the scene alluded to would be beyond my pow'r—suffice it to say the spirit of the Lord was pour'd out and we receiv'd a blessing thro' our belov'd Mother Chase & sis Clarissa, by the gift of tongues.

Sat. 2d. Stop'd overnight with sis. Geen visited in the forepart of the day at H.C. Kimball's, much to my satisfaction & spent the eve. at br. Winchester's with sis. Sessions & Loisa

M. 4th Yes. return'd to br. M's—spent this day at br. Smoot's with sis. Woodruff and Markham—snow'd last night to cover the ground—the weather today will pass for winter

fr. 8th Yest. went to the Store for a dress pattern which I have in exchange for one which br. Woolley dispos'd of for me, which was a present from br. Yearsley[70]—call'd into bishop Whitney's—he came in after the close of his day's business & he, sis. W. & myself had a very interesting conversation, at least it was so to me. Spent the afternoon of this day at br. Pack's in com. with sis. Whitney & sis Markham.

sat. 9th Loisa had a fine son born yest.[71]

m. 11th The weather which has been extremely cold for several days, is more moderate

Lines on the death of three small
children of W.& P. Woodruff—

Written by her request

Mourn not for them, their bodies rest
So sweetly in the ground—
And they'll awake to life again
    At the first trumpet's sound.

Mourn not for them for they are now
    Associated where
The purest pleasures heav'n can boast
They're privileg'd to share.

Mourn not for them—they're not as when
    Caress'd upon your knee;
They now are noble spirits, and
    Disrob'd of infancy.

Mourn not for them: the helpless state
    Which they submitted to
Was for the body's sake, but more ,
    To prove their love for you.

Mourn not for them: they laid aside
    Their dignity to come
And visit you & stay on earth ·
    Until they were call'd home.

Mourn not for them: they will return
    With grace & honor crown'd
To bless your household & to spread
    Intelligence around.[72]

fr. 15th The day cold & blustering—went to Prest. Y.'s—heard Loisa's babe blest—staid a week, as I was told to do—visited at father Mayland's & made a dress cap for mother Sessions in the time—

sat 23 Yest. in returning home I call'd at bish W's— found her [Elizabeth Ann Whitney] quite ill—spent the evening very interestingly[73]

tu 26th In com. with sis. Leavitt & sis. Markham spent a pleasant eve. at father Chase's. About this time I wrote the following

To all the Ladies who reside in the
2d mansion of Prest B. Young.[74]

<In sacred union a>
Beloved sisters all unite.
In music's sweetest strains—
T'will prove a fountain of delight
While love with you remains.

Songs of the righteous, saith the Lord
Are prayers unto me—
Our spirits prove the rich reward
Of sacred harmony.

Let not a gift be buried low
That with a proper care
And cultivation will bestow
Celestial pleasure there.

What wisdom dictates for our good
Should be our steady aim;
And no excuse should e'er intrude
Where duty holds a claim.

Sweet social music has a pow'r
To soothe the troubled breast;
And at the close of business hour
To calm the nerves for rest.

Its worth the holy fathers knew
In nature's lovely prime—
The ancient mothers lov'd it too,
And practic'd in their time.

> Bright patterns may you ever prove
>   In things of noble worth;
> And may your music rank above
>   The minstrelsy of earth.
>
> Redeem the gift from long abuse
>   When by the gentiles shar'd—
> O bring it back from satan's use
>   And with it praise the Lord.[75]

Tu. Feb. 2d Went to father Lott's from sis. Leavitt's where I had spent several days, it being the first time I had visited her in this place

W. 3d Br. Markham call'd at f. Lott's & told me that Mrs. Young call'd at his house the previous eve. requesting me to be notified to come there this mor. to attend a family party.[76] Br. M. had arriv'd from Mo. last sat. having been absent more than six weeks

Th. 4th Slept with Loisa last night having return'd with her from the party last night. The party was an interesting one five of the br. Young's being present & one sis. Probably 100 persons were present in all & we supp'd at a table that would have done honor to a better cultivated country. The exercises open'd with singing & pray'r & after feasting & dancing, clos'd with an address by Prest. Young which succeeded one by father Kimball.

This eve. Vilate Y. & C. Decker were married without noise or bustle—nobody invited—I address'd the following lines to the young wedded pair

> Please accept my warmest wishes,
>   For your good, ye youthful pair;
> That the richest, choicest blessings
>   Heav'n may grant your lot to share.
>
> Peace & friendship—love and union
>   Plentious as the summer dew,
> Shall upon your op'ning pathway;
>   Gems of sacred pleasure strew.
>
> May you feel the holy Spirit
>   Freely thro' your bosoms flow;
> Till at length you shall inherit
>   All the Priesthood can bestow.

When your life, both long & happy,
    You have finish'd here on earth;
Sweetly sleep: then reawaken
    In a more celestial birth.[77]

fr. 5th Thro' the politeness of father Sessions I attended a very crowded & interesting party, at the Council House, styled the silver greys[78]

su. 7th Yest. with Clarissa & Loisa visited at Br. Pierce's—today attended meeting all day—the weather is fine.

tu. 9th Attended a blessing meeting at father Kimball's on the occasion of his son Solomon being eight days old. [*On the side.*] W. br. M. started for Mo.

sat 13th Went to bish. W.s to put a cap in rigg for her preparatory for tomorrow, which will be the 8th day in the age of her little son, but I was sick all day with chills & fever

W. 17th Invited to sis. Sabra's to celebrate her birthday; but was sick & could not attend

fr. 19th Snowstorm commenc'd

sun. 21st. Very tedious—snow last night drifted in hills several feet in height. The water is plentifully dripping thro' the tent cloth which lines our clapboard roof.[79]

tu. 23 Commenc'd writing to sis Kimball. Wm. Cutler & others about starting for Nauvoo. The church are organizing for journeying in the Spring. Some days ago a party of of [*sic*] the Sioux Indians stole a number of horses & cattle from our herdsmen up the river

fr. 26th Cold & stormy—my health better than it has been for 2 weeks past.

sat 27th Sis Hyde spent the afternoon with us. Sent a letter to S. M. K. by W. Cutler.

<mon.> March. 1st The day fine—the snow thaws some with the sun altho' the wind is quite chilly—spent the afternoon with Miss S. Maylan at C. & M.s

Wed. 3d. Sis M. & myself visited at br. Gleason's. It thaw'd so much that
the water broke into the house like a torrent & we retreated to sis.
Walkers till eve, when we return'd to a cheerful fire—a hay carpeting
on the floor—good company &c. &c. the frost stiffen'd the mud &
snow & we came home "dry shod" at late bed-time.

th. 4th. Hear'd that the cattle which are herded up the river are dying in consequence of the rushes being buried with snow which lies
on a level at the depth of 18 inches.
    The word is that the Pioneers are to start for the western location
on the 18 of this month.

<u>Acrostic for Anna Geen</u>

M=ay the spirit of contentment,
    I=n your bosom ever dwell;
S=uch as in the hour of trial
    S=weetly whispers, "*all is well.*"

A=s the blooming rose of summer
    N=e'er withdraws its fragrant breath
N=ever may your love & friendship
    A=nd your kindness cease till death.

G=reatness, goodness, light & wisdom,
    E=ndless happiness and peace,
E=vermore adorn your pathway—
    N=ever shall your blessings cease.[80]

March.

Lines for the Album of Mrs.
Margaret Whiteside

Beautious as the op'ning rosebud
    'Neath its shady leafy stem—
Pure as summer morning dew drops—
    Brilliant as the sparkling gem—

Lovely as the modest vi'let—
    Charming as the lily fair—

Rich as orient spicy odors
Moving on the twilight air.

Tuneful as seraphic minstrels—
Bright as Phebus' noontide glow;
Lady, be your own blest halo—

Such your life's encircling bow.
All your works will be rewarded—
All your goodness be repaid—
Crowns of royalty await you—
Glorious crowns that will not fade.[81]

sun. 7th Yester. the weather chang'd & the ground & water this morning are quite clos'd up.—the river safe crossing for teams, which has not been the case for 2 days past.

<u>Lines for Mother Chase: also for Mother Sessions</u>

Truth and holiness and love,
    Wisdom, honor, joy and peace—
That which cometh from above,
    In your pathway shall increase.

Thus the spirit of the Lord
    In your heart shall e'er abide;
And produce a rich reward,
    While the "still small voice" shall guide

Faith & holy confidence
    That will bear your spirit up
Shall henceforward recompense
    All the bitter of your cup.

Righteous are your heart's desires,
    And they will not be denied;
But our Father oft requires
    That our patience shall be tried.

Tho' he should at times withhold,
    Longer than your hopes expect;

You'll receive a double fold,
   When his spirit shall direct.

Therefore let your spirit rest—
   God will order all things well;
And ere long you shall be blest
More than human speech can tell

And the Lord himself will spread
   Thro' your thoughts, a holy pride
Of your chosen earthly head—
   Your protector by your side.

Mutual shall your blesings be—
   Mutual joys shall crown your way.
Thus in Time:—Eternity
   Opens to a brighter day.[82]

Mo. 8th Very cold—freezes in the house.

<u>Lines for Mrs. Wooley's Album</u>

Lady were it mine to bless you
   With the ~~most substantial~~ <purest, sweetest> joys
Nought on earth should dispossess you
   Of ~~a bliss that never~~ <one gift that never> cloys.

Be thou blest, and blest forever
   With what <u>few</u> perchance to find,
From your breast, let nothing sever
   Heav'n's best jewel, <u>peace of mind</u>.

Hold your <u>feelings</u> in subjection
   To your <u>judg'ment's</u> better sway:
Proud to yield to the direction
   Of the lord whom you obey.

Noble are the condescendsions
   Which superior spirits make:
Thus they widen their dimensions,
   And of purer joys partake

> If we're prompt to do whatever
> 　Duty claims our service here;
> We may calmly rest, and never
> 　Need indulge in idle fear.
>
> For his holy approbation
> 　God our Father will bestow;
> And the streams of consolation
> 　Sweetly to our bosoms flow.
>
> May your influence wise & cheering
> 　Wider and more widely spread,
> Till ten thousand hearts endearing
> 　Pour their blessings on your head.
>
> Be thou blest and blest forever
> 　With that gem the upright find;
> Guard it well—let nothing sever
> 　From your bosom, <u>peace of mind</u>.[83]

tu. 9th Weather a little moderated—br. M. return'd from Mo. last eve.

fr. 12th Yest. & today quite pleasant. br. L. Johnson call'd.

sun. 14th Spent last eve. in a <u>very</u> interesting manner at sis. Gheen's in com. with Mother Chase & Sessions father Kim. call'd in & gave us much beautiful instruction, after which we had some glorious communications of the spirit of God both by way of prophecy & the gift of tongues and our hearts were made to rejoice & praise the name of God.

　This day I had the privilege of attending f. K's meeting at br. Wallace's—very interesting indeed; went home with moth. Sessions to spend the night. Br. H. ~~Brownell~~ <Loveland> came in to sit awhile & related a curious circumstance of a cake which was baked a short time since in the circle of his friends, which was written on while in the process of baking & closely confin'd under a lid or cover.

tu. 16th Went to Loisa's—sis. Mary Pierce died this afternoon.

w. 17th Attended the funeral. Prest. Y. preach'd

To br. Robert Pierce & family on
    the death of Mary.

Mary's gone—she's gone: but wither?
    To the paradise of love:
Gone to mingle in the circle
    Of our friends who dwell above.

Did they not rejoice to meet her?
    They had sent for her to come,
And were waiting to receive her—
    She was freely welcom'd home.

There she is a gem of honor;
    Yes, a gem of precious worth:
She will there increase the glory
    Of her kindred on the earth.

Tho' she's gone from us, she's moving
    In a more exalted sphere:
And while she is made more happy
    Do we well to shed a tear?

Could we for one passing moment
    Death's dark mystery unfold—
Could we draw aside the curtain,
    And eternity behold,

We should chide our grief & sorrow
    And suppress each rising sigh;
And rejoice in death, the portal
    Op'ning to the worlds on high.

Therefore, bow in sweet submission.
    God has chasten'd you in love;
You will yet rejoice with Mary
    In the royal courts above.[84]

th. 18th In the mor. call'd into br. P.s and transcrib'd the following
which I had written some weeks ago by the request of Prest. Y.

A journeying Song for the Camp of Israel. Dedicated to
  Prest. Young & Lady.

The time of winter now is o'er—
    There's verdure on the plain:
We leave our shelt'ring roofs once more
    And to our tents again.

Chorus.
Thou Camp of Israel, onward move
    O Jacob, rise and sing—
Ye saints, the world's salvation prove,
    All hail to Zion's king.

We go to choice & goodly lands,
    With rich & fertile soil:
That with the labor of our hands
    Will yield us wine & oil.

Chorus. Thou Camp &c.

We go beside the mountain cliffs
    Where purest waters flow—
Where nature will her precious gifts
    Abundantly bestow.

Chorus. Thou Camp &c.

We'll find a climate pure & free
    Producing life & health;
Where steady care & industry
    Will be a source of wealth.

Chorus.

And there again we will surround
    In peace the luscious board;
And share the products of the ground
    With skill and prudence stor'd.

Chorus.

We leave the mobbing Gentile race
   Who thirst to shed our blood;
To rest in Jacob's hiding place.
   Where Nephite Temples stood.

Chorus.—

We seek a land where truth will reign
   And innocence be free—
Where lawful rights will be maintain'd
   A land of Liberty.

Chorus.—

We seek a land of holiness
   Where justice to the line,
And to the plummet, righteousness
   Will ev'ry work define.

Chorus.—

We go where virtue will be known,
   And merit meet it's due;
For Zion's pathway will be strewn
   With light & glory too.

Chorus.—

We go where hypocrites will fear,
   And tremble at the word
Of him who is appointed here
   To wield the two-edg'd sword.

Chorus.—

We'll find the land the prophet saw—
   In vision, when he said:
"There, there will the celestial law
   Be given and obey'd".

Chorus.—

We go where nations yet will come
In ships, from climes abroad:
To seek protection—and a home,
And worship Israel's God.

Chorus.—

We'll build in peace & safety there
A City to the Lord
And shout amid our toils, to share
A Latter-day's reward.

Chorus.[85]

th. 18th Spent the afternoon at br. Noble's—Sis. Ashby accompanied me back with Loisa—my health very ill. While in this visit, in conversation with Prest. Y. he said to me that br. Markham told him that he could take me on to the west as well as not; which Pres. Y. said would be a great accommodation to him as he was short on it for wagons. The present calculation is for the families of the Twelve & all others that were able to go over the Mts this season.

fr. 19th Start for home—call'd at f. Sessions, from whence she [Patty Sessions] accompanied me to B. Whitney's

sat. 20th Went from Olive's to br. M.s—quite sick

April 5th Been very sick with inflamation on the lungs— am just able to write a little & help myself &c.—New arrangements have been entered into respecting the emigration—The families of the Twelve to remain till another season. The pioneers without families are to go on some have already started, others go out to day.
    Wrote the following to br. Luke Johnson on the death of his companion Mrs. Susan M. J.

Round the grave there are no shadows—
'Tis no more a dread to die:
Death is but a friendly porter
Op'ning to the worlds on high.

Tho' the friends we dearly cherish
For a while are call'd to leave;

They have only pass'd the curtain—
   All is well—we should not grieve.

Time is onward—things eternal
   Now are stew'd along our way;
And ere long our growing vision
   Will embrace immortal day.

Mourn not for your once lov'd Susan—
   Love her still—she's gone above,
To fulfil a heav'nly mission—
   To perform a work of love.

God in kindness has appointed
   You another loving bride
And in time to come will many
   More be clinging to your side.

Then let Susan's name be honor'd,
   And her merits often told:
Let her mem'ry be more precious
   Than rich di'monds set in gold.

You will yet again behold her—
   She will be your own again;
Glorious with angelic beings
   Proudly mingling in her train.[86]

tu. 6th Conference in the forenoon adjourn'd <u>sine die</u>. after some business matters wherein the present Authorities were voted to be sustain'd except L. Wight, who was pass'd over for the time being; & bish. Miller of whom nothing was said—The pioneers some of them leave in the afternoon—others not ready.[87]

th. 8th Br. Markham started out yest. return'd to day to spend the night with his family.

fr. 9th P. P. P. arriv'd from Eng. elders Hyde & Taylor expected soon— I have been sick 3 weeks & today not able to leave my bed—Sis. Swan brought me a fine mess of <u>wild onions</u>. The weather which was cold in the forepart of the week is now fine—cattle have been brows'd for several days, in marshy places the grass affords them a fresh bite.

su. 11th Wrote the following

The Twelve,
To Prest. B. Young.

They have gone—they have gone new privations to share
Gone as Abraham went when he knew not where
They have gone like the deer when pursued in the chase
To secure to the saints a safe hiding place.

Why? O why must they go to the depth of the wild
Where benign cultivation of late has not smil'd
Wherefore thus on a pilgrimage must they go forth
And forsake all the comforts and blessings of earth?

They are call'd to be saviors, and saviors must flee
To a wilderness home for security
While the anger of nations is raging abroad—
While the Gentiles are feeling the judgments of God.

They have gone—they have gone; may the Spirits sweet
    voice
Whisper comfort and peace that their hearts may rejoice:
May an angel of presence on each one attend
To protect from all ill and preserve to the end.

And when God shall direct may they retrace their track
And to these Winter Quarters in safety come back
That the saints who shall tarry may be of good cheer
When with heartfelt rejoicings we welcome them here.[88]

12th Prest. Y. & elder K. return'd from the Camp of Pioneers

tu. 13th Mrs. Leonard & Sessions spent a few hours with us

To Mrs. E. A. W. [Elizabeth Ann Whitney]

Great & glorious was thy station—
    Greater still it is to be;
When thy right and exaltation
    Come thro' Jesus Christ to thee.

Thou hast been his loving sister—
Thou hast been his faithful bride;
For many times and places
Thou hast acted by his side.

The great Eloheim, thy father
Ever lov'd and loves thee still;
He will give thee strength and wisdom
Day by day to do his will.

Let thy heart be fill'd with comfort
Thro' this darksome, thorny way;
Father's unseen hand will guide you
Into pure, celestial day.[89]

Elder Taylor arriv'd this afternoon.

Wed. 14th Prest. Y. call'd to bid "good bye" & started out to rejoin the Pioneers

th. 15th Br. Little from Mass. arriv'd.

sat. 17th Froze very hard last night

mo. 19th The atmosphere chang'd to the soft fanning breeze of Spring. My strength returning, so that by stopping twice to rest, I went to Bishop W.s Spent the day with sis. Whit. Kim. Helen, Sarah, Sabra, &c. &c.—The Pioneers having cross'd the [Elk] Horn on the Platt [River], went on friday mor. the 12 and others having return'd from their visit at the "City" Difficulties with the Omahaws, they continuing to kill our cattle & molest the men—having strip'd & badly injur'd a man & woman at the upper herd Our breth. are seeking some measures to prevent further trouble.

th. 22d Vis at sis. Buel's—had a very interesting time in the eve. present sis Leonard, Zina, sis. Markham Sis. Sessions and Lyons call'd in the afternoon—brought me a present from S. M. K. of dress pins, stockings, hooks & eyes & sewing silk. O God bless her for this I pray thee

fr. 23d Went to br. Leonard's in the eve. had a glorious time—father Sess presided, pres. Moth. Chase. Sis. Lyons, Leonard, Buel, Sabra

To L. O. Lyttlefield on his departure for Europe

Go, brother, go forth in the spirit of Jesus
    Enrob'd with salvation, encircled with power
Go forth as a herald and publish glad tidings—
Go call to the nations—go tell them the hour.

Go, brother, be humble, hold fast your profession—
    Continue to cling to the strong iron rod:
'Twill lead thro' the mists & the clouds of thick darkness
    To the fountain of light and the glory of God.

Go, brother, thy country has chas'd thee in exile
    With an oft oppress'd people, the Saints of the Lord
Who are passing the furnace of deep "fiery trials"
    Rejoicing in hope of the "better reward".

Go, brother and tell our dear brethren in Europe
    The suff'ring & patience & faith of the Saints
Who, for righteousness' sake on the earth are but
    strangers
    But God is their Lord & their spirit ne'er faints

Go brother & say to the Saints that are faithful,
    That God is preparing a kingdom of rest;
And when they have pass'd thro' the tide of affliction
    With the fulness of blessing they'll truly be blest

Go, brother, be faithful & God will protect you
    And bear you in safety across the great deep;
And your guardian angel will bring you instruction
    And whisper sweet comfort to you when you sleep

Go, brother & when from the friends now around you
    You are breathing the air of a far distant clime
Look oft in the mirror of your recollection
    And the sweet sounding harp-strings of friendship will
    chime

May the God of our fathers preserve you from evil
    And fill you with wisdom & light evermore;

And when you, with honor, have finish'd your mission
Return you in peace to America's shore.[90]

To the Saints in Europe

Ye saints who dwell on Europe's shore
    Let not your hearts be faint—
Let each press on to things before
    And be indeed a saint.

Altho' the present time may seem
    O'erspread with clouds of gloom
The light of faith will spread a gleam
    Until deliv'rance come.

Hold fast the things you have receiv'd—
    Be faithful in the Lord—
You know in whom you have believ'd—
    He's faithful to his word.

Your brethren in America
    Are one in heart with you
And they are toiling night and day
    For Zion's welfare too.

They even now are driven forth
    To track the wilderness;
And leave the country of their birth
    For truth & righteousness.

But there's a day—tis near at hand—
    A day of joy & peace;
That day will break oppression's band
    And bring the saints' release.

Then, brethren haste to gather up—
    We shall rejoice to meet:
When we have drunk the bitter cup
    We shall enjoy the sweet.

[*In right margin:*]
And even now, the Lord bestows
    More, more than tongue can tell
Of that which from his presence flows—
    Yes, brethren! <u>all is well</u>[91]

Lines on the death of the children of Elder F. and
        Mrs. [*space*] Richa[rds]

[*On the side:*] Written for the P[*indecipherable*] in England.

They sweetly sleep—'tis their dust that is sleeping,
    Their spirits move in the courts above;
They are now round their parents keeping
    A guardian pow'r—a strong watch of love.
Cloth'd in light & with glory surrounded
    Now they live in a wider sphere;

There the mind can go forth unbounded
    Free from clogs that confine us here.[92]
Now the grave is disrob'd of its terrors
    Within its halo the saints can sing:
While they look thro' the heavenly mirror,
    Death the tyrant has lost its s[t]ing.
Ye fond parents: forget your sorrow—
    Your lov'd ones will return again;
Soon, yes, soon—'twill scarce seem till tomorrow
    Ere on earth, they come forth to remain.[93]

Mo. 26th Left sis. Buel's—call'd & din'd at f. Session's with David. Went to the <u>Markee</u>—spent the aftnoon at br. Pierce's in com. with Sis. Whitney, Kimball, Sessions, Lyons, Lucina, Pierce & Margaret. also sis. Young came in at supper time.—Spent the eve at the Markee —had a rejoicing time thro' the outpouring of the spirit of God Present sis.'s W. K. Young, Chase Sess. Lyon. Pierce Marg. Aunt Jemima & "the Girls." All hearts comforted.[94]

<u>On the death of Leonora Agnes Taylor</u>

Like a rose-bud fast unfolding
    Is the view superior charms

Leonora's form was moulding
    Beauteous, in her mother's arms,
While the fathers fondest feeling
    Sketch'd her future grace & worth
Death's cold, icy hand was stealing
    Her away from friends & earth,
Did she—could she wish to grieve them
    When she was belov'd so well?
Did she then forsake and leave them
    When on earth she ceas'd to dwell?
No: she came to be united
    Unto them & form a tie
She perform'd the work appointed
    And return'd to worlds on high.
Now that <u>tie</u> remains a union
    Stronger than the pow'r of death:
Thro' its strength she holds communion
    With her parents on the earth.
She has form'd the dear connexion
    That has won her father's name
And thro' which the resurrection
    And the Priesthood's pow'r she'll claim
Cloth'd with beauty & salvation
    She will soon appear again
And in the regeneration
    Ornament her kindred train[95]

30th Night before last slept with sis. Lyon last night with sis. Geen.

[May] 1st This afternoon had a most glorious time at br. Leon. Sis Sessions presided—present Moth. Chase, Cutler, Cahoon sis. Whit. Kim, Pitkin, Lyons, Buel Knight &c.—spoken by the spirit of prophecy that the Pioneers were well, happy, & were in council—that tomorrow they will have a greater time of rejoicing than they have ever had.

2d. This eve. sup'd at sis. Noon's with sis. Kim. Whit. Sess. Lyon Sarah A. Helen, &c. had a[s] glorious time as I ever had on earth at sis. K.'s—myself chosen to preside—the pow'rs of the world to come were truly in our midst.

To Mrs. Lyon

Go thou lov'd one—God is with you
    He will be your stay & shield;
Treasure up each precious promise
    Which his spirit has reveal'd
From <thy> father & thy mother
    Who are twining round thy heart
Also from thy older brother
    Thou art call'd awhile to part
Your companion~~'s love~~ will ~~bless~~ <caress> you
    And your sweet angelic child
With its growing charms will bless you
    Thus the hours will be beguil'd.
And thy younger brother David
    With his social ~~cheerful~~ <harmless> glee—
With the heart & hand of kindness
    Oftentimes will comfort thee
And the saints of God, who're banish'd
    From their country & their home;
Who for Jesus' testimony
    In the wilderness do roam
Will with pray'r & supplication
    Plead for thee before the throne
Of the great Eternal Father
    <Never> ~~Wherefore~~ do not feel alone
Guardian angels will protect thee
    And the spirit's still small voice
Will from day to day direct thee
    Therefore let thy heart rejoice.
O my Father! thou that dwelleth
    In the upper courts of light;
Open thou her path before her—
    Ever guide her feet aright.[96]

Chapter 4

"Truly a Glorious Time"
The Trail Diary,
June 1847–September 1849

SECURE IN THE CARE of her sister wives and her sisters in the faith, Eliza Snow had reason to feel the contentment which permeates the last entries of the first trail journal. Halfway to Zion, she had survived the worst, though she could not have known it; and, having proved her mettle thus far, she was developing confidence that she could pass the next test.

One strain, however, is discordant with the sweet peace which pervades the entries. How is Eliza to manage once Brigham Young, her distant but sure protector, has gone ahead with the Pioneer Company? "Short on it for wagons," he had asked Stephen Markham to bring Eliza along in the following company. However, to repeat with the Markhams the wretched experiences of the Iowa journey was unthinkable to Eliza. Mary Peirce, one of Brigham Young's wives, died just as her family was preparing to follow. Margarett, her young widowed sister, also wedded to Brigham, did not discourage Eliza from applying for the place thus vacated in their father's wagon. So it was that Eliza found her own better way west. The deed was symbolic: Eliza was learning to improve her life by her own enterprise. Self-determination was a heady draft for a genteel nineteenth-century woman, and Eliza was beginning to sip its flavor.

Robert Peirce had been named captain over the "Second Ten" family groups, with which his family, including Eliza, would ride. They and five other Tens formed the "Second Fifty," headed by Bates Noble. The two Fifties comprised Jedediah M. Grant's Hundred, one of the four Hundreds that would follow the Pioneers that summer. More than two thousand Saints would enter the Salt Lake Valley in 1847.

Peirce's Ten, composed of fourteen men, nine women, twelve children, and two infants, were not strangers to each other for long. More than half of them had converted together in Chester County, Pennsylvania; the rest soon became mutually acquainted. Unlike the Iowa stretch of the journey, this last part was unmarred by dissension within the Ten in which Eliza was traveling. The Peirces, especially Margarett, half Eliza's age, were sympathetic to her sensibilities and attendant to her needs. Within the Fifty, and sometimes, when they camped nearby, within the Second Fifty also, Eliza found warm associations. Phebe Chase, Vilate Decker, Elizabeth Elsworth, and Elisa Rosacrans of the First Ten; Esther Ewing of the Third Ten; Elvira Holmes and Lucinda Howd of the Fourth Ten; and Mary Noble of the Fifth Ten enter the diary frequently. Visiting from wagon to wagon was common.

Beyond the intimate groups, though, the diary recounts that all was not always peaceful. Hundreds competing for place, for space, or to be first on the trail, enlivened the first weeks of the trek, until a calm grown of weariness dictated a stable routine rather than a rush for position.

In all of this, Eliza was the observer, the chronicler. Secure that her physical needs would be met, she also could explore her inner landscape. Juxtaposed to the slowly evolving scenery of the Great Plains is the quiet growth of her own poise and self-possession.

The sorrow of Nauvoo and the discomfort of Winter Quarters had raised Eliza's awareness of the fragility of a life dependent on others. In the relatively calm routine of the journey Eliza found developing within her a solid core of confidence. It seems fitting that her last cry for her husband's support, emotional and temporal, came on the Sweetwater, just a day's travel from the top of her world, the continental divide between East and West. Brigham Young, on whom she intended to call for husbandly nurture once she reached the Salt Lake Valley, had encountered the westbound company on his way back to Winter Quarters. With translucent fear, Eliza put her question: "Who [shall] be my counsellor in the year to come?" "Eliza R. Snow," Brigham replied with challenge in his voice, perhaps to cover up his embarrassment at her justifiable disappointment. "She is not capable," Eliza breathed. "I have appointed her president," replied Young, perhaps hinting at a later application of the term. While he makes hasty arrangements for her by conferring with Robert Peirce and writing to his young wife Clara Decker Young to share her cabin in the fort, Eliza learns her most convincing lesson in self-sufficiency:

dependence, far from being a female virtue, is an embarrassment to be overcome by personal diligence. When, settled in the Valley, she trades the making of a cap for soap and "begin[s] once more to be a woman of property," the affirmation is one of confidence growing into independence.

By the end of the journal, in 1849, "merchant shops are opening in all directions," and the wilderness settlement is becoming a city of commerce. Women and men engaged in building up Zion are giving to the task the best that is in them, and are gaining knowledge and experience in the work. Eliza Snow, however weak in body, is well on her way to that strength of spirit, that "noble independence" which will exemplify the rest of her life, and, as she gains in prominence, will become a model for generations of Mormon women. "Let Woman then a course in life pursue," she wrote in 1856,

> To win respect as merits honest due,
> And, feeling God's approval, act her part,
> With noble independence in her heart.[1]

It took Eliza Snow ten years to recover her health; Susa Young Gates insists Eliza had tuberculosis from which she cured herself by taking a cold bath each morning, summer and winter alike. However, by 1867 Eliza of the trail—passive observer and quiet chronicler— had become Sister Snow, dynamic organizer and daring activist. Whatever the source of her strength—she would have attributed it to having "no whereon to lean, but God alone"—Eliza R. Snow had passed through her "dark night of the soul" to find enlightenment and power.

Trail Diary,
June 1847–September 1849

Winter Quarters of the
Camp of Israel, June 1st 1847

tu. June 1st This is truly a glorious time with the mothers & daughters in Zion altho' thrust out from the land of our forefathers & from the endearments of civiliz'd life.

This forenoon I made a cap for sis. Pierce[1]—in the afternoon visited at sis. Miller's in com. of Priscinda Zina, sis. Chase, Cristene &c. after supper sis. Whitney, Kimball, Sessions came in and we had a spiritual feast in very deed.[2]

Spent the eve. at br. Leonard's with Priscinda, Zina & Sarah—Great instruction was brought forth—br. L. spoke of the American government—its fall &c. after which the Lord manifested the contrast of the happiness of the saints and the suff'ring of the gentiles when the Lamanites go forth. Language cannot describe the scene.

W. 2d. Spent the aftn. with Lucy in Com. of Zina Loisa & Emily. E. & myself spoke in the gift of tongues—in the eve. met at Harriets had a good time—Sis. Young join'd me in a song of Zion.

th. 3d. Sis Sess. Kim. Whit. & myself spent the eve. at Sarah Ann's—had a pow'rful time deep things were brought forth which were not to be spoken.

We had a very pleasant visit at br. Leonard's present br. Joseph Y. & wife, br. Sess. & wife sis. Whitney, Kimball, &c. I blest sis. Young.

5. Fath. Sess. leave for the wilderness—I attended meet. at sis. Leavitt's

sun. 6th. Had a glorious time at sis. Young's present sis. Whit. Kim. Chase &c. I had forgotten to mention a time of blessing at sis. K's the day after we met at Sarah's sis. Sess. & myself blest Helen—I spoke & she interpreted. I then blest the girls in a song, singing to each in rotation.

In the eve. that we met at Harriet's sis. Young told me she thought wisdom for me to go to the west inasmuch as I could go so comfortably with br. Pierce. Sis. P. had mention'd her wish for me to go with them, in his absence, but he had not yet decided whether his means would admit.

m. 7th. Met at sis. Woodruff's in the aftnoon—at br. Leonard's in the eve. Moth. Cutler receiv'd the gift of tongues. Sis. Scovil prest.

tu. 8th. Met at Lyman Whitney's—staid in the eve.—had a heavy shower of rain—went home with Loisa & Z. in the mud rejoicing

w. 9th Visited with Zina, Martha, L. E. Lucy Eliza <Pris & Sarah.> After supper we had a glorious time, sis. Pierce came in—sis. Thompson, M, Young, & Frances. Before we retir'd to rest Margaret, Martha, Loisa, Susan & Lucy reciv'd the gift of tongues.

th. 10th. In the mor. met sis. Chase at Clarissa's—blest her little daughter which was born last tu. told Harriet she would get the gift of interpretation in the eve. In the aftn. call'd at sis. Woodru[*torn page*] Priscinda's & went to br. Moor's where sis Whit.'s girls met, sent for Zina Harriet came with her. Sis. Richards Rhoda, Emeline, Anna, & one of sis. M's daughters spoke in the gift for the first time. Took supper with S. Ann, while there Lucy W. came in—she receiv'd the gift We then went into sis. K's—Helen <Sarah Ann> Genet, Harriet S. Sis. K. spoke for the first time in the gift of tongues—H. Cook interpreted.

fr. 11th Sent for Harriet—we commenc'd improving in the gifts. Helen got the interpretation also sis. W. Mary Ellen spoke in a new tongue, sis. Pack also—we had a time not to be forgotten.
    In the aft. met at Clarisa's—Sis. Snow receiv'd the gift before we left Loisa's—we had a glorious time—sis. Leavitt & M. Pierce spoke in the gift & I could truly say that my heart was fill'd to overflowing with gratitude to my Father in heaven.

sat. 12th—Bade farewell to many who seem dearer to me than life & seated in the carriage with sis. P.[Pierce] M.[Margaret] & E.[Edith Evaline] I took my departure from Winter Quarters. It commenc'd raining soon after our start—one of br. P.s drivers had the misfortune to break his wagon tongue which was soon repaired—we travel'd 7 ms. The weather became fine & we encamp'd at night having 14 wagons in com. I felt a loneliness for a while after parting with my friends but the spirit of consolation & rejoicing return'd & I journey'd with good cheer.

su. 13th The day fine—we met Parly returning to town—arriv'd at the [Elk] Horn just before sunset—my feelings were very peculiar thro' the day—it verily seem'd that the glory of God rested down on the wagons (21 in No.) and overspread the prairie.[3]

Mo. 14th. Cross'd the river which is a muddy swift running stream— on a raft in the afternoon—before which sis. Smith Thom & Sess. came to our carriage—we had an interesting time—sis. P. & sis. T. spoke in tongues & many interesting things were said.
    After crossing I went to sis. Sess. tent spoke to Lucina & Mary [Sessions] about their relationship &c. & was made to rejoice in hearing them speak in the gift of tongues.[4]

tu. 15th. The brethren call a meeting around a Liberty pole which was erected yesterday for the purpose of organizing the Camp. Judg'd to be more than 300 wagons cross'd over at noon this day—This afternoon several of the sis. met in a little circle on the prairie in front of our wagons br. Pierce met with us—fath. [John] Smith stay'd until sent for on business—we had a good time altho' the prairie wind was somewhat annoying. Sis. Sess. Chase & E present.[5] [*Added later.*] Recd. a letter from S. M. Kimball.

Wed. 16th. When I left Winter Quarters Sis. Young wish'd me to write a few lines for her; in compliance of her request wrote the following

To Mrs. Mary Ann Young

Mother of mothers! Queen of queens
    For such thou truly art—
I pray the Lord to strengthen thee
    And to console thy heart.

From infancy thou hast been led
    And guided by his hand
That thou in Zion's courts may tread
    And in thy station stand.

Thou'rt highly favor'd of the Lord
    And thou art greatly blest;

Most glorious will be thy reward
　　In peace & joy & rest.

Altho' thou hast been call'd to share
　　In sorrow and distress
That thou thro' suff'ring might prepare
　　The broken heart to bless,

Thou wilt arise o'er ev'ry ill—
　　O'er ev'ry weakness too
For God will in thy path distil
　　His grace like morning dew

O let thy heart be comforted
　　And never, never fear;
The saints of God will pray for thee
　　And seek thy heart to cheer.

Yes, ever more rejoice in God
　　Amid thy toil & care—
Thy mind is pure—thy sphere is broad
　　And great thy labors are.

The Lord will pour his blessings forth
　　And thee in honor raise,
And many nations of the earth
　　Will hear & speak thy praise.[6]

This day met Mary Ellen, Mary A. & Sis. Smithies at fath. Sess.—had an interesting interview. sis. Smithies spoke in a new tongue—Mary E. interpreted. Sis. Sess. & I took a walk, call'd at P.P.P's—had a conversation with him—I sung a song of Zion to his family Sis. Sess. interpreted.

Th. 17th Call'd in the morning at sis. Thompson's tent—sis. Smith present—sent for sis. Sess. br. Lawson spoke in tongues. After sis. Sess. & I left, he sung a song & interpretation

Sis. T. also sung & br. L. interpreted bless the Lord O my soul for these bless. I went home with sis. S.—wrote in her letter to sis. Pratt. We [*unfinished*]

fr. 18th. Had a treat of the spirit in the wagon sis. Moore & sis. Sess. prt. [present]. In the aft. attended meeting at sis Beeches—most of br. Prat fam. prt.—had a refreshing time.

Sis. Sess. & I went to br. Hunter's; found sis. H. out of health—I told them I had long desir'd to bless sis. H.—went into the wagon & spoke to br. H. in the gift of tongues, sis. S. interpreted, after which br. H. sis. S. & I laid hands on sis. H's head & rebuk'd her illness & bless'd her I then sung a song to them & sis. S. sung the interpretation; Susannah present & arose & bless'd sis. H.[7]

This day br. [Daniel] Spencer's hundred leave & move forward

Sat. 19th. Our division under J. [Jedediah] Grant, leave the Horn— we soon come in sight of the com. that started yes. Near the place of their last night encampment they found the carcass of a man re cently kill'd & pick'd by the wolves—many papers were found which designated him to have been an Officer from St. Louis.—We en- camp'd on the Platte river—about 15 ms. from where we cross'd the Horn. The pole of Liberty with the white flag waving was erected by the com. that preceded us—we saw it several miles distant.

Su. 20th. This mor. heard the painful news of a combat between Jacob Weatherbee & another br. & three Indians. Br. W. was shot by one of the Indians, thro' the body, while endeavoring to prevent them robbing his wagon. Those 2 brethren had been sent back to Winter Quarters on business & were at the time of the encontre about 7½ ms. on the other side the Horn.[8] My health ill today not able to attend the general meeting, but Sis. Chase, Sessions &c, met with us at br. Peirce's wagons & we had a rejoicing time.

Our manner of encampment, which we commenc'd last night is by joining the wagons in a circle so as to form a yard for the herd; each hundred by itself.

mo. 21st. The Artillery does not arrive—we do not journey. Br. Weatherbee died yest.

tu. 22d. The Camp mov'd traveling 5 & 6 abreast—we follow up the Platte & at night encamp near it having travelled perhaps 14 or 15 ms. the road & the country delightful.

Wed. 23d. We go 2 abreast. Capt Smoot's Com. stop for the night by a small stream a mile or so in our rear; we a ½ m. in Taylor's rear & Parley 5 ms. in advance of us. Our place is very delightful—a short grass which is a sweet treat for the herd overspreads an extensive plain—the river forming almost a half circle, while rich clusters of trees are to be seen in every direction.

thur. 24th Capt. Grant's com. start at 7—pass'd J. T.s com. who rode past us on horseback & order'd J. Grant to stop. Prest. J. Young told him to drive on—J. T. came back & told our capts of tens to stop for their leaders were in rebellion—he soon past us again on his way to Parley's camp. We travelled 10 ms. stop'd at half past one in the rear of P. A meeting in the eve—matters adjusted with good feeling[9]

fr. 25th Meeting in the mor.—travel 12 ms. in 2 file as yesterday—the wind & dust almost intolerable

Sat. 26th Travel upwards of 20 ms. 2 abreast cross the looking-glass creek—encamp on Beaver—one com. cross over. rains at night

Su. 27th I have been very sick—ride on bed the last 2 days—sis. Sess. Lucina & sis. Leonard came to the wagon—the pow'r of God rested on me—my disease was rebuk'd & I prais'd the name of the Most High. The wagons are crossing the stream thro' the day—in the eve. br. Lawson, sis. T. &c. came to our place & we had another refreshing from the Lord. Praise him all ye Saints.

Mo. 28th Our time delay'd in crossing the Creek—rumor'd that a war-party of Ind. are gather'd—broke 2 wagon-tongues in our <u>Ten</u>— cross'd Indian Creek—pass'd 2 cornfields, some habitations & over-take J. T.s Division late in the eve.—some of the inhabitants visit us, one man who is appointed to aid the Ind. in building barracks &c.. Trav. about 7 ms.

T. 29th Pass'd the Pawnee town, which seem'd entirely deserted— the scenery is much more variegated than before—it is now quite rolling—cross'd a sandy bottom'd stream in sight of the Indian set-tlement—travell'd 16 ms. encamp'd in front of several wigwams: J.T. before us and P. behind

Wed. 30th The day cool. Capt. P.s Ten take the lead of J. G.s h'd [hun-dred].—soon after we start P. & the other com's come in sight—J.T. is moving on in front—we are on an extensive prairie with little shrub-bery & the Camp can be view'd at once which presents a very impos-ing sight—had the pleasure of seeing a herd of Antelopes running in every direction. Stop'd about one o'clock by the side of a stream & near its mouth. P rides forward.—thinks best to cross the Platt
   Sis. Chase, Pierce, Hendricks &c. call into br. Noble's with me— sis. N. receives the gift of tongues—Sis Hunter call'd at the car-

riage—had a good time—she said had been better since sis. Sess. & I call'd on her Trav 8 ms.

July—Th. 1st. We cross'd the Platte, or rather what is call'd Luke's fork.[10] J. T.s com. cross'd first, J. G.s follow'd & Smoot's & Spencers & when we left Parley's was crossing. We went about 5 ms. & encamp'd without wood or water, with J. T. 3 ms. in our front. Br. P. is somewhat afflicted with sore eyes.

fr. 2 Started forward, the prarie very rolling we only ascend one ridge to come in sight of another, till about 2 o'clock when our gradual descent gave us a view of the tops of trees which skirt the river before us. The teams begin to fail for want of water, a very heavy show'r revives them & turns our sandy road to mud. Travelled 6 abreast some of the time. Trav. 16 ms. Capt. Neff leads our Com.

July.
    sat. 3d. The day fine—travel'd 14 ms. & encamp late on a stream in view of the Platte—cross'd a stream in the mor.
    In the aft. go 4 abreast—come into the trail of the Pioneers—br. Russell finds a bucket which he had given to H.C.K.

Su. 4th. Rains in forenoon—meeting in the aft. Martha, Loisa & Edith come to the wagon to me L. & E. receive the gift of tongues Sis Taylor, Hunter, Smoot & call in the eve.

Mo. 5th. Trav. 12 ms. P. takes the lead of the 2 Divisions, Miller leads in our hundred we cross the stream in the mor. each 50 making a fording place, & we enter upon Grand Island & where we encamp at night; a board is found on which the Pioneers had written, computing the distance 217 ms. from W. Quarters

Tu. 6th Our Com. start at about 8 o'clock after forming on the trail, stop until P. passes—J. T. in the rear—we stop to water & bait at noon—awhile after we move on, our fifty was stop'd, said to be thro' J. T.s orders—br. Lathrop, who leads today went to J. G. to know what to do, as J. T. demanded the roads: J. G. said he would as soon give the roads as not if J. T.s teams would give us room to go out, but as they were on our right & a slue on our left it was not practicable—Perhaps 15 of T.s wagons had come along side—the rest were in the rear—J. G. told L. to go on & he went on himself with the other 50 J. T. came up

& ordered us to stop, at length the 2d 50 halted till we overtook them in the meantime J. T's wagons crowd into our path—we all stop'd for his com. to pass; except 5 wagons that waited till our Com. pass'd by them for the nearest point of timber where we encamp on the bank of the Platte with the timber all on the opposite side—br. Smoot where we stop'd at noon & P. & T. in sight several ms. in front.

I breakfasted on antelope—quite a treat.

Trav. 15 ms.

w. 7th. Capt. P. leads our 50;—after starting we were told to leave the beaten track, and each 50 break a new one—it made hard riding for me, yet I felt like submitting to "the pow'rs that be" & endure it al-tho' the 2 roads were unoccupied—after our nooning we came where br. Rich was baiting, having broken 2 wagons—we pass'd them, but perhaps an hour after, br. Lathrop came up telling br. P. that Rich demanded the road, which we took afternoon—br. P. said the command had not come to him from proper authority, it being from Grant instead of Noble the Capt. of our 50, and we went on— encamp'd a mile from the river. Trav. 14 ms.—Sis. Wiler sent me a bush with tomato's, also a flow'r resembling the Geranium—the prickly pear is common

Th. 8. Started 10 m. after 8—cross a ravine—br. P.s & T.s com. bend their course to the river, which is far to our left we cross their roads & encamp near a slue. Show'r at night. Trav. 14 ms.

fr. 9th Capt. Miller broke a wagon crossing a ravin[e] yes. & we do not start till nearly noon—the other hds [hundreds] out of sight—we go perhaps [*illegible*] & encamp on the Platte. Had meeting in br. Hendrick's wagon—2 of his daughters & B. Young's wife speak with the gift of tongues for the first time. Praise the Lord O my soul! Trav. 12 ms.

The prairie presents a beautiful appearance resembling the tame meadows where red-top is cultivated—

Sat. 10th Soon after starting cross the track of P.s & J. T.s com.—the whole Camp encamp early on the Platte which is jugd'd about a m. in width—no timber on this side—this is a buffalo country.

<Trav. 8 ms.>

Su. 11th. A public meeting at 1 o'clock Sis. Sess. Thom. Leon. Pierce & myself meet in fath. C's wagon at 4. The Lord pour'd out his spirit—Sis. Holmes call'd to see me in the eve, & spoke in the gift of tongues. We are said to be 180 ms. from W. Quarters.

Supped on buffalo. 8 kill'd at this stop. Drank well water from br. Rich's camp.

Mo. 12th. Started late in the mor. in the rear of P.s 1st 50 & alongside of his 2d; the Camp all in sight—The prairie to day is little else than a barren waste—where the buffalo seem to roam freely

Encamp at night on the side of a slue with the river a few rods beyond. Capt. N. goes in front since fr. mor. having got an addition to his team—had gone in the rear for some time in consequence of losing an ox, the night after crossing Loup Fork all goes well—Trav. 16 ms.

tu 13th. Start between 7 & 8 nothing remarkable except the multitude of buffalo paths which lead from the bluff to the river across our way. Capt. P. leads—our nooning is on a line of lakes or swamps which intercept watering at the river. Capt. N.s 50 are left in the rear at the watering & when we start are oblig'd to go to the right which Capt G. approbates Capt. L. frets &c.—P.s 1st 50 in our front—his 2d in our rear—we fall into his tracks which occasions some trouble but all is adjusted by Capt. G. who acts as Pioneer.

Trav. 14 ms. & enc. on the river in the rear of P.—Saw buffalos & wolves.

Wed 14th. Last night or rather this mor. a frightful circumstance occur'd—the herd took fright & made a rush to the op'ning where we were—they nearly upset one of Capt. P.'s wagons, crush'd two wheels for Capt. Snow—caus'd the death of Capt. K.s only cow & knock'd several horns from the oxen.

We stop over the day to repair Capt. S.s wagon—the other companies go on by rising the bluff which here forms a point with the river; except Capt Rich who remains with us & Capt. Smoot who comes up & passes the point a little before night.

Capt G. brought me a buffalo skull on which was written by the Pioneers "All well—feed bad—we only 300 ms. from W."—&c. dated May 9th. A large b[uffalo] is divided among the hd.

July

th. 15th Started this mor. in 2 com. each 50 by itself in double file—in consequence of the fright of the cattle our leaders think best to divide the herd, & form circles by fifties when we encamp. This mor. we ascend the bluff which forms a junction with the river—after wading over one sand hill after another we find ourselves again on the river Platt with a rugged bluff at our right. This eve. find beautiful springs with pure cold water—a blessing indeed. <Tr. 12 ms.>

fr. 16th. Start at 15 m. past 7—the day intensely hot—grass eat up by buffalos—when we stop for noon our 50 kill a b. & we are detain'd while the other passes on—we pass springs. Trav. 9 ms.

Sat. 17th. The cattle in Capt. S.s 50 broke out last night—20 yoke of oxen cannot be found—Some men came down the river with letters— say they met the Pioneers at the South Pass—left several brethren at a ferry 125 ms. beyond fort Laramy. Attended meeting at sis. Gates'.

Su. 19th [18] Had 2 tents plac'd together many sis. & several breth. meet. br. L. presided Sis. G. receiv'd gift of tongues yesterday in our carriage—

Mo 20th [19] A number of brethren come from P.P.s camp 25 ms. ahead—drive in an ox which they took from a buffalo herd on the other side the river—took supper with sis. Holmes—had a good season in sis. Love's tent. P. sent word for one com. to move up there. Here the South Fork unites with the main Platte.

tu. 21st. [20] After much deliberation, consultation, parleying, grumbling &c several hunters are sent to search for the lost cattle & we move on—the first 50 in front encamp on the river bank—in the eve br. Noble call'd our Com. together for a pray'r meet. which truly made our hearts rejoice.
Trav. 12 ms.

W. 22d. [21] Start after 8—a little before 12 we met 2 men from P.s camp with 17 yoke of oxen for our assistance—this is truly a land of buffalos—they are in sight all the time—an almost innumerable herd of them came over the bluff today & seem'd about to cross our Camp on their path to the river—our hunters met them & they chang'd their course, much to our gratification.
The wind blew up last night & the day is cool—quite a contrast to a few days past. We cross a beautiful stream, several rods in width with quick sandy bottoms & encamp near it—the 2nd 50 do not come up.
Trav. 15 ms.

th. 2~~4th~~2d. Start a little before 8 in the forenoon a young buffalo was beeved by our hunters it was very soon distributed among the 5 Capt.s & we went on—at about 11 a messenger came up from the 2d 50 with orders for us to stop for them to take the front, which we did when we found a proper place for baiting—our afternoon trav. was over sand-hills & cross one pretty stream—the day cool—clouds obscure the sun & threaten storm. <Trav 14 ms.>

fr. 23d. Rain'd in the night & a little this mor. We start before [6?]— trav. over sand hills cross several beautiful little streams running down from the bluffs—no wood but b. chips[11] & what we brought from afar—the cannon from the first Camp is heard and its smoke seen— The occasion is a visit of 100 Sioux, as we are informed by brethren who visit our Camp at night which is in sight of the main body, perhaps 3 ms. distant. We pass'd some initials inscrib'd on the sides of a bluff.
     Trav. 13 ms.

Sat. 24th We start about 7 come up with the main Camp before it leaves—the Indians throng us—sell some oxen to us at noon. I took a view of their town thro' a spy-glass—their tents or lodges are small of skins gaily painted—they are across the river opposite us. Joseph Y. & the others who went in search of the stray cattle return with 4 head. Ledges of rock & cedar shrubbery on the opposite side of the river. We cross'd several streams & encamp in the neighborhood of Capt. Smoot. No wood.
     Trav. 8 ms.

Su 25th. Before we start, br. P. Young & 9 others of the Pioneers come up much to our joy—it was truly like clusters of grapes by the wayside—we come up with the main Camp which outstrip us yesterday; cross a stream & encamp in Taylor's Division about 11 o'clock. I saw sis. Sess. a few minutes as we pass'd P's Camp. A meeting call'd & one letter read from Prest. Young & one from W. Richards. P. P. recommends that we travel by fifties, & those that get ready first, start first. One 50 of P.s roll on this eve. Sis. Leonard and I have a good interview in the carriage, also at br. Noble's wagon. I write a letter to W. Quarters—P. Y. talked of going but relinquish'd the idea before night. Two others going—The Ind. [Indians] rode with us this mor. The Bluff on the other side the river for a day or two past seems compos'd of rock. Our road continues over sand hills. We had considerable rain last night.
     Trav. 5 ms.

Mo. 26th. Our 50 move in the rear—start about half past [6?]—while crossing a ridge of sand hills about noon br. Dilworth broke a axletree & we are detain'd till sunset—Many Ind. pass us with tents & baggage fasten'd to mules, horses & on drays form'd of tent poles drawn by horses, mules & dogs Covers for the little ones made by fastening skins over bows which are fix'd to the upper side of the drays.—Here we have a treat of wild currants & a kind of cherry call'd choke, but much preferable to the eastern choke-cherry. Capt. N. directs us to go on at night—The moon shines beautifully & we move on with speed—come up to the Ind. tents where they come out in scores—some shake their blankets which frightens the cattle, one of Capt. P.'s broke from the yoke which occasion'd a little trouble—several came up to the carriage where I was holding the horses, sis. P. & M. being engag'd in quieting the other teams, cows &c; I made them understand that they were in danger of the horses kicking them & they withdrew We pass'd on & encamp'd a little past 11, having trav. 10 ms.

tu. 27th. Start 10 min. past 7 at 10 arrive opposite Ash hollow where we halt for the purpose of getting timber to repair wagons in case of accident. Ate our bread up for supper & have no wood, expecting to find it last night but thro' the kindness of Moth. Chase we are supplied with the addition—of b. chips & we have a good breakfast. This is the 3d time I have done so much cooking as to bake the pan-cakes since we started—the Ind. that annoy'd us last night, pass us & strike their tents & travel with us till near night when they fall in our rear & we encamp near them—a large com. on the other side the river. It commenc'd raining just as we stop'd—no time to cook supper—I am quite sick this aft.—glad to crawl to bed.
   Trav. 12 ms.

Wed. 28th. Start early—the forepart of the day very warm—clouds up afternoon & the wind blows, rains a little where we are but the storm is most ahead. We pass the 2d 50 & encamp in front. Quite cold at night but the rain over.
   Trav. 15 ms.

th. 29th. Start 20 min. past 7—the 2d 50 come in sight & we soon come nearly up with Taylor's Com. The bluffs on both sides the riv. are very picturesque—As we commence rising the hills, which are said to be the last between this & the Fort, we can see a singular appearing bluff which in an inhabited country might be mistaken for a large building; this is said may be seen in 40 ms. travel. The bluffs all day present buildings, terraces, platforms, &c. of every description. We encamp in front of the 2d 50 & in sight of Taylor.

Trav. 25 ms.

Margaret walks on range over the peaks & brought us wood, stones, & cedar boughs. Yest. we met 5 fur trappers on horseback they left their com. on the other side to learn who we were.

fr. 30th. Br. Woodard came to Capt. N. this mor.—told him he should leave the 50 unless he could either be paid for the work he had done or have his tools carried. We start ten min. past 7—the 2d 50 in sight in our rear & 2 or more comp. in front. Move rapidly on with the same tranquility as yest. except fath. Chase stopping a few min. to arrange his oxen Capt. P. drove past him. The bluffs truly present views wildly magnificent. We arrive nearly opposite the peak which we saw yest. mor. & encamp. The sun has been scorching thro' the day tho' the nights are like Oct. I went to see sis. Ewing at noon, who has been very sick for some time. Br. Hendrick's oxen which almost gave out yest. still travels on Our people saw a man across the river found him to be from California.

Trav. 22 ms.

Sat. 31st. Start about 7—the mor. cool—the middle of the day hot— met one of the Pioneers by the name of Davenport going to Winter Quarters with a Com. of fur Traders—encamp between 5 & 6 in sight of Taylor's & in sight of the chimney peak—the bluffs are stupendous & beautiful to the lovers of nature—no wood on this side the riv. & only cedar bushes on the other—Our cooking is done with fragments of flood wood & <u>buffalo chips</u>. The "chimney rock" or as I nam'd it, chimney peak is said to be precisely 20 ms. from "scotch bluff—we en- camp about 5 ms. in rear of opposite the latter. Trav. 16 ms.

August.—

Sun. 1st. We do not trav.—this is a busy day in washing, baking &c.; the feed here is good—the 2d 50 come up & encamp near us—some of our boys visit the "Scotch Bluff—report it to be a mile high & almost inaccessible—find a few pine trees & cedar shubbery, currants &c.— the two com. hold meeting at 5 in the eve. after night the Capts. meet—motion'd that B. Young go into the 2d 50 with his uncle J.

Mo. 2 Start a little aft. 7—the forenoon very hot—clouds up & is fine travelling with now & then a sprinkle of rain—our cattle are herded

out of the yard for several past nights
Trav. 16 ms.

tu. 3d The day hot—a little before night the com. halt while sis. Ewing[12] who was taken sick 2 weeks ago died—we turn'd down to the river & encamp'd near J Taylor—the 2d 50 not in sight—I had a 2d chill this forenoon—sis. P. & M. quite ill with the heat—saw a bluff which is said to be 50 ms. beyond the Fort
Trav. 15 ms.

Wed. 4th—This mor. we saw many men & horses—many female faces were lighted with unusual joy at the arrival of some of the battalion from California, looking healthy & in good spirits—we ascertain'd the Com. to be Gen. Kearney, Freemont & 14 Mormon soldiers going to Ft. Leavens<worth> for their release &c. The Gen. had brought Freemont, he being obnoxious to our interest, by prejudicing the Spaniards against us—The burial of sis. E. was attended with all the propriety circumstances would permit—after the customary dressing, the body was wrap'd in a quilt & consign'd to its narrow home without a coffin. It truly seem'd a lonely grave. Capt. P. found a wood written by the Pioneers dated 1st of June, saying 15 ms. from Ft. Laramy &c. after which we went 2 ms. & encamp'd. Today saw patches of prickly pear nearly half over the ground. Trav. 12 ms.

Th. 5th Last night, Taylor's com. which we pass'd at noon, crowded onto our herding place—the herd mix'd &c. We started this mor. after them & pass'd them & several other comp.s—pass'd a lot of Indian huts—sev. came out to meet us—all quiet.—as we came up in the rear of Rich's com, the road on the left in which we trav. being vacant, Capt. T. trav. in it: br. Duel from the right came over & crowded in 2 wagons except this, all was harmony. We encamp near the Fording place
At eve. Capt. P. returns to the wigwams or rather <u>tents</u>—finds French <u>gentlemen</u> at supper with Indian servants—the meal consisted of light bread, coffee, & meat; serv'd on the ground with tin dishes &c.—We have a <u>sprinkle</u> of rain—very dry. Indians visit us.
Trav. 12½ ms.

fr. 6th Cross the river which here has a stony bottom we cross below the old Fort—both are built of unburnt brick—we go 5 miles beyond & encamp before 12. Capt Grant having sent for us to stop till they arrive—Ch. D. & br. Ellsworth go to P. P. for permission for some to leave the Com. & go ahead—he throws the responsibility upon Capt. N. who will not take it by giving consent &c. &c. &c. The feed good on a little island—we have plenty of wood & water & before bedtime <u>we</u> flatter ourselves, (ie. sis. P. & myself) that <u>the</u> go-<u>ahead</u> feeling will be subdued & all stop & recruit the teams, repair wagons &c.—Moth. Chase & I have a treat in the eve. Jacob Cloward baptiz'd &c. My health much better. A Spaniard supp'd with us Taylor enc. on the other side the Island.

Aug. Sat. 7th. All is well—may our union increase—But some things seem calculated to call up the feelings of the human heart & show the selfishness of man. Some of us at least feel somewhat indignant in consequence of a letter from Capt. G. to P. P. stating things derogatory to the benevolent feelings of the 1st 50. whether true or false may hereafter be proven. It is nearly night when they arrive— Capt. G. sick—I took dinner with sis. Holmes & supp'd with sis. Noble

Su. 8th A little show'r at noon which is a rare thing in this country—the sisters of our com. have a meeting—Sis. Taylor & Leonard come. The Lord pour'd his spirit upon us in a copious effusion—sis. Writer [Riter] receiv'd the gift of tongues. A move made to start in the eve. but the cattle mix'd with other herds & takes too long to find them. Sis. P. blest M. at out meet. & in the gift of tongues & united our hands &c.

Mo. 9th Move on—leave the 2d 50 doing their blacksmith work with coal that father Chase burnt for us &c.—We are now among the much celebrated "black hills"—pass Hunter & find that P. P. has gone on—we stop by the river where we find a patch of grass, cur- rants & buffalo berries—the country here is rugged enough—diver- sified with scrubby pine, hemlock, cottonwood &c very thinly scat- ter'd; with bluffs presenting the appearance of well fortified castles the inhabitants of which exclude themselves from our view, altho' 2 grizly bears have been seen.—Last night had a fine shower
     Trav. 5½ ms.

tu. 10th We had a fine show'r in the night—this mor. while waiting for Capt. G. to come up that he & Prest. Y. who have trav. with the other 50; might go with us: M. baked 2 berry pies the qualities of which are yet to be tested—we had a treat of wild goose for breakfast which sis. Wiler's driver kill'd last night. The road today is very hilly & rocky but hard &

we are not annoy'd with dust Stop & dine on our pies & milk—no feed
for cattle—I rode with sis. Grant in the aft. noon—she is quite feeble—
cross'd some beautiful little streams towards night—one warm spring
in the morning—was amus'd to see the high peak which was said to be
50 ms. this side Laramy surrounded with a white cloud at some distance from the summit—we encamp 30 ms. from the Ft. [Laramie]

W. 11th. We cross the stream on which we encamp'd last night—I am
sick all day—the road rough—considerably between bluffs—enc. on
a stream near "Kimball's Spring" of <u>good cold water</u>
   Trav. 15 ms. Rich comes up

th. 12th Cross the stream & enc. find more cold springs & plenty of
wood—sis N. gives birth to a fine girl[13]—I din'd with sis. Wiler on tea
& light biscuit—the 2d 50 come up

fr. 13th. Spent the day with sis. N.—her babe not well—Taylor, &
Smoot come up—sis. Hunter calls, informs us of the hail-storm
which last eve. threaten'd us but pass'd round—she said the stones
were large as small walnuts & whiten'd the ground.

Sat. 14th. Sis. Smoot call on me in the mor. they had 10 horses & 2
colts stolen by the Ind. night before last—I din'd with sis. Leonard
on potpie—gave notice to all the 100 & met in the aft. for worship—
had a glorious time 3 receiv'd the gift of tongues—the "spirit of the
Holy Ghost" was truly pour'd out—Last eve the young people met for
a dance & br. Baker's boys & others intruded with much insolence—
they are tried this eve. before the bishop's court &c. &c.[14] This 50
burn a coal pit—the 2d 50 are having their work done that they may
start tomorrow—We are also manufacturing tar—Capt. Smoot's com.
made 50 gal.

Su. 15th The 2d 50 start—sis. Meeks sent for me—I spent sev. hours
with her—call'd on sis. Holmes—din'd with sis. Neff—vis. sis. Grant
& N. after walking to the tarpit—&c. Capt. P. loses an ox—Yest. saw
M. Forsgreen & F. Granger pass sitting in the front of the wagon—P.
& J. Young start for the Pioneers. Very blustering in the aft. but no
rain of any consequence.

Mo. 16th. A motion is made to start—when the cattle are brought up
16 are not to be found—do not find them thro' the day William is

out on foot & alone for his ox which is gone with the rest—we feel
very anxious for him on account of the large wolves & Indians. I go to
moth. Chase's—hear that pioneers have arriv'd at the upper
camps—that the City is laid out &c.—sis H. calls while we are having
a rich treat from on high. Call on sis. Meeks. find her better. Sup at
home on a rabbit pot-pie

Tu. 17th. The men go in search of the cattle the sis. meet in the grove
for prayer—we have a time not to be forgotten—Bless the Lord O my
soul, yea I do praise him for the gift of his holy spirit—before I got
out of the grove, I heard that the breth. were on track of the cattle—
went home with sis. Young read the letter from the Pioneers, by
Porter of them & br. Binder of the soldiers—The The [*sic*] letter
brought the most cheering int. dated Aug. 2d stating that they were
in the beautiful valley of the great Salt Lake that they that mor. had
commenc'd surveying the City—that it is a "goodly land" & their
souls are satisfied—the soldiers from Pueblo & the breth. from Miss.
have arriv'd & they number in all 450 souls & know not one dissatisfied.—I din'd with br. Y. & lady & L. Robinson from Rich's
Camp—Sis. P. sick in consequence of poison which is effecting her
hands & face—the sis. remember'd her in their meeting—she heard
from her son—that he was well—had not been homesick.—that
Prest. Y. was going to keep him by his side—&c which comforted her
   We have a <u>smart sprinkle</u> of rain near night—Pres. Y. Capt. Grant &
Noble rig themselves for herding—they go out & bring in the herd—
which Capt. P. recommended but was oppos'd in. My heart was made
to rejoice at seeing our 3 head Officers united in one thing—it surely
is in accordance with the prayers of the sis. This mor. Sis. G. is better—thinks the pickled pork I obtain'd of S. Ashby[15] did her good

Wed. 18th. Capt. G. started early to meet the men who are in pursuit
of the cattle—commenc'd raining about noon—Sis. P. is better—the
men do not return.

Th. 19th. Last night rain'd in the forepart—between 1 and 2 our
cattle break from the yard—the men go in pursuit & return with
them in the mor. One of Capt. P.'s not to be found—After consulting
it is thought best to move forward with what strength we have—Capt.
P. goes in search of his ox—& we are waiting after the other tens
leave. Sis. Wiler brings me a bowl of tea while writing in the horseless
buggy. The Lord bless her for all her kindness to me. My pray'r for

the Camp is that God will pour out his spirit upon us—We seem to have the most difficulty when the most officers are with us. O Lord! fill them with thy spirit—unite their hearts—incline them to seek unto thee for thy blessings to rest upon this people—may we uphold them by the pray'r of faith.

Capt. P. finds the ox that stray'd last night & we go on—ascend a hill where every team has to double. Capt. P.'s horses gone after the cattle—he fastens the carriage to a wagon, the women walk I ride with br. Hendricks. Sis. Love is run over with a heavy loaded wagon. We encamp before night on a small creek—I bake the pan-cakes for supper—rains quite a show'r before we get supper M. E. & I crawl under a wagon the rest get in &c.
Trav. 8 ms.

fr. 20th. Last night br. Love and J. Dillworth who went for the cattle return'd—said they went 10 ms. beyond Laramy—found them in possessin of the French to whom they were sold by the Ind. They were oblig'd to give one pair to get the rest Stop'd at Laramy over night, where they were hospitably treated & drove from there the next day—When about 1½ m. from the camp the cattle broke & run to our herd, where they were found this mor. Capt. P. gets an ox of br. Love to pair with the odd one & we go on in our usual style. The road is up & down hill—high peaks to be seen at the right & left—showrs falling on them & we sometimes get a sprinkle recent rains cause the way to be rather muddy. We enc. on a brisk little stream with a range of bluffs on the left—I take a walk along thir sides & scare up a <u>mighty large</u> rabbit. Sup'd with fath. & moth. Chase on rabbit-pot-pie.
Trav. 12 ms.

Sat. 21st. We start very late. J. Y.—B. Y. Grant's & Nobles teams in front—we had not gone far when to the general joy Grant Writer & another who went back to meet them with the stray cattle; came up after recruiting their strength with a repast which was left on a post at our last night encampment. Our road was round about between bluffs & over hills—the sides of the bluffs and for a distance the road was nearly the color of well burnt brick—sometimes the red of the bluffs being strip'd with nearly a chalk color, the little green shrubs & herbage gave it a romantic appearance. We stop'd on a stream at noon—pass'd over sev.—trav. till nine at night. This mor. I heard that sis. Love sat up & comb'd her hair.—This is truly a manifestation of the pow'r of God
Trav. 17 ms.

Su. 22d. Very late when we start then we wait a long while for something to be adjusted—we see the front of the Com. forming a ring on the top of a hill at about halfpast One—Capt. P. stops on the stream below: Capt. L. proposes going three ms. farther—they yoke up or rather hitch us up—ascend the hill after swallowing hasty dinner—Capt. G. and others meet Lathrop who is in front & object to the move—after much talk they drive back & form in the ring—a meeting is call'd for adjusting matters Capt. G. saying he was willing for us to travel in 10's or otherwise but wanted an understanding have it done by the general voice—some new arrangements for herding were made & liberty giv'n for any 10 to start when ready without regard to the upper authorities &c. &c. Call on sis. Love she is quite smart.

Trav. 8 ms.

Mo. 23d. This mor. sis. P. broil'd some buff. meat which Capt. M. kill'd yes. but it seem'd to have been the father of all buffalos & <u>uneatable</u>.

We start at 8 with Capt. N. in front & Prest. Y. & Capt. G. in the rear. In about 3 ms. cross a stream—come onto the Platte in about 8 ms. which seems like meeting an old friend—find an inscription "90 ms. to F. Johns" go 2 ms. cross Dear Creek, bait & dine—a dish of tea is very acceptable—The day clear—the road pretty smooth but very hilly & barren A windy thunderstorm before night.

Trav. 15 ms.

Tu. 24th. Prest. Y., B. Y. & Capt. G. take the lead—before noon br. Love breaks a wagon; We encamp about 1 o'clock—they go back for the wagon &c Br. Baker kills a buffalo. The road not bad—on our left far in the distance, a ridge or mountain rises in majesty behind the ranges of smaller bluffs between having the appearance of dense blue clouds. A show'r of hail & rain adds variety to the afternoon scenery. Trav. 8 ms.

Wed. 25th. The camp moves out in the mor. leaving Capt. P. & Capt M. in waiting for the wagon maker & the broken wagon. We start between 11 & 12. The weather <u>cold</u>—the road smooth but deep ravines pass a board saying 110 ms. from Ft. Johns—pass a ferry where the inscription says 8 ms. to another—pass another way-mark 120 ms. from Ft. Johns Encamp sun an hour high—do not reach the camp The cloud cap & bluffs on our left look dreary in a cold day. Trav. 14 or 15 ms.

Th. 26th. Come up to the crossing in 2 ms. where the rest of the 50 were just rolling out—L. Johnson & others were starting for W. Quarters—Five 50's left here last Mon. The river is of a pebly bottom—the water not over the wagon hubb. The country is very rugged with piles of red & black rock of every form & size. No wood here we encamp 12 ms from the crossing. A bluff with cedar trees is at our front 2 ms. distant. Without wood as I sat viewing the camp I thought surely the saints are a creative people for there is plenty of cooking going on. Here is a small stream or rather Slue & small springs which serve for cooking. <A buf. & ant. kill'd>

　　Trav. 14 ms.

<u>I wrote the following A Song</u> of <u>the desart.</u>

> Beneath the cloud-top'd mountain
> 　Beside the craggy bluff
> Where ev'ry dint of nature
> 　Is rude & wild enough.
> Upon the verdant meadow—
> 　Upon the sunburnt plain—
> Upon the sandy hillock
> 　We waken music's strain.
>
> Beneath the pine's thick branches
> 　That has for ages stood—
> Beneath the humble cedar
> 　And the green cotton-wood
> Beside the broad smooth river—
> 　Beside the flowing spring
> Beside the limpid streamlet
> 　We often sit and sing.
>
> Beneath the sparkling concave
> 　When stars in millions come
> To cheer the pilgrim strangers
> 　And bid us be at home
> Beneath the lovely moonlight
> 　When Cynthia spreads her rays
> In social groups we gather
> 　We join in songs of praise.
>
> Cheer'd by the blaze of fire-light
> 　When twilight shadows fall

> And when the darkness gathers
>   Around our spacious hall;
> With all the warm emotion
>   To youthful bosoms giv'n
> In strains of pure devotion
>   We praise the God of heav'n.

fr. 27th. Start in good season—the road is very smooth insomuch that Capt. P. wishes me to record the circumstance of fath. Chase riding up hill for the first time. We pass sev. salt-petre springs & the carcases of 10 or 11 cattle. We encamp in an environ with majestic bluffs—a slue-creek & a cold spring the country is very mountainous & rocky huge piles of rock lying strew'd about the barren surface, & ornamented with a red moss—Trav. 20 ms.

Sat. 28th. When the herd is brought up, nearly half are missing—A late arrangement having been made for the Capts. to take the herding by turns—last night was Capt. P.s turn—3 horsemen & 3 footmen take the back track—Capt. N. & those who have their teams go on

Our buggy was harness'd before the herd come in I was holding the horses when about 11 the horses became un manageable—took a circle round & broke the tongue which Capt. P. & L. soon repair'd—myself quite ill since a walk I took yest. lie on sis. H.s bed till the cattle arrive, which are found by that part of the com. that went forward & are met by boys sent in that direction Capt. L. having discovered their tracks—4 are missing which are brought in at 2 o'clock at night by those that went back to the Platte where we encamp'd night before last. We move in the aft.—encamp in a basin on an elevated spot where the cattle go into a mire—they are oblig'd to take them up—talk of trav. in the night—it is cloudy, rains some—they yoke all & confine in the ring.

Sun. 29th. Start while the moon is yet shining go perhaps 6 ms. where is a beautiful stream & <u>very little</u> feed & stop till half past 10 or 11 we then go on till ½ past 4 when we encamp near the Sweet-water with our broken Com. Prest. Y. & Capt. G. go on Capt. G. having sent 2 of his wag. with Capt. N. Br. H. & sis. W. thrown out of their place by starting out in front.

The ground in many places perfectly white with Salaratus[16] or Saltpetre or some other composition—the bluffs rise one above another till the farthest looks like a dense cloud—all of irregular heights

& terminating in peaks at unequal distances. The road from where we bait is very sandy & seems laid out in an opening of a rugged enclosure. Sis. P. made me a dish of tea which is very beneficial to my health, having rode with Moth. C. all the mor. not able to sit up.

Trav. 12 ms.

Mo. 30th This mor. Capt. P. had a vote call'd on the case of br. Hendrics—he is thrown out of his place by vote of [*blank space*]—we pass the camp of Capt. N. G. &c. consisting of about 20 wagons—sis. W. with them having gone ahead yes. Pass one Ferry boat near the base of Independant Rock where we cross Sweet-water Creek—Cattle are strew'd all along the road side. Find a board in the mor. sign'd W. Snow saying left here on the 29th—lost 11 oxen since we left you. The bluffs rise on either side—some say that this is a commencement of the "pass"—we stop between 1 & 2 in an environ thro' which runs the Sweet-water—a singular opening in the bluff which rises perhaps a mile in height on one side—The 2d 50 three ms. ahead almost disabled by the loss of cattle

Trav. 12 ms.—sandy road

Tu. 31st. Start at 7—Capt. L's wagon breaks and we stop at the first encampment—a basin on the side of the river with good feed 3 of the Pueblin soldiers arrive[17]—The other part of this 50 come up at eve. The broken wheel is rigg'd in 3 hours from the time we stop'd & all is well—some baptisms attended in the eve. Br. H. in the rear of Writer—Capt. P. says he shall have his place tomorrow. Moth. C. & I have a vis.

Trav. 8 ms.

September. Wed. 1st. Start a quarter before 9 and overtake the 2d 50 a little before 12 & encamp. A meeting is call'd when an effort is made by neutralizing the strength of the teams to assist the 2d 50 who have lost 25 head since they left us—not quite all by disease, some few were return'd to other camps that had been loan'd. Capt. Snow ask'd assistance as a duty, saying he was not beholden to any man &c. &c.—Capt. G. manifested a spirit of meekness & spoke with wisdom &c. It was motion'd that the Capts. be authoriz'd to act for the com. & yoke whatever in their judgment was proper to be put to service of cows heifers, calves &c. Some thought the motion oppressive & objected but it was carried by the majority—

Trav. 5 ms.

Th. 2d. Last eve. had the pleasure of hearing from the Valley & tasting some salt from the great Lake of the Valley, by some of the soldiers & some of the Pioneers with 3 wagons that came up last night. We get ready to start in the mor. Capt. P. moves out & stops. Capt. G. & N. come up saying that J. Young said this 50 could take more load & must not go &c.—they examine the wagons at length we move on—word arrives that sis. G. is apprehensive of dying—wishes me to come back but the distance is farther than I can walk. I call'd on her in the mor.—found her sitting in bed cleaning her teeth—Her symptoms bad yet I hope & think that she will recover Capt. G. spoke as if it did not matter for this 50 to stop for the other till we get to T.'s camp which is a few ms. ahead—it seems to be by J. Y's order that we are stop'd for the <u>examination</u> after the teams were neutraliz'd. The road very sandy. hear at night that sis. G. is better—they stop 6 ms. in the rear—a show'r before night.

Trav. 12 ms. Br. Woodard comes up

Fr. 3d. A board saying 200 ms. to Ft. Johns is at our last night's enc. we start late—road very sandy for 8 ms. in the aft. we pass a straight between 2 ridges of mts.—cross the river 3 times, before which we meet soldiers & Pioneers with perhaps 18 wagons & a herd of loose oxen enc. on the riv. near the last crossing—we have pass'd the Salaratus lakes pass'd 1 yest. mor.

Trav. 12 ms.

Sat. 4th. J. Gleason parts with us I having furnish'd him a bag to carry Salaratus to sis. L., we having pass'd the springs. Br. Little takes tea with us. Br. G.'s youngest child died in bed last night—they are back 6 ms. Kill'd buf. ant. & a mt. sheep.

Trav. 7 ms.

Su. 5th. Our wash'd clothes frozen stiff this mor. on the line & bushes. The Pioneers call this a little short of 300 ms. to the Valley. [*something stricken out*] There is a mile board 230 ms. to Ft. Johns.— The day fine & the road pretty good—some of the way very sandy— the bluffs not so high & at a greater distance than for a long time. Sup on apple dumplings

Trav. 18 ms.

Mo. 6th. Capt N.s wagon which was broken yest. repair'd. Sis. W. who left sometime ago comes up in our rear. We enc. on the Sweet-water

having cross'd it 2 today & once yest. Stop about 3 ms most of the time till night—very cold & blustring. pass the 240 mile bd.
Trav. 8 ms.

Tu. 7th. This mor. I wash'd in snow the storm continued till 11. we started at ½ past 10—snow'd after intervals thro the day. All the way long hills & in places intolerably rocky—the bluffs white with snow this call'd "Wind Ridge"
Trav. 10 ms.

Wed. 8th This mor. as we were about starting Harvey P. & others came up informing us that the Pioneers were 15 ms. distant and would be with us. We went 2 ms. to a place of enc. when 2 brethren on horseback in our rear, thought best to go to the next stream; and while our wagons were many standing side by side waiting for the repair of the crossing, those men rode hastily past—the oxen took fright & almost in a moment perhaps 20 wagons were in rapid motion. Many cross'd the stream in different directions many lives were expos'd but thro' the protecting pow'r of God no one was much hurt & no wagon materially injur'd. We went a m. farther & spent the day with the Pioneers. Prest. Y. H.C.K., & A. Lyman sup'd with us. The 2d 50 came up.
Trav. 3 ms.

Th. 9th. Last night all guard was neglected, & about 40 horses & mules stolen. An arm'd com. was put on the track—late this eve. 2 horses are brought in by one of the com. The forepart of the day very cold. I spent it with moth. Chase. Had a spiritual treat wherein both rec'd great blessings. She said certain intelligence should come to me thro' the proper channel &c. We then enjoy'd a treat of tea & pan-cakes.

Fr. 10th The com. return'd with only 3 horses. Capt. P loses 1 mule. We move on after parting with the Pioneers. Last eve. a meeting was held after the Pion.s preach'd, a song sung I had written.
[*Top margin:* wrote to L. & L, & sis. S. M. K.]
Before the P.s left B. came to the carriage blest us—I ask'd who was to be my counsellor for the year to come—he said E.R S. I said "she is not capable"—he said "I have appointed her president—said he had conversation with br. P. about provision—that he will furnish me & all will be right.

Teams sufficient for both 50s to move altho' much loss was sustain'd by the 2d & it was thought necessary for us to go on to Green R. & come back for them. encamp side by side.

Trav. 12 ms.

Sat. 11th We pass or rather cross the "dividing Ridge"—pass the Pacific Springs & enc. off the road with fresh feed. The 2d 50 not quite up—The ground white with Salaratus. The day warm & sunny.

Trav. 18 ms.

Sun. 12th Soon after we start a messenger arrives from the 2d 50, with a note to Capt. N. requesting him to stop for them soon as he arrives at sufficient feed to sustain the cattle. We cross Dry Sandy & enc. on Little Sandy at night. Had a conversation with Capt. P. about matters & things of my own concerns. He said that arrangements were made to his satisfaction perfectly. Said B—m. express'd the same satisfaction for his bringing me that he had done to me before when saying that I was welcome to live in the house with Clara if I would accept it. &c. &c.—Yest. I was quite sick today begin to feel more like life.

Trav. 19 ms. pass the 300 m. board.

Mo. 13th Not much feed & we go on to Big Sandy. The ridges of Mts. so distant that it seems like a prairie country. A few scattering trees to be seen. Yest met a large com. of soldiers from Mexico.

Trav. 8 ms.

Tu. 14th Last eve. the breth. & sis. met for prayer meeting in the yard—the spirit of the Lord was there. Capt. N. open'd with pray'r, was follow'd by br. Ellsworth—The subject of stopping today for the other 50 was discuss'd in a candid intelligent & brotherly manner—br. E. motion that Capt. N. go & meet the other 50 & learn the cause of the requisition for us to stop. All seem'd to feel the necessity of wasting no time; yet they did not like to transgress the principles of order & submission. This mor. Capt. P. propos'd going to Green r. to do some repairing, while the rest come up—call'd for his 10—a discussion ensued—all conclud to wait—Capt. N. & Porter go to meet the Com.

The mts. very grand—ridge rising after ridge in front of me—the clouds sometimes obscuring the distant ridges.

I vis. sis. G. who seems improving a little sis. L. nurses her. The breth. meet & Prest. Y. explain'd the cause of wishing to see us—that B. told him to keep the com.s together till we get to Green R.—that he compar'd us to a kite & he now cuts the string & lets us go &c.

Wed. 15th We go 2 ms. & cross the B. S.[Big Sandy] river—pass the 130 m. board being 200 ms. from the Valley when cross the riv. The road very smooth most of the day—the mts. at great distances on either side. The land in the forenoon undulating—in the aft. regularly discending plain—Come to the riv. & follow it 2 ms. & enc. off the road on the stream.
Trav. 21 ms.

Th. 16th. Trav. 6 ms. on a broad descending plain then cross the Green R. a beautifully clear stream with a row of cotton-wood on the north side go 3 ms. & pass 7 wagons from Taylor's com. of whom are the 2 Brenners:—go 1 m. far. down the riv. & enc. Yes. & today we pass the country where the P's were taken sick sev. of our com. slightly attack'd with mt. fever
Trav. 10 ms.

fr. 17th This mor. Capt. P. propos'd being cut loose from the 50 which was done by vote of the Capts; after which being ready first, he took the lead. We trav. without water; come to a guide bd. directing to feed—go 1 m. & enc. on the Muddy—Capt.s L. K. & N. go on by taking the right hand which is 5 ms.
Trav. 15 ms.

Sat 18th Find the herd without diff. tho' not herded, find br. B's 3 wag. in 3 m. & come to the other enc. in 5—concluded best to spend the day in good feed. Find plenty of currents.
Trav. 5 ms.

Sun. 19th. Start late—come to a beautiful enc.—cross a stream—see the 7 wag. in front & the 2d 50 in the rear—in a short distance cross the Black Fork—Br. W. goes ahead to find pasture. Capt. M. & G. go on to hunt. Capt. N.'s carriage breaks down—Capt. P. rides before the com. We pass some splendid bluffs—pass the 370 m. board—enc. on a small stream with a shade of trees & shrubs. A br. arrives from the Valley in 4 days.
Trav. 14 ms.

Mo. 20th. Warm—the dust very unpleasant br. breaks a wagon—enc. in the sand by a stream.

Trav. 8 m.

Tu. 21st Start at 9—bait at 12 by a creek—pass Fort Bridger a short distance & enc. The Com. of Y enc. near—I am quite sick—Our people traffic with the French & Ind.

Trav. 8 ms.

Wed. 22d. The cattle cannot be found till too late & the majority move to stop till morning—The day spent in trafficking—the 2d 50 come up—Last night br. Vance arrives—speaks of a frost there that injur'd the crops. I am quite sick in the forenoon—much better in the eve. Moth. Chase & I have a rich treat in the carriage—with a promise of new int. [intelligence] if diligent & submissive.—Br. Love lost an ox—Capt. P. buys a pair & a cow & calf

Th. 23d Saw J. Y. from the Valley—Last night a dance was attended in one of the Frenchmen's houses by many from each 50, both old & young—Prest. J. Y. & wife not excepted.—it continued till nearly 2 after which a hooting was kept up till morning by the drunken natives—

We pass'd a spring—a very small run—a curiously variegated landscape & enc. on a stream—call'd Muddy that was nearly dry. The dust intolerable

Trav. 13 ms.

Fr. 24th. My health better—finish a garment for sis. P.—We start late—the pow'r of the air rules & the dust is worse than intolerable—find the 7 wag. of T's enc. at the springs when not finding sufficient water, we go on—leave Writer & Dilworth & the 2d 50 in sight—cross a mt. pass popple groves—a soda spring & the 30 m. b. from Bridger—go 1 m. beyond & enc. by Springs 1 m. from B[ear]. Riv. with a beautiful moon-light, about 8 o'clock.

Trav. 18 m.

Sat. 25th. We go to Bear R. where a consultation is had & some are desirous to stop & do some blacksmithing—part conclude to go on to Cash [Cache] Cave & hunt—Capt. P. goes ahead—we meet Capt. M. who said that a part of T's com. pass'd the Cave last eve.—no chance for game. Rich's com. having clear'd the ground—met C.

sick with mt. fever. also men from the Valley with 4 pr. of cattle. Pass some stupendous bluffs of pebble stonerock on one side the "narrows" which we pass'd before we cross'd the stream on which we enc. Capt.s P. L. & K. come up also Capt. N. in the eve.[18]

Trav. 11 ms.

Sun. 26th. Leave our enclosure which might puzzle a querist where we come in & where we were to go out; which we do by rising a long winding hill, from the top of which we see the mts. of the Valley. We enc. about noon across a small stream opposite a high bluff in the side of which is a curious opening in solid rock call'd Cash Cave Heard that sis G. died this mor.[19]

Porter & J. G. arrive in the eve. bring word that have had no frost in the V. to injure much &c. <Writer & D. come up>

Trav. 5 ms.

Mo. 27th. We trav. most of the day in a Canion or narrow op'ning between 2 ranges of mts. Capt. G. passes us with a horse team—going to the V. to bury his wife. Br.& sis. Leonard with him—Capt. P. & L. enc. together. Neff stops in the rear—K. on ahead—Our place is delightful—the mts. being in a half circle on either side & variegated with indescribable beauty; rising in a kind of majesty that could but inspire feelings of sublimity in a contemplative mind. pass the 60 m. b. from B. [Bridger]

Trav. 13 ms.

Tu. 28th Go on in the same range—pass curious mts. which delight me, mostly of a fine brick color on the right hand & rising perpendicularly & on the left covered partially with surf. with Cedar & willow bushes between the ridges. Pass sis Taylor stopping at Weber's Fork—pass the river & go 2 ms. Cross the creek that emp. in the W. 4 times.

Trav. 14 ms.

Wed. 29th. Last eve. was delightful—this mor. cold with a sprinkle of rain, a strange occurance, C. D. & Ellsworth stop to hunt—in a few rods we enter "Platt's [Pratt's?] Pass"—the road rough—sideling & thro' thickets of willow—pass the 80 m.b. & enc. on a fine stream call'd Canion Creek, after crossing one 3 times The middle of this & the 2 last day too warm for the cattle. Some of T's com. where we stop—we saw the mts. of this side the Valley.

Trav. 11 ms. The 80 m.b. on top 5 m. hill.

Th. 30 Cross'd Canion Creek 8 times—the road sideling, cradling, stumpy, bushy, &c We enc. on a side hill about 1 m. ahead of the 90 m.b.—Capt. L. passes us also sis. T. but her camp stops in our rear. The buggy is found insufficient to go any farther.

    Trav. 6 m.

October.

    Fr. 1st Left the carriage & an ox that gave out yesterday—I rode in the black wag. sis. P. M. & Edith walk—very, very dirty, thro' brush & timber—up the Mt. to Bellows Peak where we met J. T. who ask'd me if I had lately seen my face, his own being behind a black mask (the soil having chang'd)—we then went slash mash down over stumps, trees &c. &c. enc. in the Canion a little in rear of Capt. L. & sis. Taylor. Thankful for our deliverance thus far.

    Trav. 10 ms.

Sat. 2d Cross a stream 19 times—which is dry in some of its beds—the vegetation & shubbery is very much chang'd; here is oak, maple, and elder, ozier &c. About 4 we come in view of the Valley looking like a broad rich river bottom—it rains & a breach made in the side of our wag. cov. torn by the brush admits both rain & dust, but being in sight of home we make our way to the Fort—I am too sick to enjoy the scenery but a good cup tea prepar'd by sis P. refreshes me, also a vis. from sis. Sess.[20]

    Trav. 14 ms.

Su 3d This mor. seat myself by a doby [adobe] fire-place outside the body of a log house—breakfast with br. P.s sup with sis. Leonard—have my things put into Clarissa's room, who said Prest. Y. wrote her that I would live with her.[21]—The breth. have meet. P. & T. prest.—the Ep. [Epistle] of the Twelve read & sanction'd by the breth.

Mo. 4th. Last night slept in Capt. G's wagon with sis. Leonard—breakfast with sis. L., sup with her & C. in Clara's room—this is the commencement of my living with C.[22]—Commence writing to send to W. Q.

Tu. 5th Finish 11 letters to send to W. Q. by J. Thorn who is selling his substance to return with family.[23] Wrote the following to Mrs. Mary Ann Young.

May the streams of consolation
    Ever to your bosom flow;
And the bitter draught of sorrow
    Be no more your lot to know.

Blessed be your habitation
    The abode of peace & rest;
Yes with all that is a blessing
    I would fondly have you blest.

We anticipate the period
    When you to the Valley come
Haste & leave your Winter-Quarters—
    Here you'll find a better home.[24]

Wrote the following to sis. Whitney, Kimball, Sarah A. & Helen,

Now my spirit oft is with you,
    Yes, my heart oft lingers there—
That you all may reach the "Valley"
    Is my constant, earnest pray'r,

Here, a quiet, heav'nly spirit
    Seems all nature to pervade—
All the <u>saints</u> are well contented
    But the "hangers on," afraid.

All is well—is well in Zion—
    Zion is the pure in heart:
Come along, ye holy women,
    And your blessings here impart.[25]

Wrote the following, & presented it to br. G. who took supper with us.

On the death of Mrs. Caroline Grant.

Calm as mildest summer ev'ning
    When the stars serenely shine—
When all nature is most tranquil,
    Was the death of Caroline.

Brightly glow'd her lamp of reason
    While her last life-pulses beat—
Nobly she resign'd her spirit—
    Surely death to her was sweet.

One of her two lovely daughters,
   That which on her bosom lay;
To precede her mother's exit
   Like a dew-drop pass'd away.

Soon, ah soon, the parent follow'd
   To the better world on high
And with such sweet resignation
   One might even wish to die.

Well I lov'd her, and my heart clings
   Fondly to her image still,
And my feelings would have held her
   E'en beyond my Father's will.

He, in meting out our portions,
   Granted her the better lot—
She was privileg'd to go where
   Pain & sickness enter not.

Tho' she died upon the mountains
   Trav'ling to the place of rest;
She reposes in the Valley—
   In her burial, she is blest.[26]

Wed. 6th. I went to the warm spring thro' the kindness of sis. J. Y. &
Susan Hunter who took us in the carriage—felt quite refresh'd[27]

Th. 7th I finis'd sis. P.s cap—The last of the camp arrive
Capt. Kimball, Wicks & others leave here for Goodger's [Goodyear]
40 ms. distant[28]

fr. 8th. A posse of 5 men, the Martial Higgins at the head, go out to
bring back those families by order of the Council.[29]

Sat. I am quite ill—sis. Chase administers to me—we are blest.

Su. 10 By decision of Council Ira Miles comes for a bl. of flour which
is deposited in the Store-house where Clara & I live; Fath Chase objects—goes to see Prest. J. Smith—at length a rehearing is propos'd
& the excitment ends. A preaching is attended fore & aft. noon—I
sat in Ellen's door & heard P. P.—din'd with Lorenzo Young's—in the
eve a meeting held to organize according to the Epistle—the posse

return'd with a promise from Wicks, Kimball Babcock & Gardner that they would return to the Fort—The weather is quite warm.

Mo. 11th The case of the flour decided in favor of Ira—fath Chase came with him & said it was given up without his consent, Clara saying she should not give hers—that if they take it they must &c. The other flour is divided to the family <u>none for me</u>.—Several of the Battalion from California arrive—br. Rosacrans among the number. I made a cap for sis. J. Young for which she paid me in soap, 1 lb.& 15 oz. so much I call my own. I now begin once more to be a woman of property.

Tu. 12th I din'd & supp'd with sis. Sessions. Some of the Batt. [Battalion] arrive.

Wed.13th Made a cap for sis. Allen br. Grant made me a rich present of tea, for which I pray the Lord to bless him—spent some hours with sis. Taylor.

Th. <Sis. J. Young gave me some fresh meat.>

fr. 15th Vis. Ellen & M. C.—din'd with them with much happiness

Sat. 16th This mor. a hard frost it is quite cool. I made a cap for sis. P. M. presented the fol.

To Eliza

I love thee; and I'll n'eer forget
    The time we've spent together
Thro' many toilsome scenes of wet
    And storms of windy weather.

I love Thee: & my heart entwines
    Around thy noble spirit—
May ev'ry joy on earth be thine
    Long life if thou desire it.

I love thee: & may thee be blest—
    May heaven smile upon thee
And may thy health & strength increase
    And may thy days be many.

I love thee: & O may thy life
   Be one of peace & pleasure;
And may thy heart be fill'd with light
   And blessing without measure.[30]
                Margarett Whitesides

Su. 17th, Too cold for me to sit out at meeting. I feel greatly blest both tem. & spiritually. Mrs. L. Young brought me more than 1 lb. sugar & Mrs. P. ½ pint of tea & a few doz. Crackers for which I praise the Lord.

     To Margarett.

I love thee with the tenderness
   That sister spirits love—
I love thee, for thy loveliness
   Is like to theirs above.

I love thee for thy modest worth
   Is like a diadem—
Thou surely art of noble birth—
   Thou art a precious gem.

I love thee for the kindness show'd
   To me in feeble health,
When journeying on a tedious road—
   I prize it more than wealth.

I love thee and thou shalt be crown'd
   With blessings not a few
Joy, peace & plenty shall surround
   Thy path, like summer dew.

The holy Spirit will inspire
   Thy pure & gen'rous heart
And to thy sweet, poetic fire
   Its heav'nly aid impart.[31]

Mo. 18th I had the pleasure of mounting a horse which was much satisfaction altho' I lost the anticipated ride to the Spring. in the afternoon sis. Taylor call'd for me & I accompanied her to visit a sick girl, Eliza Stewart to whom sis. Smoot, Sessions & I administer'd. Sis. T. & myself having taken tea & pancakes with sis Smoot sis. T was call'd away.

Tu. 19th I made a loaf of light bread, which I had not done for a long time.

Wed. 20th. The day is unpleasant, rains & snows. My strength is gaining so that I do quite a wash. I feel very thankf[ul]

Br. Scofield inserts a 4 light window on the west side C's house which is a blessing I feel truly blest of the Lord.[32]

Th. 21st The weather is fine but cool. I made a <u>large</u> loaf bread, which C. bak'd.

fr. 22d. C. & I visit sis. Leonard, after a good supper which we enjoy'd in the spirit of the Lord, we have a spiritual treat, sis. Sess. & L. joining us.

Sat. 23d. Slept with sis. Sess. after partaking a treat of pudding & milk, breakfast with her & L. after which we call on sis. Savage, sis. Wallace, administer to E. S. & spend the aft. happily with sis. Noble blest her, the babe &c. C. & I sit awhile in br. P.'s in the eve. He made me a present of 2 lights of glass for the east side of our house.

Su. 24th Transcrib'd the following from a slip in my journal.

> To Mrs. Caroline Grant written on
> hearing of the death of her little child

> Mourn not for that sweet gem that's gone
>   Altho' you priz'd it dear:
> The resurrection morning dawn
>   Is drawing very near

> It was your own & yours 'twill be
>   In seasons yet to come:
> Yes, in the next eternity
>   'Twill ornament your home.

> Her spirit's mould was loveliness
>   Replete with placid charms:
> She's gone in perfect holiness
>   To rest in Jesus' arms.

> 'Twas a sweet child—a precious gem—
>   A rose-bud borne away:
> That beauteous on the parent stem
>   Will bloom in future day.[33]
>   Sept 4th, 1847.

I went to meeting—Prest. J. Smith & others impress'd the necessity of the prompt execution of the laws & counsels of the High Council—the necessity of getting grain into the ground—dealing honestly with the Indians &c.—In the eve. sis. Peirce came in—inquir'd respecting my provisions—I told her I had none but I felt satisfied that the Lord would open the way for me that I knew there was an arrangement made, but it had fail'd &c. she said she was mortified that they could not supply me, but could not.—My trust is in God.

Mo. 25th Sis. Noble & Rosacrans spent the aft. with us. I am very thankful for the strength I have to work, can do my part of cooking—Br. & sis. P. came in the eve. Clara at V's wagon—br. P. talk'd about my provis. I told him I believ'd the Lord would give me strength to work & I was not asham'd to ask all I see for work for provisions, &c. we could be as economical as any body He said do not starve—be economical & when that is gone which you have let us know it. I told him the worst feeling I had was that I was living on C's rations &c. he told me to feel that it is a much my own as hers, & if I did not feel at home come to his house

Tu. 26th Went with sis. Sess. who supp'd with us, to visit E. Stewart—found her better—went to br. N's. sis. Smoot spent the eve. with us very lively.

Wed. 27th After receiving liberally of sis. N. who is truly a mother in Israel with whom I breakfasted & din'd, we spent the aft. with sis. Holmes & H. carrying with me a new tin porringer basin & plate, an earthen saucer plate & creamer, also a hair comb & <2 yd of cotton drilling> & altho' I am to work for them I consider them presents & thank the Lord; to which sis. Holmes added a large saucer & sis Howd a spoon—the Lord bless them in the eve. sis. N. sent 3 pints of beans.

Th. 28th Went with sis. Sess. to br. Moore's din'd & sup'd with them, felt blest & spent the night with sis. Whitney—eat 29th breakfast with her then went to br. Love's to engage her sewing, call'd at br. M's—found them much cheer'd by our vis.—sis. M. gave me a tin cup & spoon, 4 sea biscuit, dried pumpkin linen for a pocket handkf. &c. for which I took needlework. How greatly I am blest. When I got home C. told me sis. P. had brought up my tin basin full of coffee & a quart of dried apples.

Sat. 30th. The young people take a ride to Salt Lake—The day very cold & windy—Wicks, Kimball &c. arrive having been sent for again & compell'd to come br. & sis. Sess. sent for me to come to their tent. C. & I went—had a first rate visit & feasted on 2 roasted geese.

Su. 31st The weather cold—we have a meet. in the aft. prest. sis. Sess, Leon. Lucina Chase, Peirce & J. Young <also Susanna H.> Clara being mistress of the house call'd on me to preside—we had a refreshing time.

November.
Mo. 1st Very blustring—the dust flying so that we could not see the Mts. in the forenoon—a salt rain which was succeeded by a snowstorm—sis. Sess sups with us. many of the tents having blown down & hers with the rest. She brought me 6 skeins & a spool of thread & calico to exchange for a piece of domestic gingham

Tu. 2d. Attended a meeting of the mothers in Israel at Ellen's after the close of which E. spoke in the gift of tongues—it was a rich treat. Sis. Sess presided This mor. the ground cover'd with snow

Th. 4th The day fine—we had a meet. of the young ladies in the eve. C. call'd on me to preside—we had a glorious time Present sis. Sess. Holmes, Howd, Margarett, Ellen, M. Ellen, Susan N. E. Hendricks

Sat. 6th. Lawson tried before the H.[High] Council for shooting an ox & is to restore fourfold—this week the Lord has blest me abundantly with strength to labor Beside most of the cooking, I have made 2 veils for sis. Moore, 1 for sis. Noble, done 1 cap for sis. J. Y. & 1 for sis. Sess. Sis. M. sent me 2 quarts meal a little flour. & a stranger sis. sent me 2 quts. beans—sis. P brought us her little bowl full of ginger & br. P. let us have a piece of beef.

Su. 7th We found the ground cov. with snow 3 inch. or more—had a delightful meet. of the little girls. Susan N. & Martha rec'd the gift of tongues Sarah H. improv'd upon hers which she spoke in yes. here for the first—after meet. sis. Chase blest C. & I & C. spoke in tongues & blest us. Praise the Lord O my soul!

Mo. 8th. A meeting of the young ladies at Ellens this eve. It was truly a time of the outpouring of the spirit of God

Tu. 9th Br. P. brought us a mince pie

Wed. 10th Ellen, M. Ellen & A. Benson spent the aft.n. with us—the weather is more favorable.

Sat. 13th Sis. M. & Whitney came here last eve. I told sis. Whitney it was her privilege to set the pattern in the order of our meetings in honor of the household to which she belongs & this eve. we enjoy'd a precious time in her habitation, the influence of which I trust she will realize perhaps forever. Present Moth. Dilworth Chase Sess. Leonard, Hamilton &c.

This week I have been greatly blest with strength—done all the cooking except one meal most of making 2 calico shirts for Porter— did up a cap for sis. Sess. & made 6 buttonholes for sis. P.—Sis. Chase sup'd with us last eve.

Tu. 14th. This mor. sis. Moore brought me some beef which I thank the Lord for also some sea biscuit

In the eve. sis. Writer sent me a loaf of bread & a tea cup of elderberry sauce the Lord bless her an hundred fold. Which sis. Sess. who spent the day with us gave in interpretation of what I spoke, said was our right to claim for all that we bestow either spiritually & temporally—The day fine. In the eve. had an excellent meeting at br. J. Young's—br. Cornogg confirm'd.

Wed. 17th A part of the com. for the southern expedition start to-day[34]—the day is fine—the ground cover'd with snow

Th. 18th The remainder of the com. start today making 17 or 18 in No.

Su. 21st A meet. at sis. W's D Kingsbury there. her babe 3 days old.

Th. 25th Visited sis. Love with sis. Holmes Howd, Sess. Meeks & Noble. after supp we all arose & blest her—had a good time—for some days past the breth. have been ploughing & dragging with the ground cover'd with snow. This day they commence baptizing.

fr. 26th In com. with br. Noble's fam. sis. Sess. &c. I was baptized by br. Grant who administer'd to perhaps 20. I feel this to be a great blessing from the Lord.[35] In the eve. attended meet. at sis. Whitney's sis. Rogers rec'd the gift of tongues.

Su. 28 Meet. at Clara's—she presided

Mo 29th Sis. Chase, Sess. C. & I vis. sis. P. a meet. in the eve. sev. brethren prest. sis. S. presided in the forepart when she was call'd away she confer'd the authority back on sis. P. & she bestow'd it on me the breth. spoke with much approbation.[36]

Tu. 30th Vis. Ellen, feasted & blest &c. in the eve. she presided over her meet.

Dec. wed. 1st. The weather seems like spring. Sis. Wilkie Ellen K. spent the aft. with us. after supp. they blest us & were truly fill'd with the spirit of God

Th. 2d Supp'd with sis. Higbee, sis Sess. with me. A meet in the eve. over which sis. H. presided her hus. having given her permission to do so in his absence to Eutaw Lake where he in com with others has gone for fish. A young sis. Allred rec'd the gift of tongues—br. Luddington present.

fr.3d. Din'd with sis. Chase, meeting in the afternoon

Sat. 4th Din'd at br. Meek's with sis Sess. Holmes, Howd, Love &c. had a glorious time in blessing—3 rec'd the gift of tongues after which sis. Sess. & I supp'd with sis. Scofield she call'd a meet in the eve. & presided

Su. 5th Attended public meet. outdoors the day fine.

Tu. 7th Vis. at Maj. Russels with sis. Chase & Sess. having spent yesterday at fath. Sess. & slept with her last night. Snow'd yes. stormy today

fr. 10th Vis. at br. Stratton's with M. Sess. had a very sociable time. The day very blustring—staid with sis. W. heard that the Bill for removing the poor had pass'd in British Parliament.[37]

Su. 12th Yest. so blust'ring that I spent the day with sis. W.—this mor. breakfasted with fath. Sess. rather rily times, she & I call'd on sis. Green—hear many reports calculated to discourage the sis. in their efforts for improvement, but all things will tend to the instructions of those that will be profited & hold fast to the principles of righteousness. Att. eve. meet. at J. Young's, br. Grant presided.[38]

Mo. 13th Spent the aft. & eve. at br. J. Young's. he having gone to Goodger's [Goodyear] on business—the weather fine but freezes hard at night

Tu. The Lamanite girl come to live with us—she was purchas'd last Sunday[39]

Wed. 15th Vis. with Sis. Sess. Holmes, Green &c. at br. Hickenlooper's had an interesting time—attended meet in the eve. at the schoolhouse near br. Green's—A young girl of sis. Stewart's died this mor. being the first that has sicken'd & died in the Valley[40]

Th. 16th Went from fath. Sess.'s with her to br. Noble's where we spent the day agreeably.

fr. 17th Br. & sis. Noble sup'd with us—attended meet. in the eve. at Capt. Browns. several breth. prest—sis. Wilkie presided

sat. 18th Ellen & sis. Wilkie with me in the forenoon—we all spent the aft. and eve at br. Peirce's.

Su 19th Attended a very interesting meet. at br. Whipple's—the Lord's supper was administer'd. Fath. & moth. Sess. supp'd with us. Fath C. told me he would open us some flour when necessary.

Mo. 20th Vis at br. Smithson's with Clara sis. W. ~~Brown~~ <Hunt>, &c. In the eve. att. meet. at Bish. Higbee's—five breth. present.

Tu. 21st Vis. at br. ~~Brown's~~ <Hunt's> with sis. Ses, Wilkie, Clara, Ellen & Casper, after sup. we all arose & bless'd—had a meet. in the eve. sis. ~~B~~. Hunt presided.

W. 22d Vis. at sis. Brown's with sis. Wilkie Sess. Ellen, Clara, Ostrander, &c. sis. B. presided over her meet in the eve, breth present.

Th. 23d At br. Writer's to dinner with sis. Peirce, Sess. Chase, Hunter &c. after d. we arose & bless'd the mistress of the feast, she presided over her guests in the afternoon—we had a good time,—sis. Gates nam'd our meet.'organiz'd parties.' In the eve. went to br. J. Brown's to hear Parley. he did not come. Gen. Rich preach'd.

Sat. 25th Att Christmas party at br. L. Young's—prest Fath. J. Young & wife, fath J. Smith & wives, br. Peirce & wife & br. Grant, after a splendid dinner at which we freely & sociably partook of the good things of the earth fath S. bless'd the babe of sis. Y. I serv'd as Scribe. br. G. pray'd & dedicated the house to the Lord &c. In the eve Edith had an organiz'd visit of the little girls at Clara's Moth C. presided.

Su. 26th P.P.P. had an appointment to preach at br. Writer's but in consequence of a private council on account of the increasing of an insubordinate spirit & a disposition to leave the place; he could not attend. The people met but as none of the brethren was willing to carry on meeting, br. W. told his wife she might have a meet. for the sisters—she wish'd me to preside for her.—we had a good time; being honor'd with the presence of many brethren.

In the eve. att. where P.P. presided was much edified by him

Mo. 27th, Attended meet. at br. Willis—present fath J. Smith—the order of our meeting was laid before him &c. he gave us good instruction—said he would attend with us again—bless'd us &c.

Tu. 28th. Vis. at br G. Gates with sis. Sess. Chase, P.P. Pratt, L. Hancock & others br. P. edified us with the subject of the velocity of the motion of bodies when surrounded by a refin'd element &c.

Wed. 29th A dinner at sis. Crisman's after which we arose & bless'd— a meet. in the eve. sev. breth. present.

Th. Vis. Mary Forsgreen, who set a suppertable that did honor to her mother Kimball.[41]

fr. 31st Dinner party at sis. Howd's the sis. bless'd her & sis Holmes.

Sat. Jan. 1st 1848. A dinner party at br. Millers after dinner Moth. M. arose express'd her wish for the sist. to proceed in their order of blessing, having call'd them in by the consent of her husband—requested sis. Sess. to pray Sis. Sess. arose & said she was subject to sis. M. while under her roof & was willing to act in accordance &c. she pray'd after which I arose & bless'd sis M. & was follow'd by sis. Holmes, Howd, Sessions, three of sis. M's daughters, (two of whom rec. the gift of tongues), Love, & Abbott.

—five breth present 4 of whom spoke br. Jackman remarking that there was more intelligence in the hearts of the sis. that aft. than in the hearts of all the crown'd heads of Europe by the request of his wife, br. M. dismiss'd the meet.—sent for Clara & spent the eve. at fath. Sess.

Su. 2d Att. fam. meet. at br. Whipples—the Lord's supper administer'd

Mo 3d. supp'd with Ellen

tu 4th. By request spent the day at br. Grant's in assisting with my journal in making up the history of the Camp from W. Quarters

Wed. 5th Staid till aftnoon at br. G's—at 2 att. meet at bish. Higby's Wedding in the eve at br. Hendrick's in good style—good order & with good feelings. P.P.P. officiated.[42]

Th. 6th spent the day at elder Taylor's—he adjusted his Camera Obscura for our amusement[43]—his conversation very interesting— he compar'd our getting along in this kingdom to going down the Mo. river on a raft, where the snags before beheld at a distance, seem'd thick & impassable but a way was found to row past them as they approach'd them one by one & when it became dark he always tied up his raft & lay still till the day dawn'd

The weather is fine—the ground wet. New Years day the laws were read & sanction'd for the good order of this place.

Sat. 8th A young ladies meeting at sis. Howds

Mo. 10th Din'd at br. Kotchner's—meet. at 2 o'clock at which br. K. presided—the weather is like the op'ning of spring

fr. 14th Spent the eve. at br. Noble's on the occasion of his birth-day

Sat 15th This mor. Vilate D. [Decker] gives birth to a fine daughter.

fr. 21st My 44th birth-day—staid at fath. Sess. last night having visited sis. Whitney the day before & this day spent with sis. Noble—din'd on coffee & pancakes with molasses & sup'd on biscuit made of flour ground in the Valley, butter, tea, dried beef, peach-sauce, sweeten'd fried cakes & custard pie.

To Elder Jackman on the death of his wife.

Children weep o'er disappointments
    But the chosen of the Lord
Ne'er should think the dispensations
    Of his providence are hard.
All things are of his appointment—
    All things move by his decree:
Our great Father acts in wisdom
    None so good or wise as he

Let thy heart no more be ling'ring
    After the departed one
She has now return'd to finish
    What was previously begun.
Tho' she has been call'd to leave you,
    You will in her labors share
And you would not mourn her absence
    Did you know her mission there

The fond mem'ry of her virtues
    Should be cherish'd ever dear:
Yet your heart & your affections
    Now belong to others here.

O'er her grave the roses flourish
    Which your hand has planted there
And their sweet & luscious fragrance
    Oft perfumes the ambient air.

Death to her was sweet—'twas glorious
    When the bright angelic train
Bore her free triumphant spirit
    To the blest abode again.[44]

Sat. 29th Cold & snowy—vis. sis. Hamilton

Mo. 31st Spent the day at moth. Dilworth's the eve. at fath. Smith's

Feb. fr. 4th. Celebrated sis. Sess. birth-day with br. & sis. Abbott. in
the eve. carried a cap to moth. Smith which I had made her yest. att.
meet. at br. Savage's—after a hard struggle, we had a good time

Alas! that saints of God can be so full of selfishness as to sacrifice
the source of others' happiness to gratify their own enthusiastic notions. Strange that any should seek to shorten the arm that has been
extended to lift them out of affliction

Sat. 5th Att. meet. at br. Miller's

Sun. 6th The day fine—P. P preach'd on the square

<u>To Elder Levi Hancock.</u>

Farewel brother Levi! go forth on your journey
   We'll pray for your peace & prosperity too
Altho' the long distance is tedious & lonely,
   The Lord God of Joseph will see you safe thro'

   Chorus.
The Lord thy God loves thee—thy spirit is humble.
   In Israel's welfare thy heart does delight.
Thou yet will be crown'd with a fullness of blessing
   A fulness of wisdom, of glory & might.

The angels that guard you to your understanding;
   Will words of intelligence freely impart
And often the streams of divine consolation
   From the fountain of goodness will flow to your heart.
   Chorus.—

Thou wilt not long be absent from this pleasant Valley
   Where yet for a season the saints will abide;
Yes: & when you return bring the wife of your bosom
   And those little prattlers that sport by her side.
   Chorus.—

Bring them here to 'the Valley where health is full
      blooming
   Where quietude reigns & the spirit is free;
Where the earth in due time will produce an abundance
   And where the rich treasures of knowledge will be.
   Chorus.—

And when thro' the blessing of God the Eternal
    You reach Winter-Quarters this favor confer
Go visit my sister & what is instructive
    Concerning the Valley, please say unto her.
    Chorus.—

O yes, when you feel that the noblest of spirits
    Of all the creations of God you're among
Present my best wishes & love to the households
    Of Whitney & Kimball & President Young.
    Chorus. The Lord &c.[45]

Th 10th Sister's pray'r meet for father Smith

fr. 11th Bish. Houtz died this afternoon

sat. 12th Meet. at br. Hendrick's

su. 13th Ellen K. gives birth to a son.[46]

tu. 15th Meet. at br. Allen's.

Th. 17th. Last night had a fine rain it seems like spring.

fr. 18th. This mor. the ground is cov. with a sheet of snow—Went to Mrs. M. Smith's & in com. with fath. & Moth. Sessions had my Patriarchal Blessing.[47]

sat. spent the day at fath. S's making caps

su. 20th The 3d time of trial before the High C. [Council] of the case between Peirce, Brown, Ellsworth & Decker.
    Sis. Allen died sat. mor.[48]

mo. 21 Att. meet. at W. Snow's—staid with sis. Smoot.

tu. 22d. One of br. Snow's twins died—F. K. Shed died suddenly suppos'd by eating poisonous vegetables.[49]

Wed. 23d The weather thought to be the coldest we have had in the Valley. I vis. at br. Abbotts with sis. Crandall staid at fath. Sess.

Th. 24th Din'd at sis. Shackley's meet. in the eve. fath. Pettigrew & Hancock prest.

su. 27th A little boy by the name of Oakley kill'd by a log rolling from a saw-pit—put in motion by Indians attended meet. at br. Smoot's. Spent the eve. in com. with fath. & moth. Abbot. Sess. Pettigrew &c. very interestingly indeed. The weath. a little moderated

Mo 28th Wrote the following

On the death of Franklin K. Shed

The angel of death with a sudden blow
In the season of youth has laid him low
In a time when the heart's warm springs were rife
With the hopes & the prospects of future life

He was well belov'd by the wise & good
For his heart was noble—his mind imbued
With the principles of truth & light—
In the ways of Wisdom he took delight

For the Gospel's sake he had left behind
The friends that around his heart entwin'd
His soul was inspir'd with the noblest love
He pursued the course which the heav'ns approve.

With the saints of God he was truly blest
And with them he had found a place of rest;
And then from the hand of oppression free
He sung the sweet echo of Liberty

With a friendship true & a love sincere
To the youthful circle he still is dear;
And the mirror of mem'ry long will hold
His impression there in its native mould

But there is one whose affectionate heart
More acutely than others feels the smart
A fair maiden mourns in her loveliness
O'er his loss whom she felt her life would bless

Yet the morn of the resurrection is near
When in greater perfection he'll reappear;

Yes Franklin & Mary Jane will meet
When happiness will be more complete.

Now his form is laid in the grave to rest;
While his spirit returns to the home of the blest
And from thence to the spirits in prison sent
With salvation's tidings as Jesus went.

Therefore dry your tears & weep no more
For with him the toils of this life are o'er
In the regeneration he will come
Cloth'd with glory, pow'r & immortal bloom.[50]

March 7th Brethren started for Winter-Quarters

tu. 14th The breth. restart yest. or today having return'd in consequence of the road being impassable. They calculate to take Weber Canion road.

fr. 17th Heard that 3 of the 6 who start'd in the winter for W.Q. were met by a man from Ft. John—they were in sad condition having kill'd one of their horses & eating it—their feet badly frozen—the other 3 had gone on.

Sat. 18th Made the 4th cap for sis. Sess. for this month. The weather is colder having chang'd from warm spring; some gardens put in get a little frosted

Su. 19th Snows—wrote the following

> To Mrs. Eleanor B. Bringhurst.

My heart is full of friendship—but for thee
It has a holier feeling than that name
Identifies. The recollection of
Thy countenance from the first time
My eyes beheld thee—whispers something to
My thought and feeling which I never can
Describe. 'Tis undefinable so long
As mind or understanding shall remain
As circumscrib'd as now. But when I think
Of thee, a thrill of near affinity
O'erspreads my senses & I truly feel

Within my bosom a strong kindred tie
As tho' we'd been associated in
Existence, ere we condescended to
Our present state of being. Lady, yes.
When our small understandings shall expand
And with the recollection of the past
Some knowledge of the future be inspir'd
We'll find a thousand kindred ties that form
Amalgamation's wreath, & which are twin'd
And intertwin'd, combining & combin'd
Connecting noble spirits here & there
O'er all the face of earth—from earth to heav'n
And still extendinging [*sic*] on from world to world
Unto creation's undefin'd extent.
 Then let our hearts expand & let our minds
And acts approximate towards the point
Of true perfection, that we may attain
To an association glorified
On planets more exalted & refin'd—
Among intelligences long since dear.
And let us cultivate the sacred ties
Of love & friendship here that will abide
Time's rugged changes & eternally
Endure.[51]

W. 22d Very, very windy

Th. 23d Att. the funeral of Lorenzo D. son of L. & H. Young.[52]

March. fri 24th This mor. the ground is cover'd with quite a deep snow.

Tu. 28th The storm continues sometimes rain & then snow most of the houses are leaking profusely. Ours kept dry till this eve; but pour'd down thro' the night without intermission.[53]

Wed. 29th Continues to storm till nearly night. C. is at her mothers Charles & V. [Vilate] breakfast with me while the rain drops in our dishes.

Th. 30th Ch. & V. breakfast & sup with me.

fr. 31st Sis. Scofield washes & I get supper. We feel thankful for the storm altho' it causes a deal of work

April sat. 1st The day is fine, I iron'd most of the day.

Wed 5th Att. meet. at fath. Chase's Clara came home last night. she is gone to day—does not att. meet.

Th. 6th A number of the sisters celebrated the anniversary of the Church at Adoline Benson's in prayer for the saints in W.Q. & elsewhere when I return'd. C. was absent.

fr. 7th Spent the aft. at Susan H's in com. with sis. P. S. T. H. br.s T. H. & P. spent the eve. with us.

Sat. 8th Rains & snows all day

April sun. 23d I rode out with br. & sis. Higbee call'd at P.P.P.—he seem'd to be in a very uncomfortable frame of mind

May Th 4th Has rain'd successively for 12 days which terminated this mor. in a hard freeze unfavorable to vegetation which has been growing finely.

Wed. 10th The day beautiful—growing warmer after several days of frost & cold. Saw sis. H. at fath. Sess.—she thinks a com. of horsemen, one of whom is J. Redden is on this side Laramy. Br. P. with sis. P. & Ellen call'd for me to join them in a carriage ride, when at the distance of perhaps 5 ms. to our unspeakable joy, we met the California boys, 7 of them, part of the com. having gone to the Bay & part being back with their cattle which are expected in 3 or 4 weeks.[54]
    Last sat. was a Council which excited some feeling. P.P. was chief spokesman.

Mo. 15th The farmers are getting most of their planting done. Buckwheat, beans &c. sow'd in April, is kill'd by the frost

Tu. 16th Last friday sis. Taylor, Hunter, P. & G vis. us

W. 17th Quite an Indian alarm—in consequence of Jim Oneship [Wanship] being kill'd by a Eutaw[55]

Th. 18th Hancock, Ellsworth & others start with teams to meet the immigrants. Yest. Ellsworth & wife, Scofield & wife, Charles & wife & J. Green din'd with us.

Radishes, lettuce &c. begin to grace the table

Su. 21st I breakfasted on bread & butter radishes, lettuce & pepper-grass. Att. a Bishop's court—case between Peirce & Higgins.

Tu.23d. Another com. starts with <35> wagons to meet the immigrants

May. su. 28th This morning's frost in unison with the ravages of the crickets for a few days past produces many sighs & occasions some long faces with those that for the moment forget that they are saints[56]

June. sat. 10th The crickets continue their destructiveness. Rosacrans, Hunt & others start on horseback to meet the brethren.

Th. 15th Frost in some places to injure vegetation, yest. mor. & this mor. I am quite sick—sis Gates ministers to me with kindness. Sis. Taylor spent the aftnoon with us—said she sup'd on green peas last eve.

Su. 18th Att. meet. Eld. Taylor preach'd very interestingly

July. 29th Att. a genteel party at br. Peirce's on the occasion of Harvey being 21—wrote the following:

> Robert Peirce's oldest son
> This day being twenty one,
> While we celebrate the day
> Thus to him in friendship say
>
> Like the morning vernal dew,
> Happiness your pathway strew
> Like the brilliant orb of day
> Wisdom crown your future way.
>
> Friendship's streams around you flow
> Cheering you wher'er you go
> And affection's gentle smile
> All the ills of life beguile.

Virtue like a golden gem
Growing from the parent stem
Deeply rooted in your breast
Never can be dispossess'd.

Noble principles of truth
Deeply rooted in your youth
Cultur'd thro' life's op'ning stage
Will with honor crown your age.

May prosperity attend
All your efforts to the end—
Endless life & glory bles[*unfinished*][57]

31st Started with sis. [Elvira] Holmes for the mountains.[58]

Aug. 5th The mail carriers met us on the Weaver [Weber] river & favor'd me with a letter from Lorenzo & intelligence from the Camp in general. We cross'd the river & went on, occasionally stopping to pick currants, until within 4 ms. of Cave Rock, when some of our party, (which consisted of br. Howd W. Sperry, 3 of Capt. Millers daughters, D. [L?] Miller, br. Tullers [Fellers?], br. Wolfe & sons sis. H. & myself;) visited an Indian camp about 2 m. & ½ distant <&> purchas'd some dried meat, & we started on our way back to pick currants until the servisberries should ripen

After the com. had supplied itself with c. [currants] we came to the W. [Weber] where we found 2 fam. encamp'd & picking servis b. Our party stop'd from mon. till wed. noon, & started for home in com. with Ellsworth & Hancock who came up with us on Mon. from the Platte: & arriv'd in the Valley on fr. the 18th.

Wed. 23d Spent the aftnoon with sis. Gates—taken sick in the eve.

Sept. 20th. Prest. Young & family arriv'd in the Valley—they supp'd at E. Ellsworth's—I had the pleasure of joining them at the table tho' scarcely able to sit up—having been sick from the 23d of Aug.—[59]

Oct. 23d I took up my residence with br. & sis. Holmes, Clara having previously gone to live with Lucy & Margaret P. [having] taken the place[60]

24th The ground is whiten'd with snow for the first time.

Sat. 28th Att. the blessing of E. Bainbridge's child by Prest. Y. present Mrs. Y. bro & sis. Kimball & others

Nov. tu. 1st [Tuesday, October 31] Call'd to administer to sis. Ritter's sick child—Spent the eve. at Margaret's with sis. Taylor & Smoot—br. T. supp'd with us.

Nov. Wed. ~~2~~1st Prest. Y. invited me to a carriage ride with him—we din'd at his house after conversing on some particulars.

Th. ~~2~~3d Spent the eve. very pleasantly at Prest. Y's with most of his wives. The weather cold.

Th. 9th An eve. party for the new room[61]

Su. 12th It has been very pleasant till this mor which is rainy & snowy a little—the mts. white

Dec. 1st The mail arriv'd from Winter Quarters.

Su. ~~4th~~ 3d Quite cold—letters read publicly—Lyman Wight, Hawes, Miller &c. disfellowship'd. B. call'd after meeting—I went to L's snow'd fast in the eve.

Mo. 4th Rode to br. Neff's—the wind blew a gale before ~~I~~ we arriv'd. I staid till wed. The cold intense

fr. ~~23~~ 22d Vis. at Br. Gibb's,

Sat. ~~24th~~ 23d Commemmorated the birth of Joseph Smith. The weather continues cold with the exception of 2 or 3 pleasant days, since the first of the month.

Mo. 25th Christmas, I staid at home & read news-papers which Prest. Y. sent me, he having call'd last eve: br. F. Richards at that time presented me with copy of an Address written by Lyon

Jan. su. 7th [1849] I gave Prest. Y. copy of Address I had written for br. R.[62]

Wed. 17th I am quite sick. had a chill last eve

Th. 18 Rode to L.'s had an interesting time in celebration of their wedding day. The party was yest.[63]

fr. 19th Vis. with sis. Whitney at Mary Ann K.'s The weather fine but continues very cold

Su. 21st Prest.—call'd to return the Address

Feb. 17th [18] B call'd in the mor. meet. out of doors—has been 2 sunday's previous.

Tu. 19th [20] Went to L's yest.—Adoline's son b. this mor.[64]

Th. 21st [22] had an interesting vis with H.C.K.

Su. 24th [25] Very sick yest. & today—B. administer'd to me—felt reliev'd for which I thank the Lord.

Mo. 25th [26] Has been thawing for several days—the mud drying some—cattle have hard times—B. propos'd a carriage ride to his house in few days

Tu. 26th [27] Very snowy

March 1st th. The storm over—expedition sent against the Eutaws[65]— B's folks move out of Fort

March 2d fr. B. call'd to see me—the trial of Ira Watt in H. Council[66]

12th mo. Election of civil Officers for Territorial Government.[67]

fr. 16th Seems like the breaking of winter—storms a little almost every day. gave B. 30 doll. pr m. a colony is getting up for Eutaw valley—

Su. 18th Sis. Rosacrans bade me farewell for California. Starts tomorrow

tu. 20th The ground cov. with snow again

su. 25th fine weather the last 2 days. The breth very busy sowing wheat—The meet. remov'd to the Council house in a bower[68]

April fr. 13th Amasa L. & Porter R. Start for California—see them at Bish. W's having rode home with sis. Kimball last tuesday. Wed. B.Y. come for me to visit his family, which he commenc'd organizing for living together. I spent the night & he took me to Br. K's the next day—told me to go home from there & he should soon come & move me up. He call'd this eve. with Loisa, Margaret & Clara

sat. 14th The Eastern mail starts today. Spent the eve. with Christene acc. with sis. P. W. & Ellen

su. 15th The day fine, had an interesting preach from br. K. in the aft. return'd to the Fort in the eve.

April Su. 22d Yes. we had a little shower, a little cooler, but the weather has been quite warm. Wednesday the thermometer was at 80 th. at 83.
  The crickets were thick in places—have done some injury to vegetation during the week. Bridge done over Canion Creek.

Mo. 23d Went to warm spring with sis. Noble. Heard of the death of Sarah Ann's child, died this mor.[69]

Tu 24th Rec'd a few lines from Helen.[70]

Th 26th The first general <u>Fast</u>—meeting at 1, o'clock[71]

Sat. 28th Meet. to organize the "Legion" Heard of an assault on Oneship by a party of Ind.[72]

May 4th fr. Dr. Bernhisel & others start for the States. Wed. 2d We had a fine soaking rain, Yest. fast, which is to be att. every 1st Thursday in month—Wrote letter to S.M.K. Frost this mor.

Su. 6th Beautiful day—rain'd a little last night. All things prospering

Su. 13th Last mo[nday]. I walk'd to L's & wed. vis. at Sessions with mrs. Kimball, Helen, &c. & rode home with them. Ira married[73]

su. 20th A heavy rain last wed. cloudy & cold since this mor. frost in places rainy in the afternoon

Wed. 23d. Commenc'd raining yest.—a snow today covers the ground—it looks like winter.

fr. 25th Yest. the ground was considerably froze but the mor. being cold & cloudy the freeze did but little injury to veg. Cornelia came for me & I rode to Cotton-Wood today[74]

Mo. June 4th Return'd from Cotton-Wood & stop'd at Lorenzo's

Mo. 11th Last tu. night had a fine rain today return'd to br. Holmes

tu. 12th The funeral of br. Baldwin att.[75]—some frost this mor.

sat. 16th A trial against Perrigreen Sess. yest. & today—adjourn'd till tomorro[76]

tu 19th People with pack animals arrive from the States going to California.[77] They expect wagons in 2 or 3 days. This eve. I rode to Prest. Y.s in carriage

Th. 21st return'd home.

Su. 24th Convers'd with a man from Indiana who arriv'd yest. in 2 months from St Josephs with ox teams. The weather is now hot. Some green peas

Wed. 27th This day is 5 years since Joseph's death! I rode in the forenoon with br. & sis. Lott. in the afternoon read Joseph's lectures to a circle of ladies.[78]

th 28th Mov'd to Prest. Y.s Log. row

July. 1st [Almon] Babbitt arriv'd with U.S. Mail

wed. 4th Vis. in com. with B-m & wife & sis Call at br. Crosby's

July 1849
    fr. 6th Vis at Heber's—read introductory letter of Charles H. Miller to br. K. by J. B. Backenstos. The description br. M gave of the panic for the gold mines is truly astonishing

tu. 24th. Celebration of arrival of Pioneers[79]

Th. 26th Br. Babbitt starts back with mail. I wrote to Lucius, sis. Hyde & Kimball.

Su. 29th Last eve. vis. at Bish. Higbee's Prest. Y. H.C.K. & many others present this mor. br. Egan arriv'd with Mail—

Aug. 8th [7] wed. Br. Egan's com. arrive[80]

Th. 16th Vis. with several emigrants at Br. Peirce's. Merchant shops are open in every direction.

Eliza R. Snow Family Members

Eliza Roxcy Snow compiled a catalogue of her immediate family and published it in *Biography and Family Record of Lorenzo Snow* (Salt Lake City: Deseret News Company, 1884), 488-95. This listing is based on her catalogue, augmented from other sources, including Valoie R. Hill's *Ancestors of Lorenzo Snow* ([Camarillo, CA]: privately published, 1973); H. F. Cummings and Leon Y. Pond, "Descendants of Richard Snow of Woburn, Mass.," photocopy of typescript, LDS Family History Library, Salt Lake City; Ancestral File, LDS Family History Library, Salt Lake City; Simsbury, Connecticut, cemetery, and Orrin Harmon, "Historical Facts Appertaining to the Township of Mantua . . . Portage Co., Ohio," holograph, Western Reserve Historical Society, Cleveland, Ohio.

Paternal Grandparents:
Oliver Snow II
 born: Ashford, Windham, Connecticut, 25 March 1749
 married: (1) Rebecca Wadsworth, 4 July 1771
 married: (2) Roxana (Roxeylane) Taylor
 died: Auburn, Geauga, Ohio, 5 August 1844

Rebecca Wadsworth
 born: Becket, Berkshire, Massachusetts, or Ashford, Windham, Connecticut, 12 May 1747
 died: Becket, Berkshire, Massachusetts, 18 May 1784

Maternal Grandparents:
Jacob Pettibone, Captain
 born: Simsbury, Hartford, Connecticut, 20 December 1750/51
 married: Rosetta Barber, 13 January 1778
 died: Simsbury, Hartford, Connecticut, 18 October 1807

Rosetta Barber
  born: Simsbury, Hartford, Connecticut, 15 May 1758
  died: Simsbury, Hartford, Connecticut, 10/18 April 1810

Parents:
Oliver Snow III
  born: Becket, Berkshire, Massachusetts, 18/28 September 1775
  married: Rosetta Leonora Pettibone, 6 May 1800
  died: Walnut Grove, Knox, Illinois, 17 October 1845

Rosetta Leonora Pettibone
  born: Simsbury, Hartford, Connecticut, 22 October 1778
  died: Walnut Grove, Knox, Illinois, 12 October 1846

Significant Aunts and Uncles:
Jacob Blair
  married: Charlotte Snow
  died: Mantua, Portage, Ohio, 9 April 1807

Charlotte Snow
  born: Becket, Berkshire, Massachusetts, 19 August 1782
  married: (1) Jacob Blair
  married: (2) Horace Granger
  died: Auburn, Geauga, Ohio, 19 May 1851

Franklin Snow
  born: Becket, Berkshire, Massachusetts, 27 January 1779
  married: (1) Lydia Olcott, 28 November 1804
  married: (2) Ann Conant
  died: Avon, Lorain, Ohio, 24 November 1864

Siblings:
Leonora Abigail
  born: Becket, Berkshire, Massachusetts, 23 August 1801
  married: (1) Enoch Virgil Leavitt, ca. 1820
  married: (2) Isaac Morley, before 19 December 1843
  died: 11 February 1872

Percy Amanda
  born: Mantua, Portage, Ohio, 20 April 1808
  married: Eli McConoughey, 27 September 1833
  died: Henry, Illinois, 27/28 August 1848

Melissa
  born: Mantua, Geauga, Ohio, 24 July 1810
  died: Mantua, Geauga, Ohio, 16 December 1835

Lorenzo
  born: Mantua, Geauga, Ohio, 3 April 1814
  married: (1) Charlotte Squires
  married: (2) Mary Adaline Goddard, maternal first cousin
  married: (3) Sarah Ann Prichard
  married: (4) Harriet Amelia Squires
  married: (5) Eleanor Houtz
  married: (6) Caroline Horton
  married: (7) Mary Elizabeth Houtz
  married: (8) Phebe Amelia Woodruff
  married: (9) Sarah E. Minnie Jensen
  died: Salt Lake City, Utah, 10 October 1901

Lucius Augustus
  born: Mantua, Geauga, Ohio, 31 August 1819
  married: Eliza Walker
  died: January 1898

Samuel Pearce (Pierce)
  born: Mantua, Geauga, Ohio, 22 August 1821
  married: (1) Josephine Elizabeth Scott
  married: (2) Mary Wilmot
  married: (3) Ella Jane Knapp
  died: Santa Barbara, California, 13 December 1909

Other Significant Relatives:
Cornelia Eliza Leavitt, daughter of Eliza's sister Leonora
  born: Warren, Ohio, 5 January 1825
  married: Amasa M. Lyman

Lucia Leavitt, daughter of Eliza's sister Leonora
  born: ca. 1823
  married: Almon Whiting, 10 October 1853
  died: Manti, Iowa, 20 May 1862

LeRoi Clarence Snow, youngest son of Lorenzo
  born: Brigham City, Box Eider, Utah, 26 August 1876
  married: (1) Maude Ford

married: (2) Burma Celia Thompson
died: Salt Lake City, Utah, 31 December 1962

Lury/Lura/Lucy Snow, daughter of Eliza's uncle Franklin
born: Mantua, Portage, Ohio, 1807
married: Lucius Scoville/Scovil, 18 June 1828
died: Nauvoo, Hancock, Illinois, 27 January 1846

Calvin Squires, brother of Lorenzo's wife Charlotte
born: Newbury, Geauga, Ohio, 1830
died: 2 July 1901

Charles Porter Squires, brother of Lorenzo's wife Charlotte
born: Newbury, Geauga, Ohio, 26 August 1827
married: Sarah Peters
died: 5 May 1872

Appendix 2

Register of Names,
Eliza R. Snow 1846–1849

This listing of people named in the trail diaries, 1846–1849, is provided with apologies. No one can know for sure which Emily is meant, or which Br. N. is referred to in Eliza Snow's minute and often abbreviated jottings. But for those for whom it matters, I have attempted to identify as many as possible with any degree of assurance. Where I have erred, I beg tolerance and invite correction.

The sources from which I have drawn identifications are varied. And since I may have compared several sources to ascertain one date, I have not documented them individually. In general, however, the following have proven useful: Davis Bitton, *Guide to Mormon Diaries and Autobiographies* (Provo, Utah: Brigham Young University Press, 1977); Journal History of the Church (Archives, Historical Department, The Church of Jesus Christ of Latter-day Saints); Andrew Jenson, *Latter-day Saint Biographical Encyclopedia* (Salt Lake City: Andrew Jenson History Company, 1901-35); Kate B. Carter, comp., *Our Pioneer Heritage* (Salt Lake City: Daughters of Utah Pioneers, 1958); Brigham H. Roberts, ed., *History of the Church of Jesus Christ of Latter-day Saints,* 7 vols. (Reprinted, Salt Lake City: Deseret Book Company, 1978); Marvin E. Wiggins, comp., *Mormons and Their Neighbors,* 2 vols. (Provo, Utah: Harold B. Lee Library, Brigham Young University, 1984) Susan Easton Black, *Membership of The Church of Jesus Christ of Latter-day Saints: 1830–1848,* 50 vols. (Provo, Utah: Brigham Young University Religious Studies Center, 1989); Augusta Joyce Crocheron, *Representative Women of Deseret* (Salt Lake City: J. C. Graham & Company, 1884); Edward W. Tullidge, *The Women of Mormondom* (New York: Crandall and Tullidge, 1877); *The Woman's Exponent* (Salt Lake City, 1872–1914).

The annotations and entries in edited diaries of other Latter-day Saints have helped, particularly those of Juanita Brooks in *On the*

Mormon Frontier: The Diary of Hosea Stout, 1844–1861, 2 vols. (Salt Lake City: University of Utah Press and Utah State Historical Society, 1964) and Juanita Brooks with Robert Glass Cleland, *A Mormon Chronicle: The Diaries of John D. Lee* (Salt Lake City: University of Utah Press, 1983). Dean Jessee's, Jeffery Johnson's, and Todd Compton's compilations about the wives of Joseph Smith and Brigham Young have been essential, as have Jessee's meticulous identifications in his *Papers of Joseph Smith,* 2 vols. (Salt Lake City: Deseret Book Company, 1989, 1992) and his *Letters of Brigham Young to His Sons* (Salt Lake City: Deseret Book Company, 1974). LDS Church Historical Department compilations by Melvin L. Bashore and Linda L. Haslam, especially "Mormon Pioneer Companies Crossing the Plains (1847–1868) Narratives" have been generously shared.

Besides these are innumerable facts gleaned from individuals and from the compilations in the extensive Family Search data base of the Family History Library of the Church of Jesus Christ of Latter-day Saints. In these, as in all such records, to err is human, but to have tried, divine. I am grateful for the Latter-day Saints who care about their forebears.

I have tried to catalog persons named according to their relationship with Eliza Snow, here abbreviated as ERS. The forms in brackets [] are the various names and abbreviations by which she identified them in her diaries. Question marks indicate unavailable dates or questionable identifications.

ABBOTT, LEWIS (1796–?) and ANN MARSH (1800–1849) [**Mr. and Mrs. Abbott, fath. and moth. Abbot**] Traveled across the plains in the First Hundred of 1847 with their three children. Reference could, however, as easily be to: ABBOTT, RUFUS (1784–?) and ANNA ABBOTT (1787–?) who came in the Second Fifty of the First Hundred.

ADAMS, GEORGE J. (1819–1880) [**G. J. Adams**] Mercurial, charismatic 1840 convert, alternately called on significant missions and disciplined for adultery and apostasy. He refused to follow Brigham Young, eventually disguised his Mormon connections, and in 1866 led a group of Messianic believers to Jaffa to found a colony in anticipation of the return of the Jews there. The colony failed, and Adams died in obscurity in Philadelphia.

ALLEN, LOLA ANN CLAWSON (1806–1848) [**Sis. Allen**] Born in Dryden, New York. Traveled in the third ten of Jedediah M. Grant's Hundred. Married Elihu(e) Allen. On 20 February 1848 Eliza noted Lola's death the previous day.

ALLEY, SARAH B. (1819–1846) married Joseph Bates Noble in 1843 in Nauvoo. She died at Winter Quarters on 28 December 1846.

ANDREWS, OLIVE [?] (1818–?) [**Olive**] Born in Livermore, Maine. Sealed to Joseph Smith, married to Brigham Young in 1846. She had a son "Chancy," born about 1843.

BACKENSTOS, JACOB [**Col. or J. B. Backenstos**] Hancock County sheriff who defended the Mormons against mobs in the 1840s.

BAINBRIDGE, ELIZABETH MAHALA HENDRICKS (1927–?) [**E. Bainbridge**] Born in Kentucky to James and Drusilla Dorris Hendricks; married Fred R. Bainbridge in Winter Quarters in 1847. Her child was blessed by Brigham Young, 23 October 1848.

BARNEY, LEWIS (1808–1895) [**Br. Barney**] Born in Niagara, New York, and baptized in 1840. Traveled to Utah with the Pioneer Company, and entered Salt Lake Valley 22 July 1847.

BEAMAN, LOUISA (1815–1850) [**Loisa B., Loisa**] Was sealed to Joseph Smith in 1841 and married to Brigham Young in 1846. All of her five babies, Brigham Young's sons, died as infants.

BENSON, ADELINE BROOKS ANDRUS (1813–1844) [**A. or Adoline Benson**] Was born in Windsor, Connecticut. She married Ezra T. Benson 27 April 1844 as his second wife.

BENSON, EZRA T. (1811–1869) [**Br. Benson**] Born in Mendon, Massachusetts, and joined the church in 1840. Six years later, he was ordained an apostle by Brigham Young. Married sisters Pamelia and Adeline Andrus. Benson traveled with the Pioneer Company to the Salt Lake Valley in 1847.

BENT, SAMUEL (1778–1846) [**Father Bent**] Born in Barre, Massachusetts, and was president of the settlement at Garden Grove, Iowa, where he died.

BRINGHURST, ELEANOR BITLER or BEITLER (1816–1888) [**Eleanor B. Bringhurst**] Eleanor and her husband Samuel were from the Chester County, Pennsylvania, group. He traveled with the Second Hundred; her name is unlisted among the 1847 pioneers. Under date 21 March 1848 ERS inscribed to her a poem describing the "near affinity" of the two women.

BUELL, PRESENDIA LATHROP HUNTINGTON (1810–1892) [**Sis. Buel**] joined the church in Kirtland in 1836. She married Norman Buell about 1827. After he apostatized, she was sealed to Joseph Smith in 1841 and married Heber C. Kimball in 1846. She began a school for children at Cutler's Park (Winter Quarters) in 1846, and the following year came west with her son Oliver.

CAHOON, WILLIAM FARRINGTON (1813–1883 or 1897) [**Br. W. Cahoon**] Son of Reynolds Cahoon; born in Ashtabula County,

Ohio, and baptized in 1830. A former member of Zion's Camp, he arrived in Utah in 1849.

CASPER, SARAH ANN (1828–1882) [**Sis. Casper**] Emigrated to Utah in the second fifty of Jedediah M. Grant's Hundred.

CHASE, ISAAC (1791–1861) [**Father or F. Chase**] Adopted son of Brigham Young. Traveled in the same fifty as ERS from Winter Quarters.

CHASE, PHOEBE OGDEN (1794–1872) [**Mother or M. or Sis. Chase**] Married Isaac Chase in 1818. Crossed the plains with him and two of their children.

CRISMAN, MARY HILL (1814–1892) [**Sis. Crisman**] Born in South Carolina. Emigrated with her husband, Charles Crisman, and seven children in the second fifty of Jedediah M. Grant's Hundred.

CUMMINGS, JAMES WILLARD (dates unknown) Probably born in Maine to James Cummings and Susannah Willard. Was called to leave Winter Quarters in 1847 to persuade the Oneida Indians to go west with the Saints. Traveled with the Markham group in Iowa.

DALTON, CHARLES [?] (1810–1891) [**Capt. or Br. Dalton**] Born in Wysox, Pennsylvania; married Mary Warner 1842.

DALTON, MARY ELIZABETH WARNER [?] (1826–1856) [**Sister Dalton**] Born in Manchester, New York; married Charles Dalton in 1842. She was called "Mistress of the quilting" on the plains.

DANA, CHARLES ROOT (1801/02–1868) [**br Dany**] Spent the winter of 1846–47 at Mt. Pisgah before going east to gather funds for the church for emigration purposes. His first wife, Margaret Kennedy, died during the family's exodus to Utah in 1850.

DECKER, CHARLES (1824–1901) [**C. Decker**] Born in Phelps, New York, and married Brigham Young's daughter Vilate Young in Winter Quarters in 1847. A brother to Clara Decker Young, he brought the Indian orphan Sally to his sister in 1847.

DECKER, VILATE YOUNG (1830–1902) [**Vilate Y., Vilate D.**] Daughter of Brigham Young and Miriam Works. Eliza celebrated with a poem Vilate's marriage to Charles Decker in Winter Quarters on 4 February 1847, and noted the birth to the couple of "a fine daughter" born in Salt Lake City on 15 January 1848.

DILWORTH, ELIZA WOLLERTON (1793–1876) [**Moth. Dilworth**] Converted in Chester County, Pennsylvania, and emigrated to Nauvoo and to Utah, leaving her husband Caleb unconverted in Pennsylvania. Related to the Riters [**Writer**] and the Bringhursts. The Peirces, the Yearsleys, and the Gheens were also from Chester County.

DILWORTH, JOHN TAYLOR (1825–1905) [**Br. Dilworth**] traveled to Utah in ERS's company of ten with his mother, Eliza Wollerton Dilworth, and sister Maria Louisa Dilworth. Other siblings in the Jedediah Grant Hundred included Rebecca Riter, Ann Dilworth Bringhurst, and Mary Jane Dilworth. They were part of the Chester County, Pennsylvania, group.

DIMICK, ALBERT (1831–1866) [**Albert Dimick**] Drove a wagon for the Markhams for a time. He lived in Spanish Fork after arriving in Utah. On 26 June 1866, during the Black Hawk War, he was fatally wounded in a skirmish and died two days later.

EGAN, HOWARD (1815–1878) [**Br. Egan**] Born in Ireland and immigrated to Canada as a young boy. Baptized with his wife in 1842, he traveled to Utah with the Pioneer Company, then returned to Winter Quarters to accompany his family to the Valley in 1848.

ELLSWORTH, EDMUND LOVELL (1819–1893) [**Br. Ellsworth**] Traveled in the Pioneer Company, but his wife Elizabeth Young, Brigham Young's eldest daughter, and their two children came with Jedediah Grant's company. In 1849 he was appointed deputy marshal in Salt Lake City.

FAIRCHILD, ELIZABETH (BETSY) (1828–1910) [**Sis. Fairchild**] A plural wife of Brigham Young, having married him, as did ERS, 3 October 1844. She traveled briefly with the Peirces in 1847.

FORSGREN, MARY [**M. or Mary Forsgreen**] While not a plural wife of Heber C. Kimball, she came under his care in 1848 while her husband was in the Mormon Battalion.

FULLMER, DAVID (1803–1879) [**Br. Fulmer**] Baptized in 1836, he was captain of a Hundred from Nauvoo to Garden Grove and became the presiding elder there after Samuel Bent died in 1846.

GATES, JACOB (1811–1892) [**G. Gates**] Led a company of ten in Jedediah M. Grant's Hundred. Married Mary Minerva Snow. His second wife, Elizabeth Hutchings, died in 1846. He served in the British Mission from 1850 to 1853 and was later president of the Seventies from 1862 until his death.

GATES, MARY MINERVA SNOW [**Sis. Gates**] married Jacob Gates in 1833. Daughter of Levi and Lucina Streeter Snow of Ohio, she was a sister of Erastus and Willard Snow, and related to ERS.

GHEEN, ESTHER (HESTER) ANN PEIRCE (1801–1858) [**Hester Ann or Sis Geen or Sis Gheen**] Born to a Quaker family in Pennsylvania, she married William Gheen in 1823 and joined the LDS Church with him in 1840. A widow when she was crossing Iowa in 1846, Gheen nursed ERS, who then honored her with an elegy to her deceased husband. Her daughters were Amanda and Anna Gheen Kimball, plural wives of the apostle.

GHEEN, WILLIAM ATKINS (1798–1845) [**William Geen**] Born in Goshen, Pennsylvania; he joined the church with his wife, Esther Ann Peirce, in 1840. He died in Nauvoo, and ERS honored him with a poem.

GLEASON, DESDEMONA CHASE (1821–?), [**D. or Sis. Gleason**] She was a daughter of Isaac Chase and married John Streator Gleason. Two of her six children died in infancy.

GLEASON, JOHN STREATOR (1819–1904) [**G. or J. or br. Gleason**] was a member of the original Pioneer Company of 1847. Married to Desdemona Chase, he was baptized in 1842.

GOODYEAR, MILES [**Goodyear, Goodger**] A trader in Weber, now Ogden, before the coming of the Mormons. Church officials bought his property to allow for Mormon settlement of the area.

GRANT, CAROLINE VANDYKE (1818–1847), [**sis. G. or sis Grant**] Wife of Jedediah M. Grant, she died 26 September 1847 "over the Big Mountain," just before her company entered the Salt Lake Valley. Her baby Margaret had died three weeks earlier, but her older child, Caroline (Caddie), survived. She was the first white person buried in the Salt Lake Valley.

GRANT, JEDEDIAH MORGAN (1816–1856) [**Capt., Br., or J. Grant**] Converted to the church at age seventeen in New York, wed Caroline VanDyke in 1844, and was a member of the First Council of Seventy 1845–54. An eloquent and effective missionary, he was appointed captain of the Third Hundred, in which ERS traveled. After arriving in Utah, Grant was elected first mayor of Salt Lake in 1851 and was chosen as second counselor to Brigham Young in 1854.

HANCOCK, LEVI (1803–1882) Born in Springfield, Massachusetts, he joined the church in 1830 and was ordained a seventy by Joseph Smith in 1835. He enlisted and came west with the Mormon Battalion in 1846–47. He was returning on 18 May to bring his family from Winter Quarters when ERS addressed a poem to him.

HENDRICKS, DRUSILLA DORRIS (1810–?) [**Sis. Hendricks**] Converted in Tennessee in 1835 and brought her family West in the company with ERS after her husband was wounded and partially paralyzed.

HENDRICKS, JAMES (1808–1870) [**br. Hendricks**] traveled to Utah with his wife Drusilla Dorris and their four children in the same company of ten as ERS. Shot by a mob at the Battle of Crooked River in October 1838, Hendricks was crippled for life. In Utah he served as bishop and managed Warm Springs.

HICKENLOOPER, WILLIAM HAINEY (1804–1888) [**br. Hicken-looper**] Married Sarah Hawkins in 1837 and the couple converted to Mormonism two years later. He traveled to Utah in the First Hundred and became a city councilman and longtime bishop in Salt Lake City.

HIGGINS, NELSON (1806–1890) [**Martial, Marshall Higgins**] was baptized in 1834. A captain in the Mormon Battalion, he spent the winter of 1846–47 with the sick detachment in Pueblo, Colorado, and arrived in the Salt Lake Valley in July 1847. He later presided over the Richfield, Utah, settlement.

HOLMES, ELVIRA ANNA COWLES (1813–1871) [**Sis. Holmes, Elvira**] joined the Mormon Church in 1835 and was treasurer of the first Relief Society. Sealed to Joseph Smith, she married widower Jonathan Holmes in Nauvoo in 1842. She lost a baby in Winter Quarters. Crossing the plains in 1847, Holmes, bringing her step-daughter Sarah Elizabeth, drove her own team of oxen because her husband was serving in the Battalion. She taught in one of the first schools in Salt Lake City.

HOLMES, JONATHAN HARRIMAN (1806–1880) was a bodyguard of Joseph Smith and marched west with the Mormon Battalion of 1847. A widower with two children, he married Elvira Cowles in December 1842.

HUNTER, MARY ANN WHITESIDES [?] (1825–1882) [**Sis Hunter**] traveled to Utah in the Second Hundred of 1847, of which her husband, Edward Hunter, was captain.

HUNTINGTON, WILLIAM (1784–1846) [**Father Huntington**] was father of Zina D. H. Young and Presendia Buell Kimball. Widowed in 1839, he married Edward Partridge's widow Lydia Partridge in 1840. He left Nauvoo in 1846 and was appointed to preside over the Saints at Mt. Pisgah. He died there the same year.

HYDE, NANCY MARINDA JOHNSON (1815–1886) [**Sis Hyde**] A friend of ERS from the neighboring town of Hiram, Ohio. She married Orson Hyde and in Utah settled in Sanpete County, where she was active in the Relief Society.

HYDE, ORSON (1805–1878) [**Orson or Elder Hyde**] Ordained an apostle in 1835 and designated president of the quorum in 1847. Born in Oxford, Connecticut, he joined the church in 1831 in Ohio. He married Nancy Marinda Johnson.

JACKMAN, LEVI (1797–1876) [**Elder or Br. Jackman**] Joined the church in 1831 and entered the Salt Lake Valley in 1847 with the original Pioneer Company. In January 1848 ERS wrote a poem for him on the death of his wife, Angeline Myers.

JOHNSON, LUKE S. (1808–1861) [**L. Johnson**] A captain of ten in the 1847 Brigham Young company. Ordained an apostle in 1835, he was excommunicated for apostasy in 1838 but was rebaptized just prior to coming west. The son of John Johnson of Hiram, Ohio, he grew up as a neighbor of the Mantua Snows. Nancy Marinda Hyde was his sister.

KIMBALL, AMANDA TRIMBLE GHEEN (1830–1904) [**Amanda Geen**] Joined the LDS Church in 1841 along with her sister, Ann Alice Gheen. A plural wife of Heber C. Kimball, she came west from Winter Quarters in 1848. Her life was closely connected with her sister Ann's, also a plural wife of Kimball.

KIMBALL, ANN ALICE GHEEN (1827–1879) [**Anna Geen**] Converted to the Mormon Church in 1841 and three years later married Heber C. Kimball. In 1848 she left Winter Quarters for Salt Lake. ERS included in her diary an acrostic poem for "Anna Geen," written at Winter Quarters in 1847.

KIMBALL, CHRISTEEN GOLDEN (1824–1896) [**Christene**] A plural wife of Heber C. Kimball, by whom she had four children. After emigrating to Utah in 1848, she took in boarders and sewed for the ZCMI co-op store to support her family, who by this time, according to son J. Golden Kimball, "had been boosted out of Father's mansion. . . . "

KIMBALL, DAVID KIMBALL (1846–1847) Born just a month after his parents Heber C. and Sarah Ann Whitney Kimball left Nauvoo. ERS recorded his birth on 8 March, but did not mention his death seventeen months later.

KIMBALL, HAZEN (1812–?) Led a company of ten in the first fifty of Jedediah M. Grant's Hundred.

KIMBALL, HEBER CHASE (1801–1868) [**Father or Elder Kimball, HCK or H**] Born in Sheldon, Vermont, and later moved to Ontario County, New York, where he married Vilate Murray and worked as a potter. He joined the Mormon Church in 1832 and served several missions after being ordained an apostle three years later. He helped Brigham Young prepare the Mormons to move west and was a key leader of the 1846–48 exodus. He was first counselor to Brigham Young from 1847 until his death.

KIMBALL, HIRAM S. (1806–1863) [**Br. Hiram Kimball**] Husband of Sarah Melissa Granger, he joined the church in 1843 in Nauvoo and followed his wife and children to Utah in 1852. Called on a mission to the Sandwich Islands in March 1863, he was killed en route when the ship on which he was a passenger exploded.

KIMBALL, SARAH ANN WHITNEY (1825–1873) [**Sarah, Sarah A., or Sarah Ann**] was a daughter of Newel K. and Elizabeth Ann Smith Whitney. She married Joseph Kingsbury, was sealed to Joseph Smith in 1842, and she later became a plural wife of Heber C. Kimball and had seven children by him, the first of whom was David, who was born and died on the trail.

KIMBALL, SARAH MELISSA GRANGER (1818–1898) [**Sister K., S.M.K.**] was founder of the sewing group which became the Relief Society in Nauvoo in 1842. She brought her mother and two children to Utah in 1851. She was secretary to Relief Society president ERS in 1880 and was elected a vice-president upon the society's incorporation in 1892. A women's suffrage activist, she served as the first president of the Utah Suffrage Association and an honorary vice-president of the National American Suffrage Association.

KIMBALL, SOLOMON FARNHAM (1847–1920) Son of Heber C. and Vilate Murray Kimball, he was born 2 February 1847 at Winter Quarters, at which time his mother wrote a verse ending "May he be the father of many lives. But not the Husband of many Wives." ERS witnessed his blessing eight days later.

KIMBALL, VILATE MURRAY (1806–1867) [**Mrs. Vilate Kimball, sis. Kimball**] married Heber C. Kimball in 1822 and joined the church two weeks after he did. She arrived in Utah in 1848 along with her husband's subsequent wives and their families. She had ten children.

LEONARD, ABIGAIL CALKINS (1795–?) [**Sis. Leonard**] traveled in the second fifty of Jedediah M. Grant's Hundred with her husband, Lyman Leonard. Seven years earlier, in 1840, she had defended him against a Jackson County, Missouri, mob that had tried to kill him. She hosted many of the blessing meetings of the women in Utah in the late 1840s.

LEONARD, LYMAN (1793–1877) was the husband of Abigail Calkins.

LITTLE, FERAMORZ (1820–1886) A nephew of Brigham Young, he married Fannie Decker, sister to Clara Decker, in 1846. He converted to Mormonism after emigrating to Utah in 1850. A successful businessman in the lumber industry and in banking, Little served as Salt Lake City mayor for three consecutive terms, beginning in 1876. He and his daughter Clara [**Claire**] accompanied ERS and others to Europe in 1872.

LOVE, ANDREW (1808–1890) [**Br. Love**] fled Illinois mobs in 1846 and wintered at Keg Creek. He traveled west in Jedediah M. Grant's Hundred. After arriving in Utah, he was called to the Iron Mission in 1850. He supervised the building of a wall and/or dam at Salt Creek (Nephi).

LOVE, NANCY MARIA BIGELOW (1814–1852) [**Sis. Love**] married Andrew Love in Illinois in 1834; converted to the LDS Church in 1844. She traveled with her husband Andrew and five-year-old daughter Elizabeth Angeline in the Third Hundred. She was run over by a wagon, and miraculously healed on the journey.

LYMAN, AMASA MASON (1813–1877) [**A. Lyman**] joined the church in 1832 and was ordained an apostle in 1842. He married, among others, ERS's niece Cornelia. He arrived in Salt Lake with the original pioneer group in 1847. Lyman was excommunicated in 1870 for preaching false doctrine.

LYMAN, CAROLINE ELY PARTRIDGE (1827–1908) Sister to Eliza Partridge Lyman, she was sealed to Joseph Smith and afterward became a plural wife of Amasa Lyman in 1844. She accompanied her husband to Utah, then to California and back in 1851; but she later separated from him and reared her five children alone. In 1874 she became the first Relief Society president in Oak Creek, Utah.

LYMAN, CORNELIA ELIZA LEAVITT (1825–1864) [**Cornelia**] Daughter of ERS's sister Leonora, she had two sons by her husband Amasa Lyman, one of whom was born in the San Bernardino, California, colony her husband had been called to establish. When she died, her sons were raised by other wives of Lyman.

LYMAN, ELIZA MARIE PARTRIDGE (1820–1886) [**E. or Eliza or Eliza P**] She was sealed to Joseph Smith in 1843. The eldest of three sisters who then married Amasa Lyman, she was born in Painesville, Ohio. She crossed the plains with her sister Caroline in 1848 and, after arriving in the Valley, supported her family by teaching school and working in a co-op store.

LYON, SYLVIA PORTER SESSIONS (1818–1882) [**Sis. Lyons, Lyon**] Daughter of Patty Bartlett and David Sessions, she married Winsor Lyon in 1838 and was sealed to Joseph Smith in 1846. Arriving in Utah with her brother Perrigrine in 1854, she bought a farm and later became one of Heber C. Kimball's wives.

LYON, WINSOR PALMER (1809–1849) was a pharmacist in Nauvoo who had previously been an Army physician. The husband of

Sylvia Sessions, he gave his consent for her to be sealed to Joseph Smith. She later left him to go to Utah.

MARKHAM, CATHARINE ANN JONES (dates unknown) [**Cath.**] Wife of Warren Markham, she traveled with his family across Iowa in 1846, giving birth en route.

MARKHAM, DAVID (1835–1902) [**David**] was the youngest son of Stephen and Hannah Hogleboon Markham.

MARKHAM, HANNAH HOGLEBOON or HOGABOOM (1804–1892) [**Sis. M or Sis. Markham**] Stephen Markham's first wife and mother of Warren, Whiting, and David Markham. She shared the family's wagon with ERS from Nauvoo to Winter Quarters, but remained in Winter Quarters until 1850. Family records indicate Hannah left Stephen in the 1850s and moved with their three sons to California, where she remarried.

MARKHAM, STEPHEN (1800–1878) [**Col. or br. M. or Markham**] was raised in Geauga County, Ohio, where he joined the church in 1837 and became Joseph Smith's bodyguard. He first arrived in Utah in 1847 with the original pioneer group and returned there in 1850 leading a company of fifty which included wife Hannah Hogleboon and their three sons.

MARKHAM, WARREN (1824–?) [**Warren, W.**] Eldest son of Stephen and Hannah Hogleboon Markham and husband of Catherine. ERS records the growing dissatisfaction between herself and the Markham family and specific confrontations with Warren.

MARKHAM, WILLIAM WHITING (1829–1903) [**Whiting**] Son of Stephen and Hannah Hogleboon Markham.

MILLER, GEORGE (1794–1856) [**Bishop, Bish., Bp., or br. Miller**] An early convert to Mormonism, was president of the Nauvoo House Association and a bishop in Nauvoo before breaking away from the church. After receiving a vision that James Strang should be Joseph Smith's successor, he went to Michigan and turned all his property over to the Strangites.

MORLEY, ABIGAIL LEONORA SNOW LEAVITT (1801–1872) [**L. or A.L.L. or Sis. Leavitt**] ERS's oldest sister, reared in Mantua. She married Enoch Virgin Leavitt of Warren, Ohio, but later left him, returning with her two daughters, Cornelia and Lucia, to Mantua. She joined the church in 1831; moved to Kirtland, thence with her family to Missouri, then Illinois. She married Isaac Morley and immigrated with him to Utah and Sanpete County.

MORLEY, ISAAC (1786–1864) [**Father, fath, or I. Morley**] Joined the church in Ohio in 1830 and was patriarch at Far West, Missouri, when Governor Lilburn Boggs's extermination order forced Mormon evacuation to Illinois. In 1846 he took his family to Mt. Pisgah; in 1848 they emigrated west, subsequently leading the party that founded Sanpete County settlement. His third wife was ERS's sister Abigail Leonora.

NEFF, AMOS H. (1825–1914) was a captain of ten, which included his parents and five siblings, in Jedediah M. Grant's Hundred. He married Martha Dilworth in 1848 and soon after opened the first merchandise store on record in Utah history. He later served a year in prison on polygamy charges.

PACK, JOHN AUSTIN [?] (1809–1885) [**Br. Pack**] emigrated to Utah with the original Pioneer Company, returning to Winter Quarters in 1847 to lead his family to Utah. He built the first dance hall in Utah.

PAGE, JOHN EDWARD (1799–1867) [**John E. Page**] was a successful missionary to Canada, and was ordained an apostle in 1838. He followed James J. Strang when Strang broke from the Mormon church in 1844. Page subsequently became first counselor to Strang in the Strangite church.

PEIRCE, HANNAH HARVEY (1802–1872) [**Sis. Peirce, or Pierce; Sis. P**] Wife of Robert Peirce, she was originally a Quaker from Pennsylvania. Two of her nine children had died in Pennsylvania, another in Nauvoo, and her daughter Mary at Winter Quarters before she and the remaining family reached Utah in 1847.

PEIRCE, MARGARETT(E) WHITESIDES (1823–1907) [**Margaret, M., Margarett**] Second daughter of Robert and Hannah Harvey Peirce. Widowed only seven months after marrying Morris Whitesides in July 1844, she was sealed to Brigham Young in 1846 on the same day as was her sister Mary. Margaret and ERS, sister wives and traveling companions from Winter Quarters to Utah, were close friends, though ERS was closer in age to Margaret's mother.

PEIRCE, MARY HARVEY (1821–1847) was the eldest child of Robert and Hannah Harvey Peirce and was sealed to Brigham Young on 22 January 1846 before leaving Nauvoo to come west. Her death at Winter Quarters on 16 March 1847 made possible a place for ERS in the Peirce wagon.

PEIRCE, ROBERT (1797–1884) [**Capt. P, br. P**] was born in Pennsylvania of Quaker ancestry. Married in 1821 to Hannah Harvey, he moved his family to Nauvoo in 1841 and assisted financially in building up Nauvoo. Peirce was captain of the ten in which ERS traveled from Winter Quarters to Utah.

PRATT, ORSON (1811–1881) [**Orson Pratt**] Joined the church in 1831 at age nineteen and was ordained an apostle four years later.

Traveling west with the Pioneer Company, he was the first of the Mormons to enter Salt Lake Valley. An effective missionary and published author of both religious and scientific books, Pratt also served as church historian and recorder for seven years.

PRATT, PARLEY PARKER (1807–1857) [**P. P., or P. P. P., or P. P. Pratt**] joined the LDS church in 1830, and introduced Sidney Rigdon to the church. Ordained an apostle in 1835, he served many missions in the states and in England. Persecution of the Mormons in Missouri led to his own eight-month imprisonment. In 1840 he helped establish the British periodical *Millennial Star,* which he later edited; he also published many books and tracts throughout his life. Leader of a company of Saints to Utah in 1847, he was elected to the legislative council when Utah became a territory. He was murdered 13 May 1857 near the Arkansas-Indian Territory border while serving a mission.

RICH, CHARLES COULSON (1809–1883) [**Br. or Gen. Rich**] Husband of Sarah DeArmon Pea Rich, he presided at Mt. Pisgah during the winter of 1846–47. He led the fifth company to leave Winter Quarters for Utah in 1847. He was ordained an apostle in 1849 and along with Amasa Lyman later negotiated the purchase of the San Bernardino ranch in California.

RICH, SARAH DEARMON PEA (1814–1893) [**Sis. Rich**] Married Charles C. Rich in 1838 in Missouri. A member of the Nauvoo Relief Society and a close friend of Emma Smith, she traveled to Utah in her husband's "Guard" company in 1847 with her five sister wives and five children, three of whom were infants.

RICHARDS, FRANKLIN DEWEY (1821–1899) [**Br. F. Richards, Br. R.**] was born in Richmond, Massachusetts, and baptized in 1838. He married Jane Snyder in Nauvoo, and filled a mission to England. He was ordained an apostle in 1849, and immigrated to Salt Lake in 1848. Among other positions, Richards served twice as mission president in England and as church historian. He was also probate judge in Weber County from 1869 to 1883.

RICHARDS, JANE SNYDER [?] (1823–1912) [**Sis. Richards**] married Franklin D. Richards on 18 December 1842. Two children— Wealthy, born in Nauvoo, and Isaac—died in 1846 on the trail between Nauvoo and Winter Quarters. In Ogden, Utah, she became the first stake president of the Relief Society, serving also as counselor in the general presidency of the organization. She was an active suffragist.

RICHARDS, JENETTA (1817–1845) Born in England, she met and married Willard Richards while he was on a mission in Britain. The mother of three children, one of whom died in infancy, she died in Nauvoo at the age of twenty-eight.

RICHARDS, WILLARD (1804–1854) [**Dr Richards**] was baptized by Brigham Young, his cousin, in 1836. He was secretary to Joseph Smith and was with him in the Carthage jail when Smith died. He became a counselor to Brigham Young in 1847. He was a Tomsonian (herbalist) physician.

RITER, LEVI EVANS (1805–1877) [**Writer, br. Writer**] One of the Chester County, Pennsylvania, converts, he and his wife Rebecca traveled from Winter Quarters in the same company of ten as ERS.

RITER, REBECCA WOLLERTON (1815–1894) [**Sis. Writer**] came west with her husband Levi Riter and their three children in 1847. She was a daughter of Eliza Wollerton Dilworth, who also traveled in the Peirce ten.

ROCKWELL, ORRIN PORTER (1815–1878) [**P. Rockwell or Porter** (not to be confused with Porter Squires, who appears mainly in notations relating to the Mt. Pisgah area)] He was a scout in Orson Pratt's advance group in the Pioneer Company, and his considerable influence with Native Americans often benefitted the Mormon pioneers. Rockwell later worked with the Overland and Pony Express riders and was deputy marshal of Salt Lake City.

ROCKWOOD, ALBERT P. (1805–1879) [**Col. Rockwood**] One of seven presidents of the Seventies in 1845, he accompanied the Pioneer Company to Utah in 1847. He served as warden of the territory's penitentiary for fifteen years.

ROGERS, AMOS PHILEMON (1820–1846) [**Amos Rogers**] Born in Portage County, Ohio, he was a nephew of Noah Rogers. He married Anna Matilda Doolittle in Nauvoo, and their one daughter, Amanda Jane, was born in Council Bluffs four months after her father's death on the Iowa trail. Anna Matilda married Amos's brother Samuel Hollister Rogers in Utah in 1850; they had six children.

ROGERS, NOAH (1797–1846) [**Br. N. Rogers**] Born in Connecticut, Rogers with his wife Eda Hollister, their two children, and Noah's brother Noble had moved onto a lot at Oliver Snow's Mantua, Ohio, farm in 1825. In 1828 they moved to Shalersville, where they joined the Mormon Church. ERS mentions Noah's death in 1846 at Mt. Pisgah. His wife and nine children continued on to Utah.

RUSSELL, AMASA [?] (1793–1863) [**Maj. Russels**] was born in Vermont and was a captain of ten in the Fourth Hundred of 1847.

SAVAGE, MARY ABIGAIL WHITE [?] (1823–1904) [**Sis. Savage**] traveled with the First Hundred of 1847.

JOSEPH S. SCOFIELD [?] (1809–1875) [**Br. Scofield**] A carpenter, he was a valued member of the Pioneer Company that entered the Valley in July 1847.

SESSIONS, DAVID (1790–1850) [**Father, fath., f. Sessions, or f. Sess.**] joined the church in 1834 and immigrated to Salt Lake in 1847 with his wife, Patty Bartlett Sessions.

SESSIONS, PATTY BARTLETT (1795–1892) [**Sis., mother, moth. Sessions or moth. Sess.**] Known as the mother of Mormon midwifery, she delivered 3,977 babies during her career. Often called on to aid the sick during the overland journey, Sessions later became prominent in the Female Council of Health, and was known in Farmington, Utah, as a businesswoman and philanthropist.

SESSIONS, PEREGRINE or PERRIGRINE (1814–1893) [**Perrigreen Sess.**] The son of David and Patty Bartlett Sessions, he led a company of fifty in the First Hundred of 1847 in which his parents, wives, and children traveled.

SHERWOOD, HENRY G. (1785–1862 or 1867) Nauvoo city marshal, he was healed by Joseph Smith of malaria in the early Nauvoo days. He served as commissary general for the Pioneer Company. He drew the first survey of Salt Lake City and in 1852 went to San Bernardino, California, as surveyor for the church.

SMITH, BATHSHEBA W. BIGLER (1822–1910) was the first wife of George Albert Smith, attended the 17 March 1842 first Relief Society Meeting, and served in Utah as general president of the Relief Society, 1901–10, and as matron in the Salt Lake Temple.

SMITH, GEORGE ALBERT (1817–1875) was baptized in 1832 and seven years later was ordained an apostle—the youngest in the church. He immigrated to Utah in 1849 with his family and served as church historian until his appointment in 1868 as first counselor to Brigham Young.

SMITH, JOHN (1871–1854) [**fath J. Smith, fath S., Prest. J. Smith**] was uncle of Joseph Smith, president of first Salt Lake stake, and presiding patriarch.

SMOOT, ABRAHAM O. (1815–1896) [**Capt. or br. Smoot**] was bishop in Winter Quarters. He led the largest company of 1847, the Fourth Hundred, to Utah. The first justice of the peace in Utah, he served as mayor of Salt Lake City from 1856 to 1866 and of Provo from 1868 to 1880. Smoot was also president of the board of trustees of Brigham Young Academy.

SMOOT, MARGARET T. MCMEANS (1809–1884) [**Sis. Smoot**] Baptized in 1834, at the time a widow with one son, she converted and traveled to Missouri. She married Abraham O. Smoot in 1838. She resided in Salt Lake City until 1872, then moved to Provo where she became president of the Utah Stake Relief Society in 1878.

SNOW, ERASTUS (1818–1888) traveled with the original Pioneer Company. He and Orson Pratt were the first two Mormon pioneers to enter the Salt Lake Valley in July 1847. Snow was ordained an apostle in 1849. In 1850, while on a mission to Denmark, he helped to translate and publish the Book of Mormon in Danish. He was a distant cousin to ERS.

SNOW, MELVINA HARVEY (1811–1882) [**Sis. Snow**] The first wife of Willard Snow, she crossed the plains with him and two of their children. ERS notes the death of Helen, one of the couple's twins born in Utah in 1848. Of the nine children Melvina bore, only three grew to adulthood.

SNOW, WILLARD (1811–1853) [**W., br., or Capt. Snow**] Another distant cousin of ERS, and the brother of Erastus Snow, Willard was baptized in 1833, and in 1837 married Melvina Harvey. In 1846 he also married her sister Susan, who accompanied them across the plains. Snow was captain of the second fifty in Grant's company. He died at sea while serving a mission to Scandinavia.

SPENCER, CATHERINE CURTIS (1811–1846) [**Caroline C. Spencer**] married Orson Spencer in 1830 and died in Winter Quarters 13 March 1846, leaving six children. The children, the oldest of whom was fourteen, fended for themselves until their father returned in 1849 from his mission, even crossing the plains in 1848.

SPENCER, ORSON (1802–1855) A college graduate and theologian, Spencer was baptized in the early 1840s by his brother Daniel. After his first wife, Caroline Curtis, died, he served as mission president in Britain from 1847 to 1849 and came to Utah in 1849. Appointed chancellor of Salt Lake City's Deseret University in 1850, Spencer died in St. Louis after completing his fourth mission for the Mormon Church.

SQUIRES, CALVIN (1830–1903) [**Calvin**] was a brother of Charlotte Squires Snow, Lorenzo's wife.

SQUIRES, CHARLES PORTER (1827–1872) [**Porter** (appears only in the Mt. Pisgah section of ERS's journals, 1846; otherwise this reference is to Porter Rockwell)] Born in Geauga County, Ohio, his sister Charlotte was one of Lorenzo Snow's first wives.

STRANG, JAMES J. (1813–1856) was excommunicated from the Mormon church in 1844. Claiming to be Joseph Smith's successor, he founded the "Strangite" church and led his followers to the islands in northern Michigan. Shot 16 June 1856 in an assassination plot, Strang died eleven days later.

TANNER, JAMES MONROE (1844–1846) was the son of Sidney and Louisa Conlee Tanner and is the child whose death ERS mentions in March 1846. His mother and an infant brother also died later that same year.

TANNER, SIDNEY (1809–1895) immigrated to Utah in 1848 and to California in 1851. His first wife, Louisa Conlee, died in September 1846 during the exodus from Nauvoo.

TAYLOR, JOHN (1808–1887) [**Elder, Br., or J. Taylor; J. T.**] was the successor to Brigham Young; third president of the Mormon Church. He was wounded in Carthage jail when Joseph Smith was killed. Returning from a short mission to England, he led a company of British Mormons to Utah in 1847, and crossed to Utah in the Second Hundred. Taylor died while in hiding from persecution for polygamous cohabitation.

TAYLOR, LEONORA CANNON (1796–1868) [**Sis. T. or Sis. Taylor**] was the first wife of John Taylor, and was born on the Isle of Man. She met and married Taylor in Toronto, where Parley P. Pratt converted them. By the time they reached Winter Quarters, Leonora had borne four children, one of whom, Leonora Agnes, died an infant in 1843. ERS wrote a poem commemorating the child's death.

TURLEY, THEODORE (1801–1871) was a Methodist lay preacher when he was baptized a Mormon in 1837. He immigrated to Utah in 1849 and to San Bernardino in the early 1850s. His wife Frances A. Kimberly and her namesake daughter died at Winter Quarters. The boy mentioned in ERS's diary entry of 13 May 1846 was 3-year-old Jonathan.

WHITNEY, ELIZABETH ANN SMITH (1800–1882) [**Mrs. E.A.W.; Sis. Whit or Whitney**] First counselor to President Emma Smith when the Relief Society was first organized in 1842, she married Newel K. Whitney in 1822 and came to Utah in 1848. She was respected as "Mother Whitney" for her charity, and was known for her singing in the gift of tongues. She was mother of eleven children.

WHITNEY, HELEN MAR KIMBALL (1828–1896) [**Helen**] Daughter of Heber C. and Vilate Murray Kimball, she married Horace Whitney 4 February 1846 and bore eleven children, seven of whom survived to adulthood.

WHITNEY, HORACE KIMBALL (1823–1884) was the husband of Helen Mar Kimball. He was born in Kirtland, Ohio, and was in the first group to reach the Salt Lake Valley. Printer and later manager of the *Deseret News,* he was also a member of the Deseret Dramatic Association.

WHITNEY, NEWEL K. (1795–1850) [**B. Whitney**] was baptized in Ohio in 1830 and became a close friend of Joseph Smith. He was appointed bishop at Kirtland in 1831 and later at Winter Quarters in 1846. He was married to Elizabeth Ann Smith Whitney, and later married others.

WIGHT, LYMAN (1796–1858) [**L., Lyman Wight**] was an apostle from 1841 to 1848. He went to Texas with George Miller and a small company of Mormons. Excommunicated in 1848, Wight remained in Texas until his death.

WOODRUFF, PHEBE WHITTEMORE CARTER (1807–1885) [**Sis. or P. Woodruff**] joined the church in 1834 and married Wilford Woodruff in 1837. Four of their nine children lived to maturity, but between 1840 and 1846 she lost three. After serving a mission with her husband in England, she arrived in Salt Lake City in 1850.

WOODRUFF, WILFORD (1807–1898) [**Elder or W. Woodruff**] Fourth president of the Mormon Church, which he joined in 1833. Ordained an apostle in 1839, he was a member of the first group to enter the Salt Lake Valley. Woodruff served as church historian from 1881 until his appointment as church president in 1889. In September 1890 he issued the "Manifesto" discontinuing official sanction of the practice of polygamy. His first wife was Phebe Carter Woodruff.

WOOLLEY, EDWIN DILWORTH (1807–1881) [**Br. Wooley or Woolley; E. Wool or Wooley**] Born of Quaker parents in Chester County, Pennsylvania, he married Mary Wickersham in 1831. He was baptized in 1837 and brought his younger siblings to Nauvoo. In 1848 he came to Utah, where he was a merchant, legislator, and Mormon bishop.

WOOLLEY, MARY WICKERSHAM (1808–1859) [**Mrs. Wooley**] was the first wife of Edwin D. Woolley and mother of eight children.

YEARSLEY, DAVID DUTTON (1808–1849) [**Br. Yearsley, Br. Y.**] was born in Chester County, Pennsylvania, and married Mary Ann Hoopes as his first wife. They had eight children, all of whom survived to adulthood in Utah. He crossed Iowa in Heber C. Kimball's company, sometimes traveling with the Markhams. Yearsley crossed the plains to Utah in 1847, returning the following year to Winter Quarters, where he died a year later.

YOUNG, ABIGAIL "NABBIE" HOWE (1766–1815) was Brigham Young's mother.

YOUNG, BRIGHAM (1801–1877) [**Brigham, Prest. B. Young, Prest. B.Y., B.m, or B.**] was second president of the Mormon Church and chief organizer of the emigration westward. Leading the original

Pioneer Company, he identified the Salt Lake Valley as the area in which the Saints would settle. Second husband of ERS, he married her 3 October 1844. The marriage was later ratified on 3 February 1846, the same day he stood in the Nauvoo temple as proxy for her to be sealed for eternity to Joseph Smith.

YOUNG, CLARA or CLARISSA DECKER (1828–1889) [**Clara, C.**] married Brigham Young in 1844, and accompanied him in the Pioneer Company in 1847. She and ERS shared a room in the Old Fort in 1847–48. She was the sister of Charles Decker.

YOUNG, EMILY DOW PARTRIDGE (1824–1899) [**Emily, E.**] was baptized in 1832. When her father, Edward Partridge, and a sister died in 1840, she lived with Joseph and Emma Smith and subsequently married Joseph Smith in 1843. She later married Brigham Young in 1846 and crossed the plains to Utah in 1848. She had seven children.

YOUNG, HARRIET PAGE WHEELER (1803–1871) was a wife of Lorenzo Dow Young and one of three female members of the Pioneer Company. Her daughter Clarissa Decker, by first husband Isaac Decker, was the wife Brigham Young brought in the 1847 Pioneer Company, and with whom ERS lived the first winter she spent in the Valley; and her son Charles Decker married Brigham's daughter Vilate.

YOUNG, JOHN (1763–1839) was Brigham and John and Lorenzo Dow Young's father.

YOUNG, JOHN (1791-1870) [**J Y, Y, Prest. Y or J. Y., J. Young**] was the oldest brother of Brigham, both sons of John and Nabby Howe Young. With Mary Ann he is listed in the second Fifty of the Jedediah Grant company crossing from Winter Quarters.

YOUNG, LORENZO DOW (1807–1895) [**Lorenzo Young**] was the younger brother of Brigham Young and a bishop in Salt Lake from 1851 to 1878. He married his second wife, Harriet Page Wheeler, on 9 March 1843. Two sons by his earlier marriage came in the same Hundred to Utah as did ERS.

YOUNG, LORENZO DOW, JR. (1847–1848) was the son of Lorenzo Dow and Harriet Page Wheeler Young. He was the first Mormon child born in the Salt Lake Valley.

YOUNG, MARY ANN ANGELL (1803–1882) [**Mary Ann Young**] was the second wife of Brigham Young, but was his "first wife" in plural marriage. Skilled in the use of medicine and herbs, she brought a variety of seeds from Nauvoo to plant in the Salt Lake Valley. The mother of six, she immigrated to Utah in 1848.

Notes

Editorial Methods

1. Mary-Jo Kline, *Guide to Documentary Editing* (Baltimore and London: Johns Hopkins University Press, 1987).

2. Laurel Thatcher Ulrich, *A Midwife's Tale: The Life of Martha Ballard, Based on Her Diary, 1785–1812* (New York: Random House, 1990), 35.

Introduction

1. Margaret Gay Judd Clawson, "Rambling Reminiscence of Margaret Gay Judd Clawson," holograph, Archives, Historical Department, The Church of Jesus Christ of Latter-day Saints, hereafter cited as LDS Church Archives. Thanks are due Jean Greenwood and Kathlene Fife Jackson, who transcribed the text.

2. Margaret, Duchess of Newcastle, "A True Relation of my Birth, Breeding and Life," *The Lives of William Cavendish, Duke of Newcastle, and of his Wife, Margaret Duchess of Newcastle,* ed. Mark Antony Lover [Lower] (London: John Russell, 1892), 309–10. As quoted in Domna C. Stanton, *The Female Autograph* (Chicago: University of Chicago Press, 1984), 14.

3. Sidonie Smith, *A Poetics of Women's Autobiography* (Bloomington and Indianapolis: Indiana University Press, 1987), 100.

4. Clawson.

5. Davis Bitton, *Guide to Mormon Diaries and Autobiographies* (Provo: Brigham Young University Press, 1977).

6. Patricia Cooper and Norma Bradley Buferd, *The Quilters: Women and Domestic Art* (Garden City, NY: Doubleday, 1978), 20.

7. Obert C. Tanner, ed., *A Mormon Mother: An Autobiography by Annie Clark Tanner* (Salt Lake City: Tanner Trust Fund and University of Utah Library, 1969).

8. "The Journal of Rhoda Ann Dykes Burgess," typescript in the author's possession.

9. Eliza Roxcy Snow, "Sketch of My Life," *Relief Society Magazine* 31 (April 1944): 209.

10. Seeing the cryptic diary through her historian's eyes, Ulrich comments: "Yet it is in the very dailiness, the exhaustive, repetitious dailiness, that the real power of Martha Ballard's book lies." Laurel Thatcher Ulrich, *A Midwife's Tale: The Life of Martha Ballard Based on Her Diary, 1785–1812* (New York: Alfred A. Knopf, 1990), 9.

11. Emma Lorena Barrows Brown, Diary, 1872–1882, in private possession; typescript courtesy of Kristen Hacken South. Forthcoming in *BYU Studies*, 1995.

12. Ellen Spencer Clawson to Ellen Pratt McGary, 4 November 1856, as published in S. George Ellsworth, *Dear Ellen: Two Mormon Women and Their Letters* (Salt Lake City, Tanner Trust Fund and University of Utah Library, 1974), 33.

Chapter 1

Introduction

1. Stenhouse, *A Lady's Life*, 19.

2. MS 12 (15 July 1850): 219.

3. From the Provo, Utah, *Enquirer*, as quoted in *Woman's Exponent* 6 (1 January 1878): 119.

4. I am indebted to Ronald W. Walker for his thorough study of the Godbeite conspiracy, and more particularly for superb articles on both Tullidge and the Stenhouses: "The Stenhouses and the Making of a Mormon Image," *Journal of Mormon History* 1 (1974): 50–72; and "Edward Tullidge: Historian of the Mormon Commonwealth," *Journal of Mormon History* 3 (1976): 55–72.

5. Fanny Stenhouse's memorized tirades against the Mormon leaders, described as "smoothly and clearly enunciated" lectures, attracted large audiences in the eastern states as well as in the West. See *Salt Lake Herald*, 3 July 1874.

6. E. W. Tullidge to B. W. S. [Bathsheba W. Smith], 18 January 1875, LDS Church Archives.

The Sketch of My Life

1. Oliver Snow was born 18 September 1775 in Becket, Massachusetts. Leonora Rosetta Pettibone was born 22 October 1778 in Simsbury, Hartford County, Connecticut.

2. The Tullidge text reads: "It was about the year of our Lord 1806 that Oliver Snow, a native of Massachusetts, and his wife, R. L. Pettibone Snow, of Connecticut, moved with their children to that section of the State of Ohio bordering on Lake Erie on the north and the State of Pennsylvania on the east, known then as the 'Connecticut Western Reserve.' They purchased land and settled in Mantua, Portage county."

Edward W. Tullidge, *The Women of Mormondom* (New York: Tullidge & Crandall, 1877), 26.

3. Obviously a slip: there were not seven but three sons in the family. The children were, in order of birth,

Leonora Abigail	b. 23 August 1801
Eliza Roxcy	b. 21 January 1804
Percy Amanda	b. 20 April 1808
Melissa	b. 24 July 1810
Lorenzo	b. 3 April 1814
Lucius Augustus	b. 31 August 1819
Samuel Pearce	b. 22 August 1821

4. Oliver Snow was elected county commissioner in 1809, which office he held until 1815, by which time Eliza would have been just eleven. However, he later served several terms as justice of the peace; as a contemporary observed, "It was rarely the case whilst he resided in Mantua that he was not holding some township office." Orrin Harmon, "Historical Facts Appertaining to the Township of Mantua, . . . Portage Co., Ohio," manuscript, p. 115, Western Reserve Historical Society, Cleveland, Ohio.

5. A hat made of the straw from an Italian variety of wheat (hence Leghorn/Livorno), braided and then sewn. The Portage County Fair, held at Ravenna, the county seat, was enthusiastically attended by the Snows; both Oliver and his brother Franklin served on committees at least one year.

6. Of all the Mantua schoolteachers during Eliza Snow's childhood years, Ezekial Ladd is the one who best fits the description here. He taught there the 1812–13 term. Harmon, "Historical Facts," 129.

7. Tullidge saw a close connection between what he considered Eliza Snow's "Hebraic" lineage and her poetic gifts. In this he also saw in her supposed Jewishness the roots of her patriotism. "The classical reader," he wrote, "will remember how the struggle between Greece and Turkey stirred the soul of Byron. That immortal poet was not a saint but he was a great patriot and fled to the help of Greece. Precisely the same chord that was struck in the chivalrous mind of Lord Byron was struck in the Hebraic soul of Eliza R. Snow. It was the chord of the heroic and the unique. Our Hebraic heroine is even more sensitive to the heroic and patriotic than to the poetic,—at least she has most self-gratification in lofty and patriotic themes." Tullidge, *Women of Mormondom*, 30.

8. "Missolonghi," Ravenna *Western Courier*, 22 July 1826; "Adams and Jefferson," Ravenna *Western Courier*, 5 August 1826.

9. Both Oliver Snow, Sen., and Jacob Pettibone enlisted; the former served from April to July 1777, the latter from May to October 1775 and again in November 1776, when he was taken prisoner at the surrender

of Fort Washington, New York Island. Henry P. Johnston, ed., *The Record of Connecticut Men in the Military and Naval Service During the War of Revolution, 1775–1783* (Hartford: Case, Rockwood and Brainard Co., 1889), 49, 123.

10. The 1820s were a time when, as one author suggests, "many Americans began to ask: 'Why are the gods no longer heard and seen?'" Klaus Hansen, *Mormonism and the American Experience* (Chicago: University of Chicago Press, 1981), 20. The creed of the Campbellite Disciples of Christ, which the Snows espoused ca. 1828, proclaimed "the sufficiency of the revealed will of God for all purposes of 'faith and practice,'" in effect denying the continuing prophetic function. A. S. Hayden, *Early History of the Disciples in the Western Reserve* (Cincinnati: Chase and Hall, 1975), 237.

11. The Tullidge text identifies "the Campbellite church"; the more correct name is "Disciples of Christ." The role of Sidney Rigdon, who with Alexander Campbell and Walter Scott was a leader in the Disciples church, in the conversion of the Snow family is described in Hayden's *History of the Disciples,* 240: "In the admiration of Sidney Rigdon, Oliver Snow and his family shared very largely; so, when he came with his pretended humility, to lay all at the feet of Mormonism, it caused a great shock to the little church [of Disciples] at Mantua."

12. Tullidge, *Women of Mormondom,* 61, has Eliza Snow claiming to have heard of "the mission of the prophet Joseph . . . in the autumn of 1820," an obvious slip. With the 1830 publication of the Book of Mormon in Palmyra, New York, Joseph Smith's public ministry began in earnest.

13. There is reason to question the 1830–31 dating here. Joseph and Emma Smith had moved in February 1831 from New York to Kirtland, Ohio, some thirty miles from Mantua. During that remaining winter and early spring, Joseph Smith did travel in the area, proselytizing and visiting, and could conceivably have been brought at that time to Mantua by the zealous Rigdon. On 12 September 1831, however, the Smiths took up residence at the John Johnson home in Hiram, four miles from the Snow farm, and during that winter of 1831–32, from 1 December until mid-January, Joseph Smith interrupted his work on the Bible revision to preach in the area. Joseph Smith, *History of the Church of Jesus Christ of Latter-day Saints,* 7 vols., ed. B. H. Roberts (Salt Lake City: Deseret Book, 1932–51), 1:239–41. This would be the more likely season for Smith's visit to the the the Snow home.

14. Tullidge reads: "However, I improved the opportunity and attended the first meeting within my reach. I listened to the testimonials of two of the witnesses of the Book of Mormon. Such impressive testimonies I had never heard. To hear men testify that they had seen a holy

angel—that they had listened to his voice, bearing testimony of the work that was ushering in a new dispensation; that the fullness of the gospel was to be restored and that they were commanded to go forth and declare it, thrilled my inmost soul.

"Yet it must be remembered that when Joseph Smith was called to his great mission, more than human power was requisite to convince people that communication with the invisible world was possible. He was scoffed at, ridiculed and persecuted for asserting that he had received a revelation; now the world is flooded with revelations." Tullidge, *Women of Mormondom*, 64–65.

15. Tullidge, *Women of Mormondom*, 64.

16. Of the events immediately preceding her baptism, Eliza Snow said in 1872: "We were not called upon to be baptized but had to ask the privilege. When I went to meeting for the purpose of asking permission of being baptized I had to battle very strongly with the powers of darkness. The evil one brought forth many strong arguments against my joining the Church, and it was with difficulty that I overcame them I finally commanded Satan to depart from me. Then my mind was again enlightened and filled with the Spirit of God, and I had firmness to ask for baptism." Minutes of the Senior and Junior Cooperative Retrenchment Association, 22 June 1872, LDS Church Archives, typescript in editor's files.

17. Eliza Snow's full account of the 27 March 1836 dedication is found in *Eliza R. Snow, An Immortal* (Salt Lake City: Nicholas G. Morgan Foundation, 1957), 54–65. Also Tullidge, *Women of Mormondom*, 80–95. Snow wrote in the Tullidge manuscript:

"I was present on the memorable event of the dedication of the temple, when the mighty power of God was displayed, and after its dedication enjoyed many refreshing seasons in that holy sanctuary. Many times have I witnessed manifestations of the power of God, in the precious gifts of the gospel,—such as speaking in tongues, the interpretation of tongues, prophesying, healing the sick, causing the lame to walk, the blind to see, the deaf to hear, and the dumb to speak. Of such manifestations in the church I might relate many circumstances." *Women of Mormondom*, 65.

18. The Tullidge text adds: "Three times a day he had family worship; and these precious seasons of sacred household service truly seemed a foretaste of celestial happiness." *Women of Mormondom*, 66.

19. Kirtland land and tax records show the deeding of a half-acre property to Eliza R. Snow on 25 April 1836 for $200. That she retained the deed is indicated by the subsequent payment of $3.00 tax each year until 1839. Milton V. Backman, Jr., *A Profile of Latter-day Saints of Kirtland, Ohio . . . 1830–1839* (Provo, Utah: Privately published, 1982), 161. Eliza Snow's older sister Leonora, who lived in the house with her daughters

Lucia and Cornelia, was not technically a widow. She had left her husband Enoch Virgil Leavitt and their son Norman prior to 1831, returning to Mantua where she joined the LDS Church. The money which Eliza Snow contributed for the temple was most likely from her inheritance from her father, claimed, as was Lorenzo's inheritance of $1,400, at the time she left Mantua.

20. Oberlin College, Oberlin, Ohio, the first coeducational college in the United States, first opened its doors in 1833. Its official records show Lorenzo Snow as having attended the "spring term" of 1836. Snow's own account, however, tells of his leaving Mantua in 1835 and being in Oberlin before 10 December that year, when his sister Melissa died in Mantua. By 12 March 1836 he was still at Oberlin, as witness his letter to his sister bearing that date. Lorenzo Snow, Personal History and Letter Book, 1839 ff., microfilm, LDS Church Archives.

21. Joshua Seixas, the Hebrew scholar hired by Joseph Smith to instruct the School of the Prophets in that language, arrived in Kirtland 23 January 1836 from Hudson, Ohio, where he had been teaching at Western Reserve College. According to Joseph Smith, *History of the Church* 2:429, he taught his last class in Kirtland on 29 March 1836. Even if Lorenzo Snow left Oberlin before the end of the spring term, there would be little time for him to study under Seixas before his departure from Kirtland. It is, of course, possible that the Hebrew scholar remained in Kirtland for a time after the completion of the course in the School of the Prophets to which the *History of the Church* refers. See correspondence between LeRoi C. Snow and Frederick Waite, LeRoi Snow Papers, in possession of Cynthia Snow Banner; photocopy in the author's files.

22. The suggestion here that Lorenzo Snow first came into contact with Mormonism through his sister's 1836 invitation is misleading. By his own account he had met and listened to Joseph Smith in Portage County, probably during the prophet's 1831–32 sojourn in Hiram. Lorenzo's experience at Oberlin was, in fact, highlighted for him by his colleagues' interest in the Mormon principles he would defend in debate with them. From Oberlin, 12 March 1836, he wrote to Eliza his initial response to her invitation: "Dear Sister. I am delighted in learning that you enjoy so much happenings in Kirtland; tho' at pressent I am not disposed to exchange my location for yours; yet if the advantages of learning there were the same I think I should be almost inclined to try and exchange. For, if nothing more it would prove quite interesting to me and perhaps not unproffitable to hear those doctrings preached which I have so long endeavored to defend and support here in Oberlin. . . . It is true I have not made many converts as I am not one myself yet I have made some of them [fellow students and teachers] al-

most confess they perceived some philosophy in your doctrines."
Lorenzo Snow, Personal History and Letter Book.

23. Governor Lilburn W. Boggs's infamous "extermination order"
had been issued 27 October 1838. On 18 November militia comman-
dant R. Wilson signed a pass permitting Oliver Snow and others from
the Adam-ondi-Ahman settlement "to pass and re-pass" in Daviess
County "upon all lawful business." Joseph Smith, *History of the Church*
3:210. Eliza Snow has here summarized from her more detailed account
as written for Tullidge:

"In Kirtland the persecution increased until many had to flee for their
lives, and in the spring of 1838, in company with my father, mother,
three brothers, one sister and her two daughters, I left Kirtland, and arrived in Far West, Caldwell county, Mo., on the 16th of July where I
stopped at the house of Sidney Rigdon, with my brother Lorenzo, who
was very sick, while the rest of my family went farther, and settled in
Adam-Ondi-Ahman, in Davies county. In two weeks, my brother being
sufficiently recovered, my father sent for us and we joined the family
group. My father purchased the premises of two of the "old settlers," and
paid their demands in full. I mention this, because subsequent events
proved that, at the time of the purchase, although those men ostensibly
were our warm friends, they had, in connection with others of the same
stripe, concocted plans to mob and drive us from our newly acquired
homes, and repossess them. In this brief biographical sketch, I shall not
attempt a review of the scenes that followed. Sufficient to say, while we
were busy in making preparations for the approaching winter, to our
great surprise, those neighbors fled from the place, as if driven by a
mob, leaving their clocks ticking, dishes spread for their meal, coffee-
pots boiling, etc., etc., and, as they went, spread the report in every direction that the 'Mormons' had driven them from their homes, arousing
the inhabitants of the surrounding country, which resulted in the disgraceful, notorious 'exterminating order' from the Governor of the
State; in accordance therewith, we left Davies county for that of
Caldwell, preparatory to fulfilling the injunction of leaving the State 'before grass grows' in the spring." Tullidge, *Women of Mormondom*, 143.

24. "In assisting widows and others who required help, my father's
time was so occupied that we did not start until the morning of the 10th,
and last day of the allotted grace." Tullidge, *Women of Mormondom*, 144.

25. Karl Wilhelm, Baron von Humboldt (1767–1835), and his
younger brother Friedrich Heinrich Alexander, also Baron von
Humboldt (1769–1859), were prominent scholars of the early nineteenth century. While Friedrich Alexander, a scientist, was more univer-
sally known, Karl Wilhelm, a philosopher, statesman, and patron of the
arts, is the more likely of the two to be the subject of the work widely

enough circulated for Eliza Snow to have a print hanging in her Lion House room in the 1870s.

26. Tullidge, *Women of Mormondom,* 145–47. To a sympathetic relative in Ohio Eliza Snow wrote from Far West: "The Gov. of Illinois says our people may come there,—they have been going all winter, and move very fast—A man just arrived from Ill. who said he counted 220 wagons between this and the Mississippi. It has been judg'd, there were eight thousand of our people in the County but the season has been a storm-less one—the most favorable for moving that we could wish, . . . " Eliza R. Snow to [Isaac] Streator, 22 February 1839, photocopy, LDS Church Archives.

27. Oliver and Leonora Snow, with Samuel and Lucius, lived variously in Monmouth, LaHarpe, Nauvoo, and Walnut Grove, Illinois, though the dates of the various moves are not specified. At the time of the move from Missouri, Lorenzo was on a mission in the eastern states, and Amanda and her family, who never espoused Mormonism, were still in Ohio. They would join her parents in Walnut Grove in 1845. I appreciate the assistance of Carol Baker Wahl in identifying "Cambell neighborhood," near Monmouth, Warren County, as the 1839 residence of the Snow parents and younger boys.

28. At least seventeen poems by Eliza R. Snow (often Eliza *K.* Snow in the newspaper) appear in the Quincy *Whig* between May 1839 and March 1841. They bear such titles as "An Appeal to the Citizens of the United States," "An Address to the Citizens of Quincy," and "To a Revolutionary Father" and contain sentiments of gratitude for the kindness with which the Saints were initially received in Illinois.

29. "It was very annoying to our feelings to hear bitter aspersions against those whom we knew to be the best people on earth." Tullidge, *Women of Mormondom,* 149.

30. " . . . with those whose minds, freed from the fetters of sectarian creeds, and man-made theology, launch forth in the divine path of investigation into the glorious fields of celestial knowledge and intelligence." Tullidge, *Women of Mormondom,* 150.

31. There is ample evidence that the town was not so ill-fated before the 1839 arrival of the Mormons as Eliza Snow suggests. Commerce, one understands from an 1835 letter of Catherine Wells, was a thriving agricultural community, "improving very fast, strangers coming continually." Catherine's mother was at that time teaching a school of "from 20 to 30 scholars," though there was no educational opportunity for seventeen-year-old Catherine. "There is a Sunday School at our house every Sunday," Catherine's brother Daniel continues, "and a bible class; also preaching every third Sunday. . . . The country is setling quite fast so that the neighbors are plenty. . . . [Commerce] improves and will I am

confident become quite a place." Catherine and Daniel Wells to Pamela Wells, 7 July 1835, Abigail Wells Papers, LDS Church Archives. The letters, edited by Maureen Ursenbach Beecher, are published in *Journal of Mormon History* 2 (1975): 35–52.

32. "It seemed for awhile as though all the traditions, prejudices, and superstitions of my ancestry, for many generations, accumulated before me in one immense mass; but God, who had kept silence for centuries, was speaking; I knew it, and had covenanted in the waters of baptism to live by every word of his, and my heart was still firmly set to do his bidding." Tullidge, *Women of Mormondom*, 295.

33. "Redeeming women from the curse" refers to a view that women, Eve's daughters, cursed for her disobedience in Eden, through their individual obedience to righteous priesthood leaders, notably husbands worthy of living the principle of plurality of wives, may be relieved of the yoke of thralldom to men, and receive, with them, "the power of reigning, and the right to reign." Eliza Snow's assessment of women's place and possibilities is summarized in Jill Mulvay Derr, "Eliza Snow and the Woman Question," *BYU Studies* 16 (Winter 1976): 250–64. The notion that plural marriage would also redeem the world from corruption references the argument that the system would eliminate the demand for prostitutes. See also Tullidge, *Women of Mormondom*, 296.

34. "When I entered into it [celestial marriage], my knowledge of what it was designed to accomplish was very limited; had I then understood what I now understand, I think I should have hailed its introduction with joy, in consideration of the great good to be accomplished. As it was, I received it because I knew that God required it." Tullidge, *Women of Mormondom*, 296.

35. Tullidge reads: "He was even combining with minions of the great adversary of truth in the State of Missouri, who were vigilant in stirring up their colleagues in Illinois, to bring about the terrible crisis." Tullidge, *Women of Mormondom*, 297.

36. Eliza Snow could not herself "keep silence." Her elegy "The Assassination of Generals Joseph and Hyrum Smith" was published in the Nauvoo *Times and Seasons* dated 1 July 1844, just three days after the martyrdom.

37. Nancy Rigdon, widowed mother of Sidney Rigdon, had joined the LDS Church in Pittsburgh when her son, in company with Luke Johnson, neighbor of the Snows, went there on a mission ca. 1836. There is no mention in Joseph Smith's *History of the Church* of her funeral in conjunction with the October conference.

38. There is no corroborating evidence of the nine births Eliza Snow "was informed" had taken place at Sugar Creek camp. On the contrary, there are accounts of women who were in the last months of pregnancy

being left behind in Nauvoo until they had given birth. Careful reading of this paragraph of Eliza Snow's account reveals that she herself witnessed none of the births of which she writes but rather relates hearsay with the apparent purpose of soliciting the sympathy of her readers. Patty Sessions, the midwife and diarist, arrived at Sugar Creek on 14 February but had been on the west bank for three days previous and thus available, had she been needed, to the Saints in the camp. She notes no births on the date referred to here. On 10 February, the day before she left Nauvoo, Patty had delivered two women there. The next live delivery she records is 25 February, followed within the week by two miscarriages. That is not to suggest that since Patty delivered no babies the night before Eliza Snow arrived, no babies were born. It would be unreasonable, however, to assume that one of Nauvoo's busiest midwives would have had no call to attend even one of nine births. Carol Lynn Pearson, " 'Nine Children Were Born': A Historical Problem from the Sugar Creek Episode," *BYU Studies* 21 (Fall 1981): 441–44, argues that Eliza had merged two accounts in her later hearing of the "nine babies" story: that in fact Jane Johnston claimed in her notarized account to have delivered nine babies in one night in a tent during the exodus of the "Poor Camp" that left Nauvoo in September of that same year. Richard Bennett, in an interview with the editor, 13 April 1983, with a roll of the Poor Camp as witness, refutes that testimony as well, saying that no births are recorded during that entire journey. Despite apparent discrepancies in Eliza Snow's account, her point is taken to serve her purpose: to demonstrate to a non-Mormon audience the difficulties encountered by women, especially pregnant women, on the wilderness trail.

39. "One of my brother's wives had one of the old-fashioned foot-stoves, which proved very useful. She frequently brought it to me, filled with live coals from one of those mammoth fires—a kindness which I remember with gratitude." Tullidge, *Women of Mormondom*, 309.

40. Eliza Snow had already written and published her account of "the tragic scene at Carthage"; that "the mob" threatened her life lest she write more is unsubstantiated. Her "Assassination of Generals Joseph Smith and Hyrum Smith" is an impassioned outcry against the injustice, mourning that "Never, since the Son of God was slain,/ Has blood so noble, flowed from human vein/ As that which now on God for vengeance calls." In Eliza R. Snow, *Poems, Religious, Historical, and Political*, 2 vols. (Liverpool: F. D. Richards, 1856; Salt Lake City: LDS Printing and Publishing Establishment, 1877), 1:142–45.

41. "Let Us Go" first appeared in the *Millennial Star* 10 (1 June 1848): 176; also Snow, *Poems* 1:146–47.

42. " . . . which does much in lengthening out our flour. Occasionally our jobbers take bacon in payment, but what I have seen of that article is

so rancid that nothing short of prospective starvation would tempt me to eat it." Tullidge, *Women of Mormondom*, 313–14.

43. Rosetta Pettibone Snow died 12 October 1846, ten days before her sixty-ninth birthday. Oliver Snow, three years her senior, had died a year earlier.

44. "Even now while I write, the remembrance of those sacredly romantic and vivifying scenes calls them up afresh, and arouses a feeling of response that language is inadequate to express." Tullidge, *Women of Mormondom*, 334.

45. This poem reprinted below under the date of 26 August 1847 is here refined. See also Snow, *Poems* 1:181–82.

46. Tullidge, *Women of Mormondom*, 335. The sad fact of deaths along the trail is poignant indeed, though not as all-pervasive as might be assumed from Eliza Snow's account. In the Third Hundred, in which Eliza Snow traveled, the only deaths noted are those of Captain Jedediah Grant's wife, Caroline Vandyke, and her baby Margaret. Perrigrine Sessions, captain of the First Fifty of Daniel Spencer's company, reported on his arrival that same fall, for instance, "all well and not a death had been while on the journey in my company of our hundred Souls yet several children were born on the way." Perrigrine Sessions, Reminiscence, photocopy of manuscript, LDS Church Archives.

47. It is unclear how old Sally was when she was brought by Charles Decker to his sister Clara Young, but she did stay with the Young family for several years thereafter. Eventually becoming a wife of the Ute chief Kanosh, she continued a life of as much gentility as she could manage in their log cabin in Millard County. She died 9 December 1878 and was buried there with full temple honors by the Mormons. See Nevada Driggs, "Sally Kanosh," *Deseret News*, 21 January 1839; see also George Crane, "Funeral of a Lamanite," *Deseret News*, 9 December 1878. Courtesy of Jeffery Johnson.

48. There are affirmations that a unique "flag of the Kingdom" was flown from Ensign Peak on 26 July 1847, but it appears certain from this statement of Eliza Snow, confirmed by Erastus Snow, that the flag that the Saints raised "on this Temple block" in 1847 was indeed the American Stars and Stripes. See D. Michael Quinn, "The Flag of the Kingdom," *BYU Studies* 14 (Autumn 1973): 105–14.

49. The "House of the Lord" here is not, as might be thought, the temple, but rather its forerunner, the Endowment House. It stood on the northwest corner of Temple Square and was in service to the Saints for endowments from 1855 to 1884 and for marriages to 1889. Records and other diaries confirm Eliza Snow's account of her long service in the offices of that house, both as portrayer in one of the roles of the dramatization and as de facto matron of the women's section.

50. Joseph L. Heywood, a Mormon, was the marshal of whom Eliza Snow approved. Appointees of the federal government—Perry E. Brochus and Lemuel G. Brandebury, justices of the Utah court; Broughton D. Harris, secretary; and Henry R. Day, an Indian sub-agent—arrived in Utah in June 1851. When they returned to Washington less than a year later, "to report the impossibility of carrying out their assigned responsibilities in Utah because of the domination of the Mormon Church over the lives and minds of the people," Harris withheld the $24,000 congressional appropriation for territorial government expenses. Eugene E. Campbell, "Governmental Beginnings," in *Utah's History,* ed. Richard Poll, et al., (Provo, Utah: Brigham Young University Press, 1978), 160–63.

51. Published singly as a broadsheet, and in Snow, *Poems* 1:217–18.

52. See Jill Mulvay Derr, Janath Russell Cannon, and Maureen Ursenbach Beecher, *Women of Covenant: The Story of Relief Society* (Salt Lake City: Deseret Book, 1992), 23–63, for the most recent published account of the Nauvoo Relief Society. For a more thorough study, see "Record of the Female Relief Society of Nauvoo," microfilm of manuscript, LDS Church Archives. Most of these minutes were kept by Eliza Snow as secretary.

53. A thorough account of the 1850s Relief Society movement is Richard L. Jensen, "Forgotten Relief Societies, 1844–57," *Dialogue: A Journal of Mormon Thought* 16 (Spring 1983): 105–25. Eliza Snow is not quite accurate in crediting the Fifteenth Ward with organizing the first Utah Relief Society. The movement can be traced to a grassroots organization headed by a Matilda Dudley to provide clothing for Indian women and children, which preceded by four months Brigham Young's 1854 encouragement for the ward-by-ward reorganization of the Relief Society. In the "Move South" occasioned by the Utah War, 1857–58, many of the societies were discontinued, not to take up the work again until 1866 when, under mandate from Brigham Young, Eliza Snow "headed up" the work as general officer. With vision and authority, she established the Relief Society as a churchwide body which survived her and still functions throughout Mormondom.

54. Again, a misremembered date. Contemporary records show the founding of the Retrenchment Association as occurring in the late fall of 1869. Susa Young Gates, in her 1923 *History of the Young Ladies Mutual Improvement Association* (Salt Lake City: Deseret News, 1911), 6, 7, 13, describes "Aunt Eliza's" role in that beginning as follows: "President Young asked Sister Eliza R. Snow to notify those of his family not living in the Lion House to assemble there on the evening of November 28, 1869, as he had important matters to present to them for action. No doubt this matter had been thoroughly discussed by him and Sister Snow, for later events showed that there was an understanding between them." And

later: "In some places these associations were organized by local authority, but generally speaking they were effected under the direct supervision of Sister Eliza R. Snow."

55. See Carol C. Madsen and Susan S. Oman, *Sisters and Little Saints*
(Salt Lake City,: Deseret Book, 1979), the best and most complete history of the Primary extant. Although Aurelia Rogers is credited with the
founding of the organization, its promulgation throughout the LDS
Church is assuredly the doing of Eliza Snow and her associates.

56. The only reference to a Palestine trip in the diaries now extant is
a note on 12 April 1846. There Eliza Snow shares with Elizabeth Ann
Whitney the thought "that my mind had been impress'd with the idea of
going to the land of Palestine & I felt to prophesy that we should yet
walk . . . upon the mountains of Judah. . . . " Joseph Smith by then had
been dead nearly two years. The "Journal" to which she here has reference could well be one now lost, or perhaps the discrepancies between
her remembered prophecy and the recorded one struck her as inconse-
quential. In 1872, at the time of Eliza's departure for the Holy Land,
Elizabeth Whitney was still living, and so could well be the "friend" who
brought it to her later recollection, as recorded here.

57. The purpose of the expedition, as expressed in Brigham Young's
letter to George E. Smith on 15 October 1872, was to "closely observe
what openings now exist [in Europe and Asia Minor] for the introduction of the gospel" and "to consecrate and dedicate [the land of
Palestine] to the Lord . . . preparatory to the return of the Jews." Quoted
in Tullidge, *Women of Mormondom*, 482.

"The dedicatory purpose of the tour was completed in the following
manner. Eliza Snow reporting: Sunday morning, March 2nd, [1873],
President Smith made arrangements with out [our] dragoman, and had
a tent, table, seats, and carpet taken up on the Mount of Olives, to which
all the brethren of the company and myself repaired on horseback. After
dismounting on the summit, and committing our animals to the care of
servants, we visited the Church of Ascension, a small cathedral, said to
stand on the spot from which Jesus ascended. By this time the tent was
prepared, which we entered, and after an opening prayer by Brother
Carrington, we united in the order of the holy priesthood, President
Smith leading in humble, fervent supplications, dedicating the land of
Palestine for the gathering of the Jews and the rebuilding of Jerusalem,
and returned heartfelt thanks and gratitude to God for the fullness of the
gospel and the blessings bestowed on the Latter-day Saints. Other
brethren led in turn, and we had a very interesting season; to me it
seemed the crowning point of the whole tour, realizing as I did that we
were worshipping on the summit of the sacred mount, once the frequent
resort of the Prince of Life." Tullidge, *Women of Mormondom*, 484.

58. *Correspondence of Palestine Tourists* (Salt Lake City: Deseret News, 1875) mainly reprints letters that the various members had sent to Utah newspapers for publication. Eliza Snow's marked reference in this description to "instructive, truthful descriptive reading matter" reflects the current official injunctions against "novel reading" and the encouragement of didactic and expository "home literature."

59. It is likely that the "casualty" which befell the manuscript for the second volume was not wholly accidental. By the time Orson Pratt, then in Liverpool and responsible for church publications there, received the manuscript in August 1857, the first volume, published the year previous, was selling so poorly that of the 3,000 books printed, 2,400 were still on the publisher's shelves. Orson Pratt to Brigham Young, 7 August 1857, Brigham Young Papers, LDS Church Archives; courtesy David Whittaker.

Four years later, George Q. Cannon, who relieved Pratt, reported that in the previous three years, "out of 2590 volumes of Sister E. R. Snow's Poems, 19 have been sold." When the second volume actually saw print, in Utah in 1877, it was received much more warmly as "the literary effusions of Zion's favorite poetess." A notice in the *Women's Exponent* 6 (1 January 1878): 117, hoped that "the Relief Societies will aid in bringing it to the attention of the people of Utah." No such support was available to the first volume.

60. Eliza Snow published during her lifetime the following volumes: *Poems, Religious, Historical, and Political*, 2 volumes (Liverpool: F. D. Richards, 1856; and Salt Lake City: LDS Printing and Publishing Establishment, 1877); *Correspondence of Palestine Tourists . . .* (Salt Lake City: Deseret News Steam Printing Establishment, 1875); *Hymns and Songs: Selected . . . for the Primary Associations of the Children of Zion* (Salt Lake City: Juvenile Instructor Office, 1880); *Bible Questions and Answers for Children* (Salt Lake City: Juvenile Instructor Office, 1881, 1883); *Primary Speaker: Recitations for the Primary Associations . . .*, 2 vols. (Salt Lake City: Deseret News, 1882–1891); *Biography and Family Record of Lorenzo Snow* (Salt Lake City: Deseret News Company, 1884; reprinted by Zions Book Store, 1975). One other small volume, *The Story of Jesus* (Salt Lake City: Bookcraft, 1945), was published posthumously.

61. The beginning of sericulture in Utah antedates the founding of the association by two decades. In 1875, when women took on the assignment, Zina D. H. Young was named president, and the encouragement of the industry and distribution of the materials was handled through the network of women in the Senior Retrenchment and Relief Society. For a more complete history, see Chris Rigby Arrington, "The Finest of Fabrics: Mormon Women and the Silk Industry in Early Utah," *Utah Historical Quarterly* 46 (Fall 1978): 376–96.

62. For the later history of the Deseret Hospital, see Ralph T. Richards, *Of Medicine, Hospitals, and Doctors* (Salt Lake City: University of Utah Press,

1953); see also Christine Croft Waters, "Pioneering Physicians in Utah, 1847–1900" (Master's thesis, University of Utah, 1976).

63. The addition of "Smith" to Eliza Snow's name followed the death of Brigham Young, her second husband, whose name she never took. The addition acknowledged publicly her first and more significant marriage to Joseph Smith at a time when such testimony was an act of faith and a proclamation of a truth others might dispute.

64. Eliza Snow wrote her poetic testimony, "Saturday Evening Thoughts," into her Nauvoo journal, 16 November 1842, in response to a letter apparently shown her privately by its author before its publication as "Letter of Orson Spencer," dated 17 November 1842 and published in *Times and Seasons* 4 (2 January 1843): 49. Spencer was replying in print to a query about the Mormons from one W—— C—— of Boston. His ten-page polemic is a defense of Mormonism and the Mormons; Snow's four-page poem is an impassioned explanation of her personal experience. It had been published three times before she included it in her *Poems* 1:3–6, and it obviously remained a favorite, for she copied it by hand into her "Sketch" for Mr. Bancroft.

65. Six years before her death, Eliza Snow first published the five-stanza "Bury Me Quietly" in the *Woman's Exponent* 10 (1 December 1881): 97. She was then seventy-seven. Her sentiments as expressed in the poem seem not to have governed those in charge of her funeral on 7 December 1887, for the Assembly Hall was lavishly draped—in white, after her published expression opposing black mourning crepe—and a long cortege followed the corpse to its burial in the Brigham Young cemetery. The verses of "Bury Me Quietly . . . " were set to music and sung by a choir at the funeral.

Chapter 2

Introduction

1. For a full discussion of what evidence exists for the historicity of the tale, see Maureen Ursenbach Beecher, Linda King Newell, and Valeen Tippetts Avery, "Emma and Eliza and the Stairs," *BYU Studies* 22 (Winter 1982): 87–96.

2. Inez Thomas, interview, 12 October 1983.

3. *BYU Studies* 15 (Summer 1975): 391–416.

4. Eliza R. Snow, "Sketch of My Life," holograph, Bancroft Library, Berkeley, California.

5. *Woman's Exponent* 15 (1 August 1886): 37.

The Nauvoo Journal and Notebook

1. Joseph Smith, *History of the Church of Jesus Christ of Latter-day Saints,* 7 vols., ed. B. H. Roberts (Salt Lake City: Deseret Book, 1932–51). The petition, signed by "about one thousand ladies," affirmed Joseph Smith's in-

tegrity and pled for his safety and their own and their families' protection. The women's petition was one of three delivered by Nauvoo citizens to counter the assertions adverse to the Prophet Joseph Smith being circulated at the time by John C. Bennett. In her later "Sketch of My Life," Eliza Snow wrote the following postscript to the event: "But alas! soon after our return, we learned that at the time of our visit, and while making protestations of friendship, the wily Governor was secretly conniving with the basest of men to destroy our leaders."

2. Joseph Smith, *History of the Church* 5:86–87. During this period Joseph Smith was arrested, released, and in hiding to avoid arrest on charges of complicity in the attempted murder of Governor Boggs in Missouri. The validity of the arrest hinged on the legality of the various writs with which Smith and Porter Rockwell were served.

3. Later published as "Invocation" in *Times and Seasons* 3 (1 September 1842): 910, and in *Frontier Guardian*, 16 May 1842; and as "Supplication," in Eliza R. Snow, *Poems, Religious, Historical, and Political*, 2 vols. (Liverpool: F. D. Richards, 1856; Salt Lake City: LDS Printing and Publishing Establishment, 1877), 1:135–36, and *LDS Hymns* (Liverpool: F. D. Richards, 1856), 394, and subsequent hymnals published to the year 1871.

4. Joseph Smith, *History of the Church* 5:95. Powers "ascertained that there was no writ issued in Iowa" for Joseph Smith.

5. Joseph Smith, *History of the Church* 5:121–23; also F. Mark McKiernan, *The Voice of One Crying in the Wilderness: Sidney Rigdon, Religious Reformer* (Lawrence, Kan.: Coronado Press, 1971), 121. The contemporary account is from *Times and Seasons*, 15 September 1842. The Eliza mentioned is Rigdon's daughter.

6. George M. Hinkle, Mormon commander of the Caldwell County militia at Far West, became the LDS counterpart of the Benedict Arnold archetype: Mormons had thought him sympathetic to their cause when he persuaded their leaders to parley with General Lucas after the issuance of the Boggs "extermination order," but instead of negotiating with them, Lucas imprisoned the Mormon men. Hinkle was later excommunicated. David E. Miller and Della Miller, *Nauvoo: The City of Joseph* (Santa Barbara and Salt Lake City: Peregrine Smith, 1974), 16–17; see also Joseph Smith, *History of the Church* 3:188–89.

7. Joseph Smith, *History of the Church* 5:110–11 reprints one such letter that reports on conditions, advises Joseph Smith to absent himself for a season, and promises Law's continued aid and loyalty.

8. This is presumably Erastus Derby, who had proven himself loyal and useful to the Prophet Joseph Smith "in administering to [his] necessities" during the traumatic August days of his hiding out. Joseph Smith, *History of the Church* 5:90–95, 106–7.

9. Another account of the attempted arrest is recorded in Joseph Smith, *History of the Church* 5:145–46.

10. Eliza's older sister Leonora, married but long since separated from her husband Enoch Virgil Leavitt, was living in Morley Settlement, sometimes called Yelrome, a Mormon community headed by Isaac Morley just north of Lima, Illinois, some thirty miles south of Nauvoo.

11. Joseph Smith, *History of the Church* 5:161.

12. Jonathan H. Holmes, a Nauvoo widower, married Elvira Annie Cowles in Nauvoo on 1 December 1842, as reported in the Nauvoo *Wasp,* 10 December 1842. The poem, with minor changes, was reprinted there under the announcement. That Eliza wrote her poem in September suggests the closeness of her friendship with Elvira, since she knew of the wedding so far in advance.

13. This is Amanda Percy Snow, Eliza's sister. She and her husband, Eli McConoughey, would eventually travel west from Ohio, where they had married before the Snows left for Missouri; but they did not do this until 1847, after Eliza had left Nauvoo for Utah.

14. This poem remained unpublished, both in Nauvoo and later in Utah. See discussion in Maureen Ursenbach Beecher, *Eliza and Her Sisters* (Salt Lake City: Aspen Books, 1991), 68–70.

15. Joseph Smith, *History of the Church* 5:167. Similar rewards were also posted for Orrin Porter Rockwell's arrest.

16. The poem is published, its first stanza deleted, as "To He Knows Who," in Snow, *Poems* 1:133. Other references to Emma's illness suggest a siege of the ague, or chills and fever, that lasted much of the fall and into the winter. See also Joseph Smith, *History of the Church* 5:166 ff.; and Joseph Smith Diary, 26 December 1842, in the hand of Willard Richards, holograph, LDS Church Archives. The place of Joseph Smith's "seclusion" is identified in *History of the Church* 5:169–72 as "Father Taylors," but its location is not specified.

17. *Times and Seasons* 4 (15 December 1842): 48; *Wasp,* 21 January 1843; *Millennial Star* 4 (May 1843): 4; and Snow, *Poems* 1:51–53.

18. "True Happiness," *Deseret News,* 16 April 1853; *Millennial Star* 15 (10 September 1853): 608; Snow, *Poems* 1:47–48.

19. *Times and Seasons* 4 (2 January 1843): 64; *Millennial Star* 4 (July 1843): 43; *The Mormon,* 23 June 1855; Snow, *Poems* 1:3–6.

20. Eliza Snow conducted the school not in what is now known as the Masonic or Cultural Hall, the building on Main Street built in 1844, but in the large second-story room in Joseph Smith's red-brick store on Water Street. It carried the Masonic identification because the Nauvoo lodge met there. Elizabeth Ann Whitney recorded that she and Bishop Newel K. Whitney lived in the store at about this time.

21. A class roll from the school reveals an attendance of thirty-seven students, ranging in age from four to seventeen years. Included are four children of Joseph and Emma Smith, five of Newel K. and Elizabeth Ann Whitney, two Partridges, three Knights, and one child of William Marks,

as well as several others with names less prominent in Nauvoo leading circles. Nauvoo School Records, LDS Church Archives.

22. Eliza gives no reason for the move out of the Smith household, although some conjecture may be valid. It is believed that the Smiths were still living in the "homestead," a four-room wooden house. Conditions there would have been crowded at best—there were four Smith children, as well as Joseph and Emma, and possibly Joseph's mother. An altercation with Emma Smith might also have precipitated Eliza's removal. More than once Eliza would find a haven with her friends Jonathan and Elvira Holmes.

23. Published in Snow, *Poems* 1:74–76 under the title "As I Believe," and dedicated to President Heber C. Kimball.

24. Lorenzo D. Barnes died in Bradford, England, 20 December 1841. Joseph Smith, *History of the Church* 5:319–20. The "transatlantic bard" is John Lyon, a Scottish convert who was also a poet.

25. The elders had traveled to Lima, or Yelrome, to speak to the Saints there about the Nauvoo House. Emma Smith also accompanied them. Joseph Smith Diary, 13–15 May 1843.

26. Judge Higbee's death of "choleramorbus" (dysentery) is noted in Joseph Smith's Diary under the date of 8 June 1843; a funeral address delivered by Joseph Smith is summarized under the date of 13 August 1843.

27. The speech is summarized in Joseph Smith, *History of the Church* 5:423–27, drawing on original accounts in Joseph Smith Diary, 11 June 1843, and Wilford Woodruff Diary, 11 June 1843, holograph, LDS Church Archives.

28. The visit here mentioned resulted in Joseph's capture at Dixon, Lee County, Illinois. The more complete account is in Joseph Smith, *History of the Church* 5:431–75, 481–88, and Joseph Smith Diary, 13–30 June 1843. The *History of the Church* narrative has Joseph and Emma Smith leaving Nauvoo on a Thursday rather than the Tuesday of this mention, but the Joseph Smith Diary concurs with Eliza's dating.

29. The poem, obviously more personal than most of Eliza Snow's verses, had been published in the *Wasp*, 10 September 1842, some nine months earlier. Although it might have been Joseph Smith himself who originally submitted it for publication—his brother William was then editor—it is likely that it was John Taylor, William's successor, who returned the poem to Eliza. In the *Wasp* the verse is signed merely "E."

30. Most likely their destination was actually Joseph Smith's farm, where Cornelius Lott was foreman. That this is Eliza's wedding anniversary, and that her companions were all involved in plural marriage by this date, suggests the chief topic of discussion.

31. Published in *Nauvoo Neighbor,* 26 July 1843; *Times and Seasons* 4 (1 August 1843): 288; Snow, *Poems* 1:127–29; *Deseret News* 6 (21 January

1857): 363; and Charles O'Brien Kennedy, *A Treasury of American Ballads: Gay, Naughty, and Classic* (New York: The McBride Company, 1954), 59–61. In preparing the *History of the Church* for publication, editor B. H. Roberts weeded the poem out of the original collection of documents, explaining his reasons to President Joseph F. Smith in a memo: the story had already been "twice told" in the narrative, he explained, and the Snow "poem" (quotation marks are his) added nothing "either of beauty or fact" to the account. "The verses are the merest dogerel," he complained, and concluded, "All that jingles is not poetry." Undated memo, B. H. Roberts Papers, LDS Church Archives.

32. A nineteenth-century definition of "unavailable" suggests meanings akin to "unavailing, useless, futile."

33. Only one poem by a "Mr. Huelett" appears in any Nauvoo papers. "Lines" by S. Huelet was published almost simultaneously in both the *Nauvoo Neighbor*, 11 December 1844, and *Times and Seasons*, 15 December 1844. The borrowing from Eliza's earlier published poem on the same subject, the martyrdom of Joseph and Hyrum Smith, suggests that the poet considered himself disciple to the more experienced poetess.

34. The poems that Eliza wrote and published in Ohio during her pre-Mormon years, 1826–1835, carried such pseudonyms as Narcissa, Pocahontas, Cornelia, Minerva, and Tullia.

35. Lorenzo had apparently visited Eliza and Leonora at Morley Settlement, from which place he likely continued to Nauvoo to report his mission/visit to Ohio.

36. Published as "To Mr. and Mrs. S., on the Death of a Child," Snow, *Poems* 1:81–82.

37. Published as "The Lord is My Trust," Snow, *Poems* 1:147–49.

38. Joseph Smith, *History of the Church* 6:47–49. Joseph Smith had proposed the release of Sidney Rigdon as his counselor, but the vote of the conference reinstated Rigdon.

39. Eliza Partridge had been sealed as a plural wife to Joseph Smith some seven months earlier. Date courtesy of Todd Compton.

40. Published as "Celestial Glory," *Times and Season* 4 (1 November 1843): 383; *Nauvoo Neighbor*, 20 December 1843; *LDS Hymns* (Liverpool, 1851), 138–39, and in subsequent hymnals; Snow, *Poems* 1:139–41.

41. The blessing as it appears in Isaac Morley's book is signed "A. Leonora Leavitt, scribe." That Eliza changed the signature in copying the blessing into her own book confirms her knowledge that her sister's sealing to Isaac Morley, later confirmed in the Nauvoo Temple, had in fact already taken place. Nauvoo Temple Records, 14 January 1846, LDS Church Archives.

42. Mary Ann Frost and Parley P. Pratt's son Nathan died 12 December 1843. He was five years old.

43. Sylvia Porter Sessions and Windsor P. Lyon had lost their second child, Philofreen[e], 2 January 1844. She was nearly three years old. Sylvia had been sealed to Joseph Smith for eternity since February 1842.

44. Eliza's accommodation with the Markhams must have proved satisfactory, for she apparently stayed there for the remainder of her time in Nauvoo. When she left in the February 1846 exodus, she traveled with the Markhams, and she stayed with them till they reached Winter Quarters. Her next extant diary accounts begin with the February move from Nauvoo, heading west.

Chapter 3

Introduction

1. Nauvoo *Times and Seasons*, 1 July 1844. Despite the date on the masthead, the paper was not published until several days later, explained the editor, in order to include a more complete account of the events. The poem appeared also in the *Nauvoo Neighbor*, 17 July 1844.

2. *Times and Seasons*, 15 December 1845; also Eliza R. Snow, *Poems, Religious, Historical, and Political*, 2 vols. (Liverpool: F. D. Richards, 1856; Salt Lake City: LDS Printing and Publishing Establishment, 1877), 1:1.

3. The far-reaching reality of family kingdoms in the Mormon mind is developed in Rex Eugene Cooper, *Promises Made to the Fathers: Mormon Covenant Organization* (Salt Lake City: University of Utah, 1990), 164–84.

4. Zina D. H. Young, as quoted in Edward Tullidge, *Women of Mormondom* (New York: Tullidge & Crandall, 1877), 327.

5. 1 Cor. 12:8–10.

6. Scott S. Dunn, "Glossolalia: Evolution of a Religious Phenomenon in Mormonism," paper presented to the Mormon History Association, May 1982. Typescript in the editor's files.

7. Minutes, Female Relief Society of Nauvoo, holograph, LDS Church Archives.

The Trail Diary, February 1846–May 1847

1. Sarah Melissa Granger Kimball, though nearly fifteen years younger than Eliza R. Snow, was probably her closest friend at this time. The two exchanged letters frequently, as noted in the diary. For a thorough and sensitive account see Jill Mulvay Derr, *Sarah M. Kimball* (Salt Lake City, Utah: Signature Books, 1982). The Hiram and Sarah Kimball home, recently restored, is located in the old Commerce section of Nauvoo, close to the waterfront, a wagon ride of less than a half-hour from where Eliza had lived at the Markhams' house. The plan to stay at the Kimballs' home may have been predicated on the need to arrive early in the morning in order to be among the first in the line at the

ferry. Of a similar occasion Louisa Barnes Pratt later wrote: "The boat was not ready to cross that night so I went to Sister Hiram Kimball's and slept." Louisa Barnes Pratt, Diary, in Kate B. Carter, ed., *Heart Throbs of the West,* 12 vols. (Salt Lake City: Daughters of Utah Pioneers, 1939–1951), 8:236.

2. Lorenzo Snow, Eliza's brother, had arrived four days earlier. His account in "Diary and Account Books, 1841–1846," photocopy of holograph, LDS Church Archives, describes the circumstances in which the Markhams and Eliza found him: "After we arived at Sougar Creek we sewed a couple of waggon covers together that were not in use and made them into a very comfortable tent. . . . There were seven in family: so with Two wagons and a Tent we made ourselves as comfortable as the circumstances of the wether would admit." The groups would all stay at the Sugar Creek camp, six miles from the Iowa shore of the Mississippi, until 28 February, though because of Markham's duties as one of the Pioneers, his family, with Eliza Snow, moved from the east to the west end of the camp on 17 February.

3. This Sister Kimball is not Sarah, who did not come west with the Saints that year, but probably Vilate, first wife of Heber C. Kimball.

4. First published in the *Millennial Star* 10 (15 May 1848): 160, after which Eliza Snow included it, under the title "Camp of Israel," in her *Poems, Religious, Historical, and Political,* 2 vols. (Liverpool: F. D. Richards, 1856; Salt Lake City: LDS Printing and Publishing Establishment, 1877), 1:161–62.

5. Bishop George Miller, an enthusiastic church leader, had been the first to bring his family across the river and would be often in the vanguard through the trek to Council Bluffs. His later defection to the Strangites in Michigan, and still later to lead his group to Texas, would hardly have been anticipated at this point.

6. Captain William Pitt's Brass Band, a group of British converts, accompanied the Saints west, not only helping build morale for their co-religionists but generating good will among the residents of towns along the way. See also 4 March 1849 entry; also *William Clayton's Journal* (Salt Lake City: Deseret News, 1921; reprint, New York: Arno Press, 1973), 3, 6–7.

7. First published in the *Millennial Star* 10 (1 July 1848): 208, and then in Snow, *Poems* 1:163–64. The phrase "all is well," which appears frequently in Eliza Snow's trail poems, echoes William Clayton's "All is Well," composed a year earlier and sung since under the title "Come, Come, Ye Saints."

8. The later organization of the Saints into companies of Hundreds, Fifties, and Tens was not yet in place at this first stage of the journey, but this loose division into Fifties under various church leaders—Heber C. Kimball, in this case—lasted until the 27 March reorganization.

9. David Kimball was born to Sarah Ann Whitney Kimball and Heber C. Kimball.

10. Richardson's Point, as identified in the entry for the same date in the Journal History of the Church of Jesus Christ of Latter-day Saints, microfilm, LDS Church Archives. The Journal History is a scrapbook compilation of church-related materials compiled and indexed by staff of the LDS Church Historian's Office.

11. Latter-day Saint scriptures since 1833 have inveighed against the use of coffee, but in the early years the injunction was taken as advice more than as commandment. See Leonard J. Arrington, "Have the Saints Always Given as Much Emphasis to the Word of Wisdom as They Do Today?" *Ensign* 7 (April 1977): 32–33. "Jonny cake," or journey cake, is cornmeal bread; "fried jole" may be either fish heads or the jowls of pork or beef.

12. Caroline Curtis Spencer (mistakenly called Caroline), wife of Orson Spencer, left six children motherless, among them Aurelia Spencer Rogers, who in 1878 would found the LDS Primary Association. See Aurelia S. Rogers, *Life Sketches of Orson Spencer and Others and History of Primary Work* ([Salt Lake City]: Geo. Q. Cannon & Sons, 1898.)

13. The reference is to schisms forming among Latter-day Saints disaffected by Brigham Young's assumption of the leadership of the church. James Strang and William Smith each claimed leadership by direct appointment of Joseph Smith prior to his death. John E. Page was disfellowshipped in Nauvoo 9 February 1846 for following Strang. See D. Michael Quinn, "The Mormon Succession Crisis of 1844," *BYU Studies* 16 (Winter 1976): 194–95, 203–4. Luke Johnson, whose family Eliza Snow had known in Ohio, had left the church; the note here represents his rebaptism at the hand of his brother-in-law Orson Hyde, another Ohio convert.

14. The Tanner baby, named James Monroe, was fifteen months old when he died. His father ascribed his death to "inflammation of the brain." Sidney Tanner to James Conlee, 13 April 1847, LDS Church Archives. Louisa Conlee Tanner, the boy's mother, would give birth at Council Point three months later, then die of fever the following September in Winter Quarters. The baby would survive her by only two months.

15. Edwin Little, a son of James and Sarah Young Little, was buried beside the Tanner baby, "on the divide between Fox and Chequest rivers." Journal History, 18 March 1846.

16. "Record of the Organisation of the Camp of Israel, . . . Shariton [Chariton] Ford, . . . March 27 . . . and 31st 1856," holograph, LDS Church Archives, courtesy Dean C. Jessee, estimates the number of wagons in the whole camp as "about three hundred."

17. First published in the *Millennial Star* 10 (1 June 1848): 176; next in Snow, *Poems* 1:146–47, under the title "Let Us Go."

18. In his *Autobiography* (1873; Salt Lake City: Deseret Book, 1972), 341–42, Parley P. Pratt acknowledges Brigham Young's reprimand for the "spirit of dissension and of insubordination manifested in our movements" but defends his actions by asserting the purity of his motives. After the council, "all things being harmonized and put in order, the camps moved on," he concludes. This was one of several such incidents in which the chain of command was misunderstood as the companies moved westward.

19. A "Law of Adoption" practiced in Nauvoo permitted members of the church to become affiliate members of the families of various general authorities. The suggestion here is that Sarah Melissa Granger Kimball, with no relationship by blood and only distant relationship by marriage, had been adopted into the family of Heber C. and Vilate Kimball. It is possible that, in the same way, Eliza Snow would claim Heber Kimball as her adopted father on 7 April 1846; that relationship, however, could as easily reference her membership in the company of which he was titular "father." See Gordon Irving, "The Law of Adoption: One Phase of the Development of the Mormon Concept of Salvation, 1830–1900," *BYU Studies* 14 (Spring 1974): 291–314.

20. Published in Snow, *Poems* 1:165.

21. Noah Webster's 1828 dictionary designates "shurk" as a New England pronunciation for "shark," meaning to live by shifts, or to pick up hastily, or in small amounts.

22. In 1872–73 Eliza Snow did visit the Holy Land as part of the mission headed by George A. Smith, sent to dedicate the land for the return of the Jews. Elizabeth Ann Whitney, then aged seventy-two, did not go with them. See Eliza R. Snow Smith, *Correspondence of the Palestine Tourists* (Salt Lake City: Deseret News Steam Printing Establishment, 1875).

23. Gimp is silk twist or edging, a small luxury that Eliza Snow, with her sewing ability, could well use.

24. Lorenzo Snow's account of this section of the journey is poignant. Traveling with his pregnant wife Harriet and plural wife Sarah Ann, who was sick with ague, through roads made impossibly muddy by preceding wagons, he was further delayed by a broken axeltree on his wagon. That repaired—it took a few days—the wagon became mired and Lorenzo had to carry everything out of the wagon to lighten its load. Finally reaching camp, they found their company, Parley P. Pratt's fifty, rested and ready to move on. Lorenzo Snow, Diary, 1841–46.

25. The expression "divide" with him or her meant to give half of one's provision to a neighbor who had none.

26. Eliza Snow had five days earlier persuaded her brother Lorenzo to transfer from Parley P. Pratt's company to Heber C. Kimball's in which she and the Markhams traveled. The letter is from their sister Abigail Leonora Leavitt.

27. Webster's 1828 dictionary identifies "shorts" as the bran and coarse part of meal, presumably either corn or wheat.

28. Brigham Young's own 22 April experience with snakebite adds detail to Eliza Snow's comment: "My horse was bitten on the nose by rattlesnake. I cut the snake into pieces and applied them to the wound. They drew out the poison, leaving the horse uninjured." *Manuscript History of Brigham Young, 1846–47*, ed. Elden J. Watson (Salt Lake City: Privately published, 1971), 139.

29. Published under the title "To Mrs. V. Kimball" in Snow, *Poems* 1:177. That Vilate Kimball had difficulty adjusting to plural marriage is apparent from many sources, notably her daughter Helen Mar's later statement that "I had, in hours of temptation, when seeing the trials of my mother, felt to rebel. I hated polygamy in my heart." Helen Mar Whitney, in Augusta Joyce Crocheron, ed., *Representative Women of Deseret* (Salt Lake City: J. C. Graham, 1884), 112.

30. This was Garden Grove, the first more or less permanent way-station, settled and secured as a benefit for Saints to follow. Lorenzo, who arrived a week later, wrote of that place: "At garden Grove we all fell to work and fenced a large field and built a number of houses." Lorenzo Snow, Personal History and Letter Book, 1839 ff., microfilm, LDS Church Archives. *Manuscript History of Brigham Young*, 149, under date 2 May 1846, reports "Some brethren making rails, others building a bridge," and later, quoting Brigham Young on page 151, " . . . let every man go to work under his respective Captain taking up his cross (his ax, maul and wedge), and let us fence the fields and plant them, and when this is accomplished we will go on to the next location."

31. The tea need not be black tea but rather may be one of many herbal preparations commonly used as medicines. See entry under 13 May, where Eliza speaks of using cranesbill tea.

32. Eliza Snow's letter "for Walnut Grove" would be to her parents and other family still living in Illinois.

33. The Sister Green is Fidelia, the wife of Thomas Green. She died near Miller's Mills, in Mercer County, Missouri. Journal History, 7 May 1846.

34. Sir Walter Scott's "Rokeby," published ca. 1813, could well have been part of Eliza Snow's personal library. It is evident from her poems, as well as from such direct statements as this, that she was well read in English literature.

35. "Spotted cranesbill" is a North American wood plant with rose-

purple flowers, sometimes called wild geranium or alum root. That it
has astringent qualities suggests that Eliza Snow's malaise was a form of
dysentery.

36. Theodore Turley, 1800–1872, see Appendix 2, Register of Names.

37. Peter Haws (Hawes) had been appointed captain of the second
company of fifty in the council on Shoal Creek, 27 March 1846. His responsibilities included the band as part of his company and duties as
"contractor." Juanita Brooks, ed., *On The Mormon Frontier: The Diary of
Hosea Stout, 1844–1861*, 2 vols. (Salt Lake City: University of Utah Press,
1964), 1:89, 136, 144.

38. The allusion to Peleg is to a patriarch named in Genesis 10:25.
The name is an interpretation of *division,* "for in his days was the earth
divided." Eliza Snow's reading of scripture, characteristic of Mormon in-
terpretations generally, was quite literal. See also her "Address to Earth,"
Snow, *Poems* 1:153.

39. Eventually the strain of living with the Markhams led to open altercation. The "one" here alluded to is likely Warren, who, in a November incident, seems to be most offensive to Eliza Snow's sensibilities.

40. As the name suggests, the guide board, inscribed with date and
mileage, would indicate the location of advance parties and provide assurance to following companies.

41. Mt. Pisgah is the name given this camp, the longest lasting of the
layover settlements between Nauvoo and Council Bluffs. Parley P. Pratt
named the spot after the biblical point from which Moses viewed the
Promised Land. See Pratt, *Autobiography,* 342; also Stanley B. Kimball,
"The Iowa Trek of 1846," *Ensign* 2 (June 1972): 36–45.

42. Arriving ahead of the main camp at Mt. Pisgah, Lorenzo found
himself assigned with "the whole camp" to "go to work ploughing, fencing and putting up houses. [He] assisted in choping and putting up
brother Pratts House logs and about that time was taken sick with the
fever." Eliza's account of his sickness is enlarged by his own later record:
"I never had such a severe fit of sickness before. . . . My friends and family had given up most all hopes of my recovery. Father Huntington, the
President of the Place called on his Congregation to pray for me. He
also with Gen. Rich and some others clothed themselves in the garments
of the Priesthood and prayed for my recovery." See Eliza Snow trail diary
entries for 15 April ff; also note 43. Lorenzo notes the arrival of his wife
Charlotte's brothers Porter and Calvin Squires, ages 19 and 16, "part of
my family from Nauvoo," who assist the family group, which now com-
bines with Isaac Morley's family, presumably because of Leonora's connection with them. Porter and Calvin (Eliza Snow later refers to him as
John) remained with the family until 1856, when Lorenzo Snow returned to Utah from his mission to Italy. Besides his wives Charlotte and

Adaline, and Adaline's three boys by her first marriage—Hyrum, age 12, Orville, age 10, and Jacob Hendrickson, age 7—are Lorenzo Snow's other wives, Sarah Ann and Harriet. Eliza R. Smith [Snow], *Biography and Family Record of Lorenzo Snow* (Salt Lake City: Deseret News Company, 1884), 92–95. The "aloy" that Eliza Snow sent her brother would be one of the aloe medications, either bitter aloes or aloe vera, used, among others things, as a purgative.

43. Patty Sessions, having been eighteen days at Mt. Pisgah, which she termed a "prety place," regretted that she must leave "many good Brethren Sisters Horn. E. Snow. Zina. Emily. and many more" to move forward. Most of all she regretted that her daughter, Sylvia Lyon, and husband would not accompany the Saints west. Patty Sessions, Diary, 2 June 1846, microfilm of holograph and typescript, LDS Church Archives.

44. Elizabeth Ann Whitney's "songs of Zion," sung in the gift of tongues, were a particularly valued manifestation of the Spirit among the women. Years later, Wilford Woodruff would record his impression of her singing, under date 3 February 1854: "During the evening Sisters Whitney and Eliza Snow called upon us and spent the evening. Before they left Sister Whitney sung in tongues in the pure language which Adam & Eve made use of in the garden of Eden. . . . It was as near heavenly music as anything I ever heard." Wilford Woodruff, Diary, 3 February 1854, microfilm of holograph, LDS Church Archives.

45. Stephen Markham's arrival in Nauvoo is noted in Journal History, 12 June 1845, in which case his journey took seven days. The main body had crossed the same distance in four months. "Adaline aunt G & H" are Eliza's maternal aunt Percy Amanda Pettibone Goddard, her daughter Adaline, and Adaline's ten-year-old son Hiram Hendrickson by her first husband. Adaline had since married Lorenzo in the Nauvoo Temple.

46. Although it was not unusual for woman to administer to the sick in the manner of a priesthood administration, with anointing and sealing "in the name of Jesus Christ," it seems more likely in this case that Eliza Snow uses the term to mean simply providing nursing care to her brother. See Linda King Newell, "Gifts of the Spirit: Women's Share," in Maureen Ursenbach Beecher and Lavina Fielding Anderson, eds., *Sisters in Spirit: Mormon Women in Historical and Cultural Perspective* (Champaign: University of Illinois Press, 1987), 117–21.

47. "Father" William Huntington and "General" Charles C. Rich were presiding officers of the Mt. Pisgah camp, an office to which Lorenzo would soon be called. The prayer "in the order of the Priesthood" refers to a ritual prayer circle, in which the endowed men, and sometimes women, wearing their temple clothing, would perform the sacred offices as a prelude to fervent prayer. A similar incident at about this time is recorded in Hosea Stout's journal. Brooks, *On The Mormon Frontier* 1:170.

48. Wilford Woodruff entered his account of the administration under date 18 June as: "I went to see Lorenzo Snow. He had been quite sick and is still. I Administered to him And He seemed better." Scott G. Kenney, ed., *Wilford Woodruff's Journal 1833–1898, Typescript,* 9 vols. (Midvale, Utah: Signature Books, 1983), 3:53.

49. The early Saints considered a renewal of the baptismal covenants to be an act of dedication which would result in restoration to health or other blessings.

50. Former Missouri governor Lilburn Boggs was indeed ahead of the Saints, en route to California. Two days after Eliza Snow wrote this account, he, with a company of emigrants, among them the Donners and the Reeds, was at Fort Bernard on the North Platte. However, he had no troops, nor did he in any way represent the threat to the Mormons that he did in 1838 when he had issued the infamous "extermination order." Bernard Devoto, *The Year of Decision, 1846* (Boston: Little, Brown and Company, 1943) follows Boggs with the others in their crossing to northern California. There Boggs finally settled, across the bay from the first party of Mormons to arrive in the West, those who accompanied Samuel Brannan on the *Brooklyn.* That the word received and recorded by Eliza Snow adds troops and malevolent intent to Boggs's journey suggests the continuing fear felt by the Saints, even in the wilderness, that their enemies were still in pursuit.

51. Braiding straw for hats was a frequent employment of women, and Eliza Snow was particularly adept at the craft. Later in Utah she would teach and encourage the women to make such hats for sale as well as domestic use.

52. In retrospect Eliza Snow will have more to say about the enlisting of the Mormon Battalion; for now, her dating and description are accurate: on 26 June 1846 Captain James Allen arrived at the camp at Mt. Pisgah with three dragoons and orders to invite the Mormons to send 500 men across the southern United States to ensure U.S. claims in California. John F. Yurtinus, "A Ram in the Thicket: The Mormon Battalion in the Mexican War" (Ph.D. diss., Brigham Young University, 1975), the most complete study of the Mormon Battalion to date, is soon to be published by the University of Illinois Press. Hosea Stout expressed the general response of the Saints thus: "We are all very indignant at this requisition and only looked on it as a plot laid to bring trouble on us as a people." Brooks, *On the Mormon Frontier* 1:172.

53. Eliza Snow is still essentially in Mt. Pisgah. "Since I left Mt. Pisgah" refers to her 27 June move, with Lorenzo, to Isaac Morley's settlement about a mile upstream from the main camp.

54. Still in connection with the enlisting of the Mormon Battalion, Eliza Snow notes the presence in camp of James C. Little. What she and

her contemporaries failed to recognize in their mistrust of the U.S. government and their resentment of the calling up of the Mormon militia was that Little's business in Washington had been to plead for just such an option—for Mormon troops to cross the continent at government expense.

55. "Hat-timber" is the straw that women would braid and then sew into hats for use or for sale.

56. Just how "growling, grumbling, devilish [and] sickly" a time it was is better described in Lorenzo's account. "The latter part of July and August witnessed a general and almost universal scene of sickness throughout Pisgah. Well persons [could] not be found to take care of the sick. . . . A great number of deaths occured and it was often difficult to get their bodies decently interd. . . . Scarcely a family escaped sickness and very few where death did not make an inroad. A general spirit of lamentation and sorrow prevaded Pisgah." Lorenzo Snow, Personal History, 51.

57. The medicines "nervine" and "anti-bilious pills" are self-explanatory. "Pepper" as a medication, according to a nineteenth-century household manual, was "chiefly employed to excite languid digestion and correct flatulence [excessive gas in the digestive tract]." *Book of the Household,* 2 vols. (London: London Printing and Publishing Company, n.d.), 2:312.

58. "Nationa Botana" is Eliza Snow's phonetic rendering of "Nishna-botna," a river near Pottawattomie Indian settlements.

59. *Manuscript History of Brigham Young,* 350, 351, records Young's visit at Daniel Spencer's camp and his return to Council Point under date 26 August 1846. He did not stay there but rode on that afternoon to Cold Spring, where he stayed "with Sister Gheen, bro. Erastus Snow, and others."

60. *Manuscript History of Brigham Young,* 353, records a "council" of Young and the High Council of the church "with the principal Omaha chiefs and about eighty of the Omahas," the purpose being for the Mormons to obtain permission to remain the winter on Omaha land.

61. The "Camp" to which Eliza Snow refers is Cutler's Park, the first headquarter camp across the Missouri River. The Winter Quarters settlement to which she here refers was established a few weeks later, three miles east of Cutler's Park, closer to the river. The Markhams, with Eliza Snow, made the move on 22 September 1846. The temporary town was organized into two main areas, each presided over by Brigham Young or Heber C. Kimball, hence "Heber's Division." Organization into wards under the direction of bishops would follow.

62. John Smith, patriarch to the church and later to become president of the Salt Lake Stake, was an uncle of Joseph Smith. The poem was first published in *Millennial Star* 10 (1 September 1848): 272.

63. The tensions in the Markham family proved stronger than the marriage and their family ties. After their settlement in Utah, and after Stephen Markham took a second wife (though not necessarily because of that), his wife Hannah left him and with her sons moved to California, where Hannah married again. Telephone interview with Agnes Markham Wood, Salem, Utah, 25 January 1983. See also Mervin LeRoy Gifford, "Stephen Markham: Man of Valour" (Master's thesis, Brigham Young University, 1975).

64. "Hester" is alternatively spelled "Esther" in church records. That Eliza Snow would plead with the widow Gheen to "mourn not" suggests more about Eliza's own sense of a brighter hereafter than her understanding of the very human need to grieve. The poem was never published. William Gheen had died 15 July 1845 in Nauvoo. Eliza Snow never finished the intended verses to Amanda and Anna (Ann Alice) Gheen; however, she did later write an acrostic to Anna, under date 4 March 1847. Presumably on presentation of that poem to Anna, Eliza learned the correct spelling of the family name. That Ann Alice and Amanda were by this time plural wives of Heber C. Kimball may have added a dimension to their friendship with Eliza Snow.

65. Brooks, *On the Mormon Frontier* 1:216–17 gives a fairly complete account of the altercation between Omaha and Iowa Indians. Eliza Snow's details seem accurate: Chief Big Head, camped with a few others north of the town, had been attacked and others injured, including a woman whose arm was amputated the next day by Dr. Cannon, a surgeon in the camp. By the time Stout, in his office as police chief, had finished his investigation, Brigham Young had moved the frightened and injured Indians into lodgings near his home.

66. These unpublished verses are also found in manuscript in the diary of Eliza Maria Partridge Lyman, 29 December 1847, holograph, LDS Church Archives. The baby, Don Carlos, born in a wagon 14 July 1846, was not quite five months old. His mother Eliza had suffered from child-bed fever, and the baby had been "very poor" from birth. "I cannot see what ails him," Eliza Lyman wrote on 6 December 1846. Six days later she recorded: "The Baby is dead and I mourn his loss. We have done the best we knew how for him, but nothing has done any good. . . . he is gone and I cannot recall him, so I must prepare to meet him in another and I hope a happier world than this. I still have friends who are dear to me, if I had not I should wish to bid this world farewell." Partridge Lyman, Diary, 9 August, 6, 12 December 1846. Eliza Lyman would give birth again 20 August 1848, on the Platt River near Fort Laramie. This time the child, Platte DeAlton, survived.

67. Again Hosea Stout provides details: Word first arrived on 12 December that an Omaha hunting party had been attacked by Sioux.

Fifty or sixty were then presumed dead. Now, interpreter Logan Fontanell reported that there were seventy-three dead men, women and children. Brooks, *On the Mormon Frontier* 1:217, 219.

68. Rosetta Pettibone Snow died in Walnut Grove 12 October 1846. Lorenzo Snow's response to the news, which, according to his personal history, he did not receive until 2 February 1847, is much like his sister's: "She was good, and virtuous benevolent and charitable to all, true and faithful in the New and Everlasting Covenant Therefore I am comforted in the thought that her spirit rests in the presence of her Great Father." The verses on the occasion of the deaths of Oliver and Rosetta Snow were never published during Eliza's lifetime, though they were later printed in the *Improvement Era,* July 1943, 435.

69. The occasion was a celebration of Hannah Gheen's birthday. Since Patty Sessions attended the party on 24 December and the dinner at the Woolleys' on Christmas day, from which "Eliza R. Snow came home with me," and then entertained at her own place the next day, it seems the friendship between the two women was deepening. Sessions, Diary, 24–26 December 1846. There are frequent references to Eliza Snow throughout Sessions's diary until early 1848. Perhaps by 25 November, but certainly by this date, the women in Eliza's circle were holding blessing meetings marked by the manifestation of spiritual gifts of tongues, interpretation of tongues, prophecy, testimony, healing, and casting out evil spirits. "Interesting" is Eliza Snow's euphemism for events of such significance.

70. Edwin Woolley kept a store at Winter Quarters. Leonard J. Arrington, *From Quaker to Latter-day Saint: Bishop Edwin D. Woolley* (Salt Lake City, Utah: Deseret Book Company, 1976), 117; see also Eliza R. Snow entry for 28 October 1846, when Woolley shipped goods from St. Louis.

71. Louisa Beaman was a plural wife of Brigham Young. Eliza would stay with the new mother and child for a week following his blessing on 15 January. The baby, named Moroni, lived only a few months. Sessions, Diary, 8 January 1847; Dean C. Jessee, "Brigham Young's Family: The Wilderness Years," *BYU Studies* 19 (Summer 1979): 488.

72. Ezra Woodruff, Phebe and Wilford Woodruff's baby, had died the day before, two days following his premature birth. Their sixteen-month-old son Joseph had died of pneumonia two months earlier on 12 November. Sarah Emma, the Woodruffs' first child, had died in July 1840 at age two. "List of the Deaths and Burials in the Camp of Israel, Cutler's Park, after September 1846," manuscript, LDS Church Archives; Thomas G. Alexander, *Things in Heaven and Earth: The Life and Times of Wilford Woodruff, a Mormon Prophet* (Salt Lake City: Signature Books, 1991), 99, 135, 136.

73. Elizabeth Ann Whitney would give birth to a boy two weeks later, on 6 February 1847.

74. There is irony in the term "mansion" for a Winter Quarters home, though the buildings erected by Brigham Young for his family seem to have been better than average in quality. *Manuscript History of Brigham Young*, 445, describes one of his houses as of November 1846: it had "doors, but no windows, and chimneys built of brick obtained from the ruins of an old fort at council Bluffs, but no floor."

75. The gift of tongues, experienced by the women during Eliza Snow's long visit with others of Brigham Young's wives, had been practiced in the church almost since its inception. That Eliza goes into such defense of its use here suggests that the practice had not been widespread and that some of the sisters were not convinced of its appropriateness.

76. The extended family of Brigham Young included by now not only several of his wives and their children but also several adopted sons and their families. The importance of this invitation to Eliza Snow, more than the content of the gathering and other similar ones, was the reinforcement it provided her of her belonging to the family.

77. Vilate Young, seventeen-year-old daughter of Brigham Young by his first wife, Miriam Works, married twenty-three-year-old Charles Decker, son by a previous marriage of Lorenzo Young's wife Harriet Decker Young. Eliza Snow published the epithalamion in her *Poems* 1:180 under the title "To Charles and Vilate."

78. The Silver Greys, the "senior citizens" of the community, were hosted by Patriarch John Smith in the Council House, a plain building, thirty-six feet square, with a good floor for dancing. After sermons from Smith and Brigham Young, encouraging dancing as appropriate recreation, the floor was cleared of benches for dancing. It was indeed "an interesting and novel sight," states the *Manuscript History of Brigham Young*, 521, "to behold the old men and women, some nearly an hundred years old, dancing like ancient Israel." That but a few of the guests were actually very old is suggested by the invitation extended to Eliza Snow, then just turned forty-three.

79. Hosea Stout details the severity of the snowstorm: "This morning the snow had blown and drifted untill it was near half way to the top of my door & I could scarcely get it opened. . . . It was decidedly one of the deepest snows that has fallen for some years & is still blowing and drifting all day, the air still full as in a snow storm." Brooks, *On the Mormon Frontier* 1:237.

80. The acrostic, an ancient verse form, had by the nineteenth century become a popular device in which the subject of the poem is addressed by the initial letter of each line spelling out her name. The irony here is that Eliza Snow here and earlier in the diary misspells the name

of her friend: "Miss Anna Geen" is Ann Alice Gheen, one of the daughters of Hester and William Gheen. The error must have been noted, since in subsequent entries Eliza Snow uses correct spelling. Never published during Eliza Snow's lifetime, the poem appeared in *Improvement Era,* August 1943, 467.

81. Eliza Snow has more than friendship bonds with twenty-six-year-old Margarett Peirce Whitesides: the young widow had since become a wife of Brigham Young, and thus was Eliza Snow's sister wife. Later this same spring, Margarett's sister Mary, also a wife of Young, died, and Eliza took her place in the family group to travel with them to the Salt Lake Valley. Until now unpublished, the poem appears in manuscript in Autograph Book, Margarett Peirce Whitesides Young, Gaylen Snow Collection, LDS Church Archives.

82. As implied in the title "Mother," or "Mother in Israel," Phoebe Ogden Chase and Patty Bartlett Sessions shared honor among the Saints for their nurturing capacity and their spiritual maturity. Both were "ordained" by Joseph Smith in Nauvoo with the right and power to administer to the sick among the Saints. Patty Sessions's diary contains a copy of the poem under date 15 March 1847. Patty's entry reads: "E. R. Snow came here last night she has done me up a cap and written me some poetry which she composed which I shall write here." She makes no mention of the poem's also being dedicated to Phoebe Chase. The poem remained unpublished until it appeared in *Woman's Exponent* 14 (1 June 1885): 2.

83. Mary Wickersham Woolley, wife of Edwin D. Woolley, stayed in Winter Quarters with her merchant husband until 1848, when they emigrated to Utah. Arrington, *Edwin D. Woolley,* 178–80. The poem is unpublished.

84. Like her younger sister Margarett, Mary Peirce had been sealed to Brigham Young, and so was sister wife to Eliza Snow. The account in *Manuscript History of Brigham Young,* 538, reads: "I buried my wife, Mary H. Pierce, aged twenty-five years, daughter of Robert and Hannah Pierce. She died of consumption." Eliza Snow later crossed the plains in the Peirces' wagon in the place made vacant by Mary's death. The poem is unpublished.

85. The "Journeying Song" that Eliza Snow here says she wrote "some weeks ago" is dated in her *Poems* 1:170–73 as 10 April 1847, the date on which Brigham Young left Winter Quarters with the Pioneer Company heading west. Manuscript copies of the song, which is sung to the tune of "Auld Lang Syne," are found in the Brigham Morris Young file and in the William Clayton Papers, LDS Church Archives. It was published twice in *Millennial Star,* 9 (1 November 1847): 366, and 12 (15 September 1850): 288; and also in *Frontier Guardian,* 29 May 1850.

86. Luke Johnson had lived in Hiram, Ohio, the neighboring town to Mantua, during Eliza Snow's young years. Their families had known each other then and continued in contact during the rest of their lives, Nancy Marinda Hyde, Luke's sister, being a close associate of Eliza Snow in Utah. Luke Johnson, once an apostle, had left the LDS Church for a time but the year previous to this had been readmitted into fellowship. He and his wife Susan Arminda [Armelda] Poteet [Pottet] were with the Saints in their westward move when Susan died. Their six children, ages twelve to infant, were cared for by Johnson's second wife, America Clark, whose first child, born the next year at Council Bluffs, was named for the first wife. The prediction or prophecy in stanza five of the poem, that "many more will be clinging to your side," saw partial fulfillment in the subsequent births of seven more children to Luke and America Johnson. The poem has remained unpublished until now.

87. Lyman Wight and George Miller were excommunicated or disfellowshipped from the church on 3 December 1848 and 20 October 1848, respectively. The conference sustained Brigham Young as "President of the Church," though the ultimate affirmation of his role did not come until October when, on his return from the Salt Lake Valley, he was named president with counselors.

88. The Pioneer Company, those men who would go ahead, formed a camp not far west of Winter Quarters, from which the leaders returned often over the next few days. They would leave from there to the Elk Horn River, where an embarkation camp was established for them and subsequent pioneers. The poem is published under the same title in Snow, *Poems* 1:173–74. That Eliza Snow uses the first person "we" in the final phrase, "we welcome them here," suggests that, since Stephen Markham had gone with the Pioneers, and she had as yet no other recourse, she at this point anticipated waiting until Brigham Young returned to be taken to the Great Basin.

89. In her address to Elizabeth Ann Whitney, Eliza Snow enunciates the doctrine that Jesus Christ is elder brother to humankind, while Elohim, God, is the Heavenly Father. "Mother Whitney," as Elizabeth Ann was called, four years Eliza Snow's senior, had borne eleven children, the last just two months earlier, 6 February 1847, in Winter Quarters. This poem is unpublished elsewhere.

90. There may well have been a literary kinship between Eliza Snow and Lyman O. Littlefield, since he was also a published writer. His "Sights from the Lone Tree," *Times and Seasons* 3 (1 November 1841): 586–87, is a lyrical prose idyll of Mormon Nauvoo that Eliza Snow might well have applauded. He served his mission in Great Britain. This poem appears in Snow, *Poems* 1:178–79 under title "To Elder L. on his Departure for Europe."

91. The 1841 hymnal printed in Liverpool published this as verses to be sung in LDS services. It was first published in *Millennial Star* 9 (15 December 1847): 379, eight months after Eliza Snow wrote it; also in Snow, *Poems* 1:83–84.

92. Webster's dictionary of 1828 defines "clog" as "Anything put on an animal to hinder motion"; or, by extension, an encumbrance, a hindrance, or an impediment.

93. While Franklin D. Richards was serving a mission in England, his wife Jane Snyder Richards, newly arrived at Cutler's Park, gave birth to a son, Isaac, who died just hours after his birth on 23 July 1846. She brought the tiny corpse to Mt. Pisgah where it was buried. Their daughter Wealthy, not yet three, died two months later, 14 September 1846, and was buried in the Mormon cemetery at Winter Quarters. I appreciate Bettie Mckenzie's calling the first burial to my attention. The poem's last couplet refers to the Mormon belief that the highest heaven will be on this earth, after the earth has been cleansed and glorified.

94. The "Markee" (marquee) was a temporary tent erected to serve as a meetingplace. The *Manuscript History of Brigham Young*, 107, refers to a council being held at "a Markee furnished for the occasion" at the camp on the Chariton; the one at Winter Quarters would soon be replaced by the Council House. "The Girls" referred generally to subsequent wives in plural marriages.

95. John and Leonora Taylor's fourth child, named for her mother and grandmother, was born in Nauvoo 1 June 1842 and died 10 September 1843. Poem published in *Millennial Star* 10 (15 April 1848): 128; also in manuscript in the John Taylor Collection, LDS Church Archives.

96. Sylvia Sessions Lyons had, with her baby and her younger brother David, been visiting her parents, Patty and David Sessions, since 21 April. Her return to her husband was painful to Patty, who wrote: "[David] and Sylvia left me on the bank of the Missouri River started for home. . . . May the Lord speed them in all safety home. May they keep the spirit of gathering with all their connections, gather up their substances and come to us again as soon as the Lord will." Sessions, Diary, 21 April, 5 and 9 May, 1847. Patty Sessions copied Eliza Snow's poem into her own journal, dividing it into quatrains and replacing "you" with "thee." It has not been published.

Chapter 4

Introduction

1. From Eliza R. Snow, "Woman," in Eliza R. Snow, *Poems, Religious, Historical, and Political*, 2 vols. (Liverpool: F. D. Richards, 1856; Salt Lake City: LDS Printing and Publishing Establishment, 1877), 2:178.

The Trail Diary, June 1847–September 1849

1. Eliza spells the name of her benefactors this way consistently until 20 June, when she seems to have learned the family's preference and changes the spelling to "Peirce."

2. Patty Sessions's account for the day reads: ". . . E R Snow is here   the girls wash some for her   she lines Carlos ha   we had a feast in the afternoon at sister Millers there we blessed and got blessed   I blessed Sister Christeen by laying my hands upon her head the Lord spoke through me to her great and marvelous things—at the close I thought I must ask a blessing at sister Kimbal's hands but it came to me that I must first bless her and show Herbers girls [wives of Heber C. Kimball] the order that duty called them to perform to get many blessings from her upon them   I obeyed   layed my hands upon her head although it was a great cross and the power of God came upon me   I spoke great and marvelous things to her she was filed   [filled] to the overflowing   She arose and blesed the Lord and caled down a blessing on us and all that pertained to her sister   Hess fell on her knees and claimed a blesing at my hands   I then blesed her   sister Chase claimed a blessing of sister Kimbal   she blesed her with me she spoke great things to her the power of God was poured out upon us. E R Snow was there with many others   thank the Lord." Patty Sessions, Diary, 1 June 1847, holograph, LDS Church Archives.

Patty Sessions's hesitation to bless Vilate Kimball suggests her sense of ecclesiastical authority: Vilate was the first wife of Apostle Heber C. Kimball, and participant with him in the Holy Order, those who had received endowments during Joseph Smith's lifetime. That she felt no such hesitancy to bless Christeen Golden, another of Kimball's wives, suggests that Patty felt social and ecclesiastical parity with her.

3. "The Horn" is the Elk Horn River, two days beyond Winter Quarters, where the Saints gathered and formed their companies for the trek. Described as a "wide and rambunctious stream," the river could not generally be forded in the spring, but wagons could be floated across, or, in this case, ferried on rafts. Merrill J. Mattes, *The Great Platte River Road* (N.p.: Nebraska State Historical Society, 1969), 130–31.

4. Lucina [1819–1904] and Mary [1829–1865] Sessions were sisters, daughters of Cyril and Sally Tiffany Call, and sister wives of Patty Sessions's son Peregrine Sessions.

5. That the women, and presumably John Smith, Joseph Smith's uncle and soon to be president of the first stake in Utah, met in a circle on the prairie suggests but does not confirm that they participated in the ritual of the "prayer circle" that would have required the wearing of temple robes and the following of established litanies. More likely the format of the meeting was the familiar one of blessing and "exercising

the gifts." Patty Sessions's terse comment reads: "We have a good meeting today. I presided. It was on the prarie. We have good times every time [we] meet." Sessions, Diary, 15 June 1847. See D. Michael Quinn, "Latter-day Saint Prayer Circles," *BYU Studies* 19 (Fall 1978): 79–105.

6. Mary Ann Angell Young, second wife of Brigham Young, remained in Winter Quarters awaiting her husband's return in the fall. She would emigrate to the Valley in 1848. This poem is unpublished elsewhere.

7. Edward Hunter, captain of the Second Hundred, traveled with his wife Mary Ann in the Second Fifty.

8. Accounts of the incident vary, but Eliza Snow's record agrees in the main with that of the *Manuscript History of Brigham Young, 1846–47*, ed. Elden J. Watson (Salt Lake City: Privately published, 1971), 560: "While Jacob Weatherby, A. B. Lambson and two women were returning from Elk Horn river to Winter Quarters the Indians shot Bro. Weatherby, who died soon after."

9. Daniel Spencer's account of the altercation is more detailed: " . . . after travelig about 2 Miles from camp B[rother] J. Taylor calld to me as he was passing & said he wished me to go a pice with him which I accordg did   he said that he had ordered B Jedadiah Grant to Stop his team and let him pass but he refused to Stop Saying that he was undr B J[oseph] Young   he then said to B Young you must Stop or I shall prefer a Charg against you for disobednc of Council   according they did not stop Taylr thn preferd a charg against B Grant and young and a councile ws held & the subject discd at Lenght by Sevrel men particulaly by B Pratt wh gav a full history of the Mod of govermnt of the Church & Camp to the entire satisfaction of the Camp accordg to ther Vote & young and Grant askd pardon of B Taylor for ther insult to him and all was amicably settled." Daniel Spencer, Diary, photocopy of typescript, LDS Church Archives. See also Parley P. Pratt, *Autobiography of Parley P. Pratt* (1873; Salt Lake City: Deseret Book Company, 1972), 358–60.

10. This is the Loup Fork of the Platte River, a particularly difficult crossing because of sand bars, quicksand, and a rapid current. Hal Knight and Stanley B. Kimball, *111 Days to Zion* (Salt Lake City: Deseret News, 1978), 43.

11. Buffalo chips, dried buffalo dung, were used as fuel.

12. Four days earlier Eliza had visited Esther Shaffer Ewing, wife of Samuel Ewing and mother of nine children, who had been sick for some time. The Ewings and the Job Sidwell family, from Little Britain, Pennsylvania, were traveling together in Hazen Kimball's Ten.

13. Mary Adeline Beaman Noble, having lost six of her seven children, here bore her eighth child, whom she named Eliza Theodocia, presumably after Eliza Snow and her husband Joseph's mother. This

child lived to maturity in Utah. Joseph Bates and Mary Noble had with them Edward Alvah Noble, their own six-year-old son, Anna Noble, and George Noble, Joseph's three-year-old son by his second wife, Sarah Alley, who had died in Winter Quarters.

14. Simon Baker had with him eight of his nine children by his first wife, Mercy Young, who had died in Montrose in 1845. His second wife, Charlotte Leavitt, who would have had the care of his four children under ten, was just twelve years older than her oldest stepson, Jarvis, who was seventeen. Presumably he and his brothers Amenzo, who was fifteen, and Albert, thirteen, are the ones accused of insolent behavior at the dance. George Leavitt, Charlotte's twenty-year-old half-brother, the boys' uncle by marriage, may also have been involved.

15. This could be forty-seven-year-old Susan Ann Ashley, in Joseph Noble's First Ten; or it could also be Susan Hammond Ashby, Captain Noble's third wife.

16. One of many forms of alkali, the white salaratus powder distilled from the groundwater in the arid soil of this region was bicarbonate of soda and could be used as a leavening agent in baking.

17. These would be stragglers from the sick detachments of the Mormon Battalion who had wintered in Pueblo, Colorado. Most of the men and their families had joined the Pioneer Company and were already in the Salt Lake Valley. See John Yurtinus, "A Ram in the Thicket: The Mormon Battalion in the Mexican War," 2 vols. (Ph.D. diss., Brigham Young University, 15), 1:250–315.

18. The advance guard of the Pioneers under Orson Pratt had traversed a particularly treacherous stretch, so the leader had backtracked to search out a better way. Finding none, he ordered his entire company to "labor on the road" to make it passable for subsequent travelers. Hogsback Summit is the present name of the spot.

19. See Carter E. Grant, "Robbed by Wolves," *Relief Society Magazine* 15 (July 1928): 355–63 for Susan Noble Grant's remembered account of the death of Caroline and her infant, Margaret.

20. Patty Sessions had been in the Valley eight days when Eliza Snow's group arrived, almost the last of the year's migration. "In the evening visited Sister E. R. Snow," Patty recorded. "She has just come in. This week has been a good time to me. My heart has been glad in seeing my sisters." Sessions, Diary, 2 October 1847.

21. In September, Brigham Young had written his nineteen-year-old wife Clara from South Pass telling her, "I wish you to live at home of sister Eliza Snow," as though the space she inhabited had been allocated to the older woman. When Eliza arrived, Clara reported to their husband Brigham that "Sister Eliza Snow is coming in the morning to live with me I was much pleased with the arrangement." Brigham Young to "My dear

Clary" [Clarissa Decker Young], 8 September 1847, and Clara Young to Brigham Young, 9 [4?] October 1847, holograph, LDS Church Archives.

22. Clara D. Young later remembered the log house being part of the east side wall of the fort. The house she moved into was about fourteen by sixteen feet, built of logs hauled from the "canons." She speaks of a roof of poles and dirt, and puncheon floors—logs split in half, laid with the rounded sides underneath. A fireplace with clay hearth and adobe chimney was in one corner. A bed in which the two women slept was built into another corner, poles attached to holes in the walls forming the outer sides, with bed-cords tightly wound around pegs in the poles. Clara's chest served them for a table. Clara Decker Young, "A Woman's Experience with the Pioneer Band," *Utah Historical Quarterly* 14 (1946): 174–76. An entry dated "Sept. 4th, 1847" and copied into the journal on 24 October obviously belongs here.

23. This would be Joseph and Lorena Thorn, who, with their two children, had arrived 25 September. Hosea Stout records their arrival in Winter Quarters on 18 December 1847, with the comment that Joseph "was dissatisfied." Juanita Brooks, *On the Mormon Frontier: The Diary of Hosea Stout, 1844–1861*, 2 vols. (Salt Lake City: University of Utah Press, 1964), 1:291.

24. Unpublished elsewhere, the poem is addressed to the senior wife of Brigham Young, Mary Ann Angell Young, who, with others of the Young family, waited in Winter Quarters until the following summer for Brigham Young to bring them west.

25. These lines to Elizabeth Ann Whitney, Vilate Kimball, Sarah Ann Whitney Kimball, and Helen Mar Kimball Whitney have been until now unpublished.

26. The poem is unpublished elsewhere.

27. One of the pleasant rituals of arrival—Brigham Young did it two days after he got to the Valley—was to visit the Warm Springs, about a mile northwest of the first fort, to bathe. The waters, Willard Richards suggested, had "valuable medicinal properties." *Manuscript History of Brigham Young,* 566.

28. Miles M. Goodyear had established holdings on the Weber River at present-day Ogden, north of Salt Lake City.

29. Against instructions, a group of four men with their families had left the fort and were headed north towards Goodyear's place on the Weber, apparently planning to settle there. William Weeks, Hazen Kimball, —— Babcock, and William Gardner, "somewhat embittered" by the too-rigid discipline of the Council, resisted return, but were finally brought in (see entry for 30 October) by a persistent marshal, identified here as Higgins but elsewhere as John VanCott. Journal History, 14, 24 October and 3 November 1847, LDS Church Archives.

30. Here Eliza realizes she has been misspelling her friend's name, but again later forgets.

31. Margarett Peirce Whitesides Young entered this Eliza Snow poem in her own reminiscences; see holograph, LDS Church Archives. It remained unpublished until it was included in the *Improvement Era* (February 1944): 113.

32. A "4 light window" was simply one with four panes of glass, a precious commodity in the wilderness. When the women first moved into their house built on the east side of the fort, Clara later remembered, it had only a wooden window which was removed during the day for light and nailed back in at night. A little "port hole" at the east end could likewise be covered. The two lights Eliza received from Brother Peirce would be sufficient for this smaller window. Young, "A Woman's Experience," p. 175.

33. Caroline and Jedediah Grant's four-month-old baby, Margaret Grant, born 19 May in Winter Quarters, died 3 September 1847. Eliza had not been able to visit Caroline the day before but had written the little poem here on a scrap of paper from which she copied it.

34. Eli Harvey Peirce and a company of seventeen others made the first expedition to California for seeds and plant cuttings. They returned the following May.

35. Rebaptism and confirmation among the Saints newly arrived in the Valley was a ritual of recommitment and rededication to their gospel principles.

36. The women's "blessing meetings" had been suspect by some since their beginning at Nauvoo. Here Eliza Snow has been careful to note the presence of men holding priesthood office whenever there were any in attendance, a reflection of the criticism which had been and continued to be levied against the practice. See her entry for 1 January 1848.

37. While no record is available of such a bill having been passed, the rumor was certainly not groundless. Great Britain in the 1840s was struggling towards passage of equitable poor laws; its population of "poor" citizens is recorded as lying between 3.5 and 4.5 percent of the total population. *Library of Universal Knowledge*, 18 vols. (New York: American Book Exchange, 1881), 15:25–27.

38. It would appear that the policy that had been established following the discontinuance of the Relief Society in Nauvoo of having no women's meetings without a priesthood holder being present had been reinstated. In reporting each of the next several meetings, Eliza R. Snow was careful to note the names of any men present. Such was the case less than two weeks later, 20 December 1847, where in reporting a meeting at Bishop Higbee's she named no women but noted "five breth. present." Two days later, she listed several women's names, and added as an

afterthought "breth present." When on 23 December the sisters met with Sister Riter presiding, Sister Gates attempted to diffuse criticism by suggesting such gatherings be called "organiz'd parties."

39. The native girl renamed Sally was brought to Clara Decker Young by her brother Charles Decker and was cared for by the Young family until she reached adulthood. She married Chief Kanosh and lived among the Pahvant tribe near the town of Kanosh, where she died in 1878. John R. Young was quoted as relating the story of her rescue as a child. He told of a disturbance in the Indian camp near his family home. He was sent to the fort, returning with Charley Decker and Barney Ward, the interpreter, and others. "It was Wanship's band," he remembered. "Some of his braves had just returned from the war path. In a fight with Little Wolf's band, they lost two men, but had succeeded in taking two girl prisoners. One of these they had killed and were torturing the other. To save her life, Charley Decker bought her and took her to our house to be washed and clothed. She was the saddest looking piece of humanity I have ever seen. They had shingled her head with butcher knives and fire brands. All the fleshy parts of her body, legs, and arms had been hacked with knives then firebrands had been stuck into the wounds. She was gaunt with hunger and smeared from head to foot with blood and ashes. After being scrubbed and clothed, she was given to President Brigham Young and became as one of his family." "Indian Women of the West," in *Heart Throbs of the West,* 12 vols., comp. Kate B. Carter (Salt Lake City: Daughters of Utah Pioneers, 1939–1951), 1:113.

40. Thirteen-year-old Mary Eveline Stewart, daughter of George and Ruthinda Stewart, died 15 December 1847.

41. Mary Forsgren, while not a plural wife of Heber C. Kimball, came under his care in 1848 while her husband was in the Mormon Battalion. Stanley B. Kimball, *Heber C. Kimball: Mormon Patriarch and Pioneer* (Urbana: University of Illinois Press, 1981), 147.

42. The wedding of Elizabeth Hendricks to Frederick Bainbridge is inexactly noted in her mother Drusilla Dorris Hendricks's reminiscence as occurring "about the middle of the winter." The marriage was apparently of short duration: discouraged by meager rations and the hard work of irrigating, Bainbridge soon left the Valley. Marguerite Allen, comp., *Henry Hendricks Genealogy, (1730–...)* (Salt Lake City: Hendricks Family Organization, 1963), 29.

43. Usually used in sketching, the camera obscura was entertaining in itself: through the aperture in a dark box, images of external objects were received with a convex lens and exhibited in their natural colors on a prepared surface.

44. Angeline Myers, Levi Jackman's wife and mother of six children, had died 24 January 1846. In November 1849 Jackman would marry

again and after that take six more wives. The poem, with its familiar admonition against mourning, is unpublished.

45. Levi Hancock, who had come west with the Mormon Battalion in 1847, was now returning to Winter Quarters for his wife Clarissa Reed and their children, the seventh of whom was born the February previous. "My sister," to whom Eliza sends greeting, is Leonora Leavitt Morley. Driven back on this attempt by an impassable road, Hancock tried again on 14 February and finally succeeded 18 May. The poem is unpublished elsewhere.

46. Ellen Sanders, the Danish immigrant wife of Heber C. Kimball who had accompanied him with the Pioneer Company, gave birth in the Valley to her first child, Samuel Chase. He would live only five months.

47. "Father" John Smith, uncle of Joseph Smith, had been sustained church patriarch and was entitled to pronounce individual blessings on the Saints.

48. Forty-two-year-old Lola Ann Clawson and her husband Elihu Allen had traveled from Winter Quarters in the same Fifty as Eliza R. Snow. Lola's death left three teenaged children and two others under five. Three of their children had died three years earlier, December 1845, in Nauvoo. Their father Elihu would die two years later, 11 October 1850.

49. Franklin H. Shed[d], a Massachusetts convert then twenty-three years old, came to the Valley in the same hundred as Eliza R. Snow, and in Willard Snow's Fifty. That he and Helen, one of the Snows' twin babies, just two weeks old, should die the same day would be doubly hard.

50. The Mary Jane of the poem has no definite identity, but she may have been Mary Jane Dilworth, six years his junior, who traveled to the Valley in the same Fifty as Shed. She would marry Francis Hammond six months from this date. The poem is unpublished.

51. A far remove from the regular rhymes and rhythms of the previous poems, the lines to Eleanor Bringhurst, who crossed with Eliza Snow in the Big Company, are freer in form, sometimes almost prosaic. It is as though Eliza Snow, with some leisure now, has become more inventive and less dependent upon the old poetic patterns. See also *Improvement Era* 47 (April 1944): 218.

52. Lorenzo Dow Young, named for his father, was the first white male child born in the Salt Lake Valley, on 20 September 1847. His mother was Harriet Page Wheeler Young. See Journal History, 22 March 1848.

53. This is the long storm of which Eliza Snow wrote later in her "Sketch of My Life." There, memory having softened the discomfort and heightened the humor of the occasion, she can recount in more detail the storm and its effects.

54. In her "Sketch," Eliza R. Snow speaks of this company of young

men who had gone to California for seeds and cuttings, from whom on their return she bought a handful of potatoes.

55. Jim Wanship ("Oneship") was the promising son of Chief Wanship, leader of a band of Ute Indians that had separated from the Utah Valley tribe to Salt Lake Valley where they merged with Shoshone Indians from the north. The incident referred to involved young Jim Wanship's mission to Utah Valley to negotiate with the Utes, during which he was killed. The action brought fear of an Indian uprising to the Mormon settlers. Courtesy Ronald W. Walker.

56. The oft-told miracle of the crickets and the seagulls is here seen as it was perceived at the time—a long and quiet test of the faith and endurance of the Saints. By Eliza Snow's account, the crickets began devouring the young crops "a few days" before 28 May 1848 and continued at least until 10 June. The two severe frosts she noted during that season worsened the chances for the remaining crops. There is no mention in her diary of seagulls devouring the crickets, although by the writing of her "Sketch" the story had been canonized into its later form as a miracle of divine intervention. See William G. Hartley, "Mormons, Crickets, and Gulls: A Look at an Old Story," *Utah Historical Quarterly* 38 (Summer 1970): 224–39.

57. The poem to Harvey Peirce stops in mid-word, as though the ink had run out or the poet had been disturbed. The quatrain requires one more line, now unavailable. The poem was never published.

58. It was not uncommon for the Saints to escape from the heat of the valley sun by taking two- or three-day trips into one of the several canyons east of Salt Lake City. That this outing lasted eighteen days suggests the importance to their food supply of the currants and "servis berries" (serviceberries, juneberries, or shaberries—the blue-black or purplish fruit of a shrub of genus *Amelanchier,* native to the region) that they could pick there and preserve.

59. It is surprising that Eliza R. Snow makes no mention here of news she would doubtless have received: that her brother Lorenzo and his family would be arriving shortly. He actually arrived, as head of a Hundred, on 22 September.

60. Eliza would stay in the Fort with Jonathan and Elvira Holmes until the following June, when she would move to a row of log houses near City Creek with others of Young's wives. She was obviously comfortable with the Holmeses, having boarded with them in Nauvoo as well.

61. Brigham Young had built a row of houses, known as the Log Row, on his property near City Creek near what is now First Avenue between State Street and Second East in downtown Salt Lake City. Presumably these are the "new room[s]" referred to here. On 1 March 1849 "B's folks" would move out of the Fort, and on 28 June 1849 Eliza Snow

would move into one of the apartments there, joining others of Brigham Young's wives and their children. Brigham Young himself lived in the White House, up the hill from the Log Row, until the late 1850s when the wives moved into the Lion House and he and wife Mary Ann Angell Young moved into the adjoining Beehive House on South Temple at State Street.

62. Eliza's long poem, "To Elder Franklin D. Richards, On his first return from Europe," appeared in the *Millennial Star* 12 (1 May 1850): 143, and later in Eliza R. Snow, *Poems, Religious, Historical, and Political,* 1:211. It contains greetings to John Lyon, the Scottish convert poet from whom Richards had brought greetings and the address referred to in the 25 December entry.

63. On 17 January 1846 Lorenzo Snow was sealed in the Nauvoo Temple to his first four wives: Mary Adeline Goddard, Charlotte Squires, Sarah Ann Prichard, and Harriet Squires.

64. Oliver Goddard Snow, Lorenzo Snow's son by his wife Mary Adaline Goddard, was later recorded as having been born 20 February 1849. Eliza R. Snow Smith, *Biography and Family Record of Lorenzo Snow* (Salt Lake City: Deseret News Company, 1884), 489.

65. Hosea Stout recounts the six-day expedition in which some thirty-five men commanded by Col. John Scott rode into Utah Valley in pursuit of a maverick group of Utah Indians who had been stealing cattle from the Mormons. Juanita Brooks, *On the Mormon Frontier* 2:344–47.

66. Ira West ("Watt"), one of the captains of ten in the move west, was accused before the Council of Fifty of "lying, stealing and swindling," and was remanded to the care of his brother. Brooks, *On the Mormon Frontier* 2:348.

67. In this first election, 655 voters elected Brigham Young governor; Willard Richards secretary; Heber C. Kimball, Newel K. Whitney, and John Taylor, justices; H. S. Eldredge, marshal; Daniel Wells, attorney general; Albert Carrington, assessor; and Joseph Heywood, supervisor of roads. Brooks, *On the Mormon Frontier* 2:348.

68. A stand in a bowery had been erected near the construction site of the Council House, not yet completed.

69. This is the second child Sarah Ann Whitney Kimball lost. Her first, David, born in Winter Quarters 8 March 1846, had died five months later; this one, David Orson, was just eight months old, having been born 26 August 1848. Kimball, *Heber C. Kimball,* 314.

70. Helen Mar Kimball Whitney recorded several such communications with Eliza Snow. "Our intimacy began the first winter after we came to this [Salt Lake] valley, we were both invalids and though we lived within half a block's distance of each other, we were unable to walk it; but we could communicate our thoughts and feelings by letter which we

often did, though paper like every other commodity at that time was very scarce; we never left any blank space. Her notes contained many things which were to me as precious treasures, which I have preserved among other choice relics of the past." "Life Incidents," *Woman's Exponent* 9 (15 April 1881): 170.

71. This instituted the monthly fast and testimony meeting, observed by contemporary Latter-day Saints on the first Sunday of each month but at this time held on Thursdays. Typically the faithful would abstain from eating for a day, donate their saving in food to the poor, and attend services for testimony bearing.

72. Brooks, *On the Mormon Frontier* 2:351, under date 28 April 1849, provides details of the incident. Wanship had been attacked a week earlier by an opposing band under Little Chief. Men on both sides were killed. Stout also records that on this date two regiments of the Nauvoo Legion, that city's militia, were reorganized in Salt Lake City under the general direction of Daniel H. Wells.

73. On this date Ira Willes married Malissa Lott, who had earlier been sealed to Bernhisel.

74. Cornelia, daughter of Eliza Snow's sister Leonora, now one of Amasa Lyman's wives, apparently lived with the rest of that family at Cottonwood, a farming community about ten miles southeast of downtown Salt Lake City.

75. Caleb Baldwin had been with the Mormon Church since the Missouri depredations and had been incarcerated there in 1837 with Joseph and Hyrum Smith.

76. Eliza Snow's friend Patty Sessions notes the trial of her son Peregrine in her diary: "Saturday 23   P G s trial cloesid to day he came off better than when he began." After some three or four sittings, reported Hosea Stout, the court found Sessions "guilty of taking advantage of the people in the sale of his corn &c." Stout adds: Sessions "is now to make restitution to all he has injured." Sessions, Diary, 23 June 1849; Brooks, *On the Mormon Frontier* 2:353.

77. This obviously notes the California gold rush, started by the 1848 discovery by Mormon Battalion veterans of gold at Sutter's Mill near Coloma, California. Leonard J. Arrington, in *Great Basin Kingdom: An Economic History of the Latter-day Saints, 1830–1900* (Cambridge, Mass.: Harvard University Press, 1958), 68, estimated that in 1849–50 ten to fifteen thousand "Forty-niners" passed through the Valley, leaving prosperity in their wake.

78. The "circle of ladies" would likely have been Joseph Smith's widows now living in the Valley, and the "lectures" were most probably the published "Lectures on Faith."

79. Lorenzo Snow was the official responsible for the celebration, and

Eliza's biography of her brother gives a very full account of the day's events. After an early morning chorus of cannon, the band, and the Nauvoo bell, the Saints assembled in a large bowery while an escort paraded to Brigham Young's residence, returning with him to the bowery for speeches and music by the band and singers. Two verses by Eliza Snow were performed, one sung by twenty-four young women, one by the Silver Greys. Picnic tables afforded lunch. In all, the celebration resembled, understandably, those July Fourths celebrated in the 1830s in Mantua, Ohio, and, for that matter, in many a New England town. See Snow Smith, *Biography and Family Record of Lorenzo Snow*, 96–107.

80. This begins the arrival of the immigrating companies for the year. Howard Egan's small group had left Iowa on 18 April 1849 and was followed that summer by five more companies, totaling about three thousand Mormons.

Index